D1707140

ATKA Island

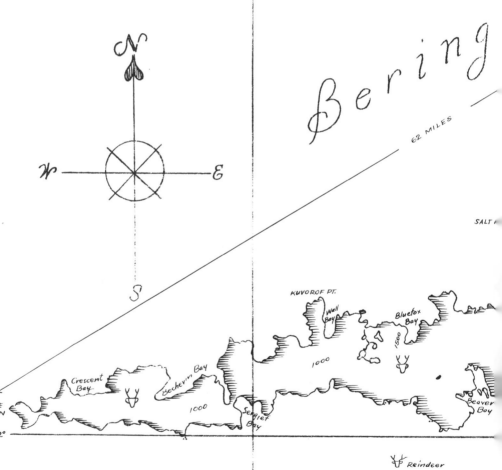

52° 30'

Bering

62 MILES

SALT

52°

KUVOROF PT.

Wall Bay

Bluefox Bay

1500

1000

Crescent Bay

Bechevin Bay

1000

CAPE KIGUN

Sergief Bay

Beaver Bay

Reindeer

Coal – (Sand Bay)

Copper (Salt Island)

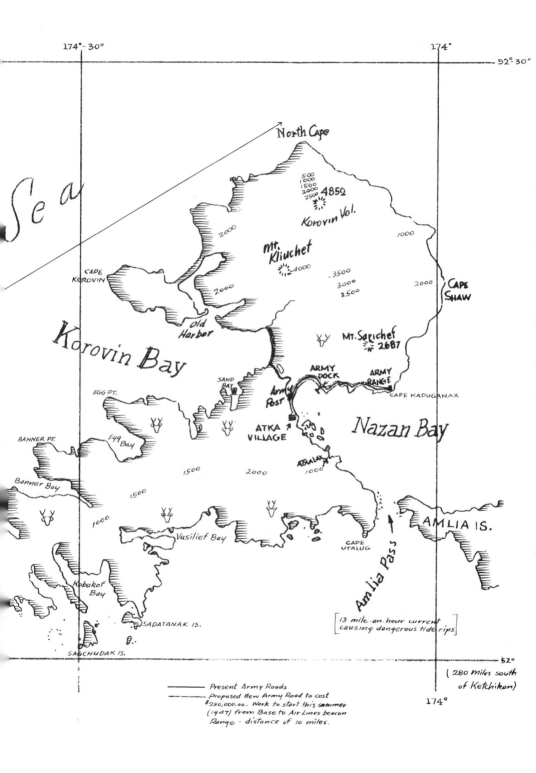

52° 30"

174°- 30"   174°

North Cape

Sea

500
1.000
1.500
2.000
2.500 4852

Korovin Vol.

2000

Mt.
Kliuchef

4000   3500
3000
2500

1000

CAPE
KOROVIN

2000

CAPE
SHAW

2000

Old
Harbor

Mt. Sarichef
2687

Korovin Bay

SAND
BAY

ARMY
DOCK

ARMY
RANGE

CAPE KADUGANAX

Army
Post

Nazan Bay

EGG PT.

ATKA
VILLAGE

BANNER PT.

Egg
Bay

ATKALAX

BANNER PT.

1000

Banner Bay

1500

2000

AMLIA IS.

1500

1500

Vasilief Bay

CAPE
UTALUG

1000

Amlia Pass

Kobakof
Bay

SADATANAK IS.

[13 mile-an-hour current
causing dangerous tide rips]

SAGCHUDAK IS.

52°

(280 miles south
of Ketchikan)

174°

—————— Present Army Roads
- - - - - - Proposed New Army Road to cost
$250,000.00. Work to start this summer
(1947) from Base to Air Lines beacon
Range - distance of 10 miles.

✲JOURNAL OF AN ALEUTIAN YEAR

☀️JOURNAL OF

University of Washington Press *Seattle and London*

AN ALEUTIAN YEAR

Ethel Ross Oliver

Introduction by Margaret Lantis

Foreword by Moses L. Dirks

Designed by Joanna Hill
Printed in the United States of America

Illustration credits: Except for Reg Emmert's photograph of Parascovia
Lokanin Wright on page 145 and the portraits of the Olivers on page 3,
all photos are by Simeon and Ethel Oliver (courtesy of Ethel Ross
Oliver). Front end paper shows a map of Atka Island, drawn by Simeon
Oliver in 1946 (courtesy of Ethel Ross Oliver).

This book is published with the assistance of a grant from the Alaska
Humanities Forum, a state-based program of the National Endowment for
the Humanities.

Library of Congress Cataloging-in-Publication Data
Oliver, Ethel Ross.
  Journal of an Aleutian year.
    1. Aleuts.   2. Aleuts—Government relations.
3. Indians of North America—Alaska—Aleutian Islands.
4. Teachers—Alaska—Biography.   5. Oliver, Ethel Ross.
I. Title
E99.A34O45   1987   979.8'4   87-18907
ISBN 0-295-96567-3

To the Aleut people,
with my sincere admiration and affection

Aerial view of Atka Island

The Shrouded Islands

Something deep hidden in me grew to love
Those bare volcanoes, those unquiet skies;
The clinging clouds and sea fogs; the surprise
Of sunshine and the misted moon that strove
To light the lonesome bays.
With blended sadness
And joy I thrilled to watch the blowing rain
And vapor blur the hills; to hear the strain
The sea wind sang or cried as if in madness.

Something in me wakened which no reason
Can ever touch, no voice can ever tame;
Something that found in each Aleutian season
A kindred waywardness.
I cannot name
The dark wild spirit, old as it is young,
That loved those islands I was long among.

Courtland W. Matthews

(Courtland W. Matthews was a young naval ensign from Portland, Oregon, stationed on Atka Island during World War II. Used by permission.)

✳ CONTENTS

✻ ILLUSTRATIONS

✳ FOREWORD

The Atka of 1946–47 no longer exists. Many things have changed since my grandfather and uncle served the village as Old Chief and young chief, respectively, and Mrs. Oliver taught school here.

Communication with the outside world has improved tremendously. In July 1976 the state telephone utility installed a small earth station to provide service to the community through a single telephone. In 1983 the service was expanded to provide house-to-house and long-distance lines. The single-sideband radio that was once the only method of communication with the outside world is now used to communicate with planes traveling to Atka from Cold Bay and Adak, and as a backup when the telephone system fails. Alaska's state-operated satellite television network provides Atka with commercial programming and with daily news from the rest of the state, nation, and the world.

Regular, scheduled transportation and mail service makes it easier to get to and from Atka. Peninsula Airways provides service from Adak twice a month, with the schedule being determined by the community. Food, clothing, medicines, and other goods arrive on the mail plane. The local store, which the Olivers had a hand in organizing through the Alaska Native Industries Co-operative, can obtain stock when needed through the postal service and the mail plane. A 3,500-foot, paved and lighted airstrip (built by the State of Alaska in 1983) and a nondirectional beacon make Atka more accessible than it ever was, even during poor weather conditions. The Bureau of Indian Affairs still provides barge services to Atka, though the *North Star* was placed in dry dock several years ago. As often as twice a year, the barge transports oil and items that cannot be brought to Atka by plane.

Atkans enjoy a higher standard of living than in the past. In 1983 eighteen new housing units were built, a mile and a half north of the village site. Many residents moved there from older houses, leaving unoccupied homes in the village. Each house is Arctic insulated and has the conveniences (refrigerators, water, sewer) that would normally be found in an urban setting. Electricity is provided twenty-four hours a day by an electric utility owned by the ANCSA village corporation, Atxam Corporation. Atka's residents have come to depend on electricity to operate the variety of appliances they have accumulated—very few people want to return to the days of the Coleman lantern!

Adak is less accessible to Atkans than it was in the past. It is now restricted and security has been tightened because of the world situation. Military planes and personnel no longer travel back and forth to Atka to help the residents. The only concession the Navy makes is allowing Atka residents, and those visiting on community business, to pass through Adak to catch a Reeve Aleutian Airways flight to Anchorage.

Medical care is provided by the Indian Health Service. There is a resident health aide and she can consult with a doctor in Anchorage if necessary. A doctor and dentist from the Alaska Native Medical Center in Anchorage visit Atka once a year. All babies are born in a hospital in Anchorage. In medical emergencies, Atka must rely on a plane to come from Cold Bay and transport patients to Anchorage; this can sometimes take up to twelve hours. At present, there are no known active cases of tuberculosis on the island.

The church is still a very important part of the community. Traditional Russian Orthodox holidays are still observed. There is still no priest residing in Atka; lay readers conduct services regularly, and a priest periodically travels to Atka from Unalaska to conduct divine liturgy and perform weddings in church, baptisms, etc.

Subsistence activities in Atka are changing. Food resources are still abundant, but the utilization of those resources has changed due to a variety of factors, including the cost of gasoline and ammunition, commercial activities, and new methods of preservation. In the past it was essential to hunt and gather food daily; now Atkans own freezers and can freeze meat and fish for later use. The local store stocks a variety of foods, including canned goods and frozen beef, chicken, and pork. No gardens are planted on Amlia Island.

Some subsistence activities of 1946–47 are still important, though no longer a way of life for Atka. In her journal, Mrs. Oliver mentions how much she enjoyed clamming. Today, the sea otters have become so numerous that they have depleted the shellfish stock, and it has become impossible to obtain a sufficient number of clams to make a meal for a family. Reindeer, too, are harder to get. Hunters have to go out in their small skiffs and travel many miles, to the western end of the island, to find them. This is a very expensive trip, too, because gasoline costs approximately four dollars a gallon. Halibut are harder to catch since commercial halibut fishing has begun around Atka.

In Mrs. Oliver's time, teachers provided technical assistance and other kinds of aid to people in need. Although the elders of the community are well aware of how valuable teachers like Mrs. Oliver were in the past, the situation has now changed. School is no longer the center of the the village's life, and teachers are not relied on to perform the variety of tasks that Mrs. Oliver took on. Residents have now assumed responsibility for providing medical care, managing the business affairs of the community, and operating the post office. Most residents now manage their own personal affairs and do not rely on teachers for help as they did in the past. Teachers are expected only to educate students.

The Atka school is operated by the State of Alaska, through a Rural Education Attendance Area (REAA). The Aleutian Region School District is based in Anchorage and operates schools in the Aleutian communities of Atka, Akutan, Cold Bay, False Pass, and Nelson Lagoon. School is in session for five hours a day, one hundred and eighty days a year, as required by Alaska State law.

The present school is very modern. Instead of Mrs. Oliver's single classroom, the school has four classrooms and a number of areas designed for special activities, including home economics, shop, and science. Sufficient texts and supplies are available. The school is equipped with computers, which the students are taught to use; the computer is also used to transmit and receive information from the Aleutian Region School District in Anchorage.

An Aleut language and culture program exists as part of the Aleutian Region School District curriculum. Every student at the Atka school receives forty minutes of language instruction during each school day. Students are taught to have more pride in their native language, Atkan Aleut. As a result, students are more aware of their culture and where their ancestors came from.

Students may attend through twelfth grade if they choose; they no longer have to leave Atka to complete high school. In the last ten years, the drop-out rate in the Atka school has been zero.

The future holds even greater changes. Atka is in the process of developing an economy based upon bottom fisheries, in ensure the survival of the community. Since it is no longer possible to rely solely on subsistence activities, a cash economy is needed. More influences from outside of Atka are expected. Throughout the Aleutian Islands there is an increase in activity related to the military and the fishing industry. Such changes will have a direct impact on the lifestyles of Atkans.

Atka was very fortunate to have a teacher of Mrs. Oliver's caliber during the difficult period of readjustment for the Aleuts whose lives were disrupted by World War II. She was sensitive to the needs of the students and the welfare of the community as a whole. She was sincere and cared about the people.

Moses Dirks

Atka, Alaska
September 1987

✳ PREFACE

On the third and fourth of June, 1942, the Japanese made bombing raids on Dutch Harbor, Alaska, the largest community in the Aleutian Islands and the site of the westernmost military installation on the North American continent. In so doing they turned the inhabitants of the Aleutian islands into innocent casualties of the war. Immediately after the raids, and without consulting the Aleuts, the United States government ordered the several native villages in the island chain to prepare for immediate evacuation, since it was feared that the Japanese planned a major invasion of Alaska.

When the Japanese bombers met with unexpected resistance in their attempt to take the military base at Dutch Harbor, they retreated to the west under the cover of fog. Their supporting task force, which had been lying to at sea, followed them. Three days later Japan invaded the islands of Attu and Kiska at the western end of the Aleutians.

The large invasion force of Japanese soldiers spread over the hills and valleys of Attu Island and swept into the little village of forty-two Aleuts and two white Alaska Native Service personnel at Chichagof Harbor, capturing it without resistance and breaking the limited radio contact between Attu and the rest of the world. The usual daily weather report from Attu was not sent to Dutch Harbor on Sunday, June 7, 1942.

For several years Chief Mike Hodikoff of Attu had reported to American government officials on the visits by Japanese ships engaged in mapping the waters and harbors of the western islands of the Aleutian Chain. He had feared a Japanese invasion, but his reports apparently had been consigned to the wastebasket or otherwise ignored.

Mike Hodikoff's fears were realized on that June day when the Japanese captured Attu. No one in the outside world knew the fate of the unprotected villagers—the first captives of the war in the Aleutians. It was only known that Japan had succeeded in invading America and had gained a foothold in the Western Hemisphere, and might at any moment attack the mainland.

While mainland Alaska hastily prepared for the worst and the western states of America instituted blackouts, the hasty evacuation of the Aleuts from the other islands in the Aleutian Chain began with the Atka villagers. Theirs was a traumatic experience.

On June 10 a Navy seaplane tender, the *Gillis*, mother ship to twenty Catalinas and a squadron of PBV-5As, anchored in Nazan Bay off Atka Village. The Aleuts moved to their usual summer fishing camps, vacating part of the village in order to provide housing for the plane crews. For three days, from their camps, the villagers watched the Japanese planes bomb their village. They watched the U.S. planes fly out in futile attempts to drive the Japanese from Kiska, and come limping back to refuel and fly out again.

The *Gillis* ran out of fuel and ammunition for its flock of aircraft and was ordered to return to Dutch Harbor. Orders were also given to bring the Atka Aleuts to a safer location. The tender *Hulbert* was to evacuate them.

On the night of June 13 most of the Aleuts were hastily rounded up at their camps and hustled aboard the *Hulbert* with only the clothes on their backs. They were prevented from going ashore for the suitcases that they had left in their homes, packed and ready for this emergency in accordance with the governmental order. The little group stood helpless and bewildered at the rail of the *Hulbert*, and wept as they watched frenzied young Americans rush about, setting fire to their precious homes and church in order to prevent the Japanese from occupying the village.

When they reached Dutch Harbor they were put aboard a grimy old transport ship and several days later the eighty-three men, women, and children were dumped at an abandoned herring saltery at Killisnoo, west of Juneau, in southeastern Alaska. Here they were practically forgotten by authorities, and death, brought on by privation and disease, took a terrible toll of their number.

Other Aleuts were taken to other evacuation camps, such as Funter Bay and Ward Cove in southeast Alaska, for the duration of the war, but none suffered the initial hardships borne by the Atkans. These indomitable Aleuts simply asked for tools and began to build a new life for themselves in their unfamiliar and alien surroundings until they could return to their island homes.

※ ※ ※

Don C. Foster, superintendent of the Alaska Native Service, a branch of the United States Bureau of Indian Affairs, came to see us at our home in Anchorage in May 1945. He was almost ready to return the Aleutian Island people to their village homes from the evacuation camps in southeast Alaska where they had been held for three years.

Atka Village had been burned by the United States naval forces at the time of the evacuation and would have to be completely rebuilt. Superintendent Foster planned to send his chief construction man, Glenn Greene, to Atka with the villagers to start the rebuilding. Mrs. Greene would go to teach the children. Superintendent Foster said he could only spare Mr. Greene until June of 1946. He needed a couple to replace the Greenes and continue the work, and he felt that my husband and I were the best qualified.

Simeon's qualifications were unmistakable. He had been born and raised on the western Aleutian Chain. He knew the people and the area. When the Japanese bombed Dutch Harbor (on his home island of Unalaska) he was living in New York, where he lectured on Alaska. Immediately he had offered his services to the Army. He was accepted and sent to Fort Richardson in Anchorage, Alaska, where he was assigned to G2—Army Intelligence. After the conclusion of the Aleutian campaign he was released from military service. In the meantime we had married and he stayed in Alaska, writing a sequel to his first book, *Son of the Smoky Sea,* and preparing for a lecture tour in the midwest during the 1945–46 season.

My own qualifications were less impressive. I had for several years been a successful teacher and held an Alaska Life Teaching Certificate. In addition, I had spent nearly twenty-five years in various parts of Alaska, much of it pioneering along the abandoned Iditarod Trail after the Alaska Railroad was completed. During these years I had built a firm friendship with and had acquired some knowledge of other Alaska native people. Simeon and I were both college graduates and were roughly the same age as the adults with whom we would be working in Atka.

After reviewing our qualifications, Superintendent Foster explained to us that couples hired by Alaska Native Service were usually designated "Teacher" and "Assistant Teacher." Although I was actually the teacher, the title would officially be Simeon's. He would sign all of the reports and correspondence as "Teacher." There was no official description for his real job, which would be to oversee the construction work and order supplies for that and to refurnish the homes, church, store, and warehouses. He was to serve as liaison between the people, the government, and the military forces stationed on the island and on neighboring Adak. My job was to look after the education of the children and the health and welfare of the Atka people.

We gladly assured Superintendent Foster that we would board the *North Star* in Seattle on June 1, 1946, ready to sail to Atka.

The year we spent in Atka was even more interesting and exciting than we expected. Much was required of us by the Juneau office of the Alaska Native Service. Mail was infrequent and one mail in April brought several official letters, all marked "Urgent—Process Immediately." Simeon selected the organization of the new Alaska Native Industrial Co-operative Association as the most urgent. The Juneau office was urging a group of native stores to form an association to do their own purchasing of supplies, and loans would have to be made to them for that purpose. The loan for Atka would be based on a survey and report on the entire assets of the village. This was the reason for the Economic Survey. Simeon and I worked together on the project, gathering data and compiling it.

There was nothing official about the journals I kept. All my life I have recorded the things of interest that I saw or did. After I came to Alaska in 1921 my journals became the source for long letters to my mother, which she shared with family and friends. While in New York in 1945 my husband and I signed a contract to write a book on our experiences in the Aleutians, but we later asked to be released from it so we could return to the lecture field. We took back to Anchorage a large file of material concerning Atka, and stored it and the journals in our home, but we did not at that time plan to use them in writing books.

In later years I felt a growing concern that so few people in Alaska and in the rest of the United States knew anything about the fact that a part of our nation was occupied by an enemy for more than a year, nor did they know that an Alaskan village was captured and the people taken to a foreign land, imprisoned, and used as slave labor, and that other villages were evacuated and the residents held in evacuation camps for the duration of the war. The United States government knew this, but the facts were not made generally available to the public. This is a part of American and Alaskan history which should not be lost. I determined to do what I could to preserve it and make it known. That was when I got out all the material we had gathered and started to write this account. My daily journals were supplemented by the government letters and directives and by personal correspondence and pictures. The Aleut names of the months, given at the beginning of each chapter, are from *History, Ethnology, and Anthropology of the Aleut,* by Waldemar Jochelson (Carnegie Institution of Washington, 1933).

In this journal, I have recorded many personal conversations with Aleuts from the islands of Atka and Attu. It is important to remember that English was a second (or third) language for all the villagers, few of whom had had much formal education. The English spoken on Atka Island in 1946–47 had evolved on two different islands over several centuries, and was influenced by English-speaking, Russian, and Scandinavian visitors. The "village English" spoken in this journal and reproduced in the appendixes should be understood in this context. I have also recorded the frequent use by villagers of the term "Japs," and some derogatory references to the Japanese. These must be understood in the context of the general political climate in the United States and its territories during and after World War II, and in light of the fact that many of the villagers had recently returned from a bitter experience as prisoners of war in Japan.

My son, Ernest Ross, did the final preparation of the manuscript, and I am indebted to him and to my sister, Veva Morgan, for their ready understanding and encouragement. Royal and Ethel Brown gave me helpful criticism and made valuable suggestions. Finally, I want to acknowledge the help I received from many Aleut friends in the village of Atka, who helped make this book theirs.

Ethel Ross Oliver

Anchorage, Alaska

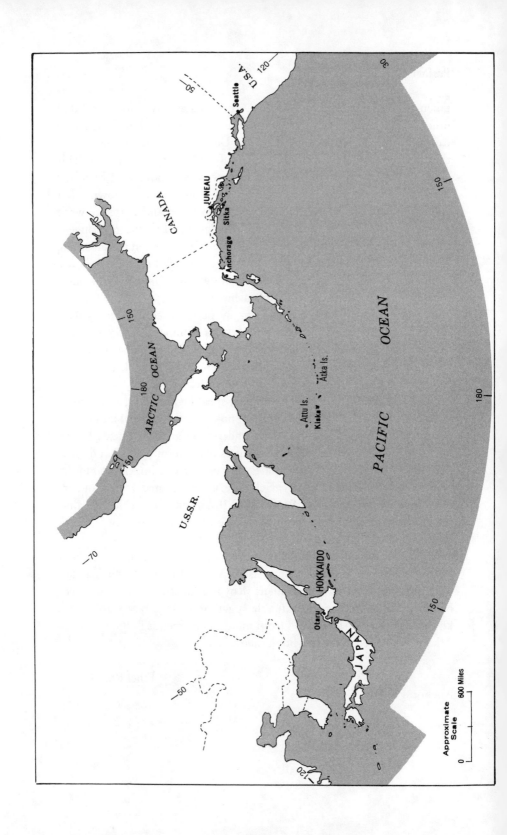

ARCTIC OCEAN

CANADA

U.S.A.

Seattle

120

50

150

90

JUNEAU

Sitka

Anchorage

150

180

150

70

U.S.S.R.

Attu Is.

Kiska

Atka Is.

PACIFIC OCEAN

180

150

HOKKAIDO

Otaru

JAPAN

50

120

Approximate
Scale

0   600 Miles

✳ INTRODUCTION

At the end of World War II, there was a relocation of peoples—a going home or going to a new life—in many parts of the world. In the western Pacific, east and southeast Asia, the United States west coast, and Central and Eastern Europe, people displaced during the war came or were brought to old and new homes. In Alaska, too, lives were rebuilt by returning populations.

The western end of the Aleutian Islands Chain, which stretches from southeast Alaska almost to Asia, was the only part of continental North America that was actually occupied by Japanese forces. In 1942, in great haste and confusion, the Aleuts of all the communities, except those closest to the Alaska mainland and the one closest to Soviet territory, were evacuated to southeast Alaska for the duration of the war. Residents of Attu, the westernmost village, had been captured in June and taken to Japan in September; personal accounts of that experience appear in this book. Attu was retaken in May 1943.

After the war, the government rebuilt the village on Atka Island, which had been virtually destroyed during its chaotic evacuation, and the returning villagers were joined there by the surviving Attuans who were brought back from Japan. In June 1946, Simeon and Ethel Ross Oliver came to Atka, to serve as, respectively, liaison with the United States government and schoolteacher. Although Ethel Ross Oliver's memoir of the first full year of life in the rebuilt village of Atka conveys the challenge and excitement of a frontier experience, it is important to remember that this far west American region had had a longer personal contact with Europeans than some parts of what is commonly called "the American West." An understanding of the prehistory and history of the area and its peoples will help to put Mrs. Oliver's account into perspective.

The Aleuts' name for themselves is Unangan or Angagin, or, in the Atka variant, Angaginas, "We the People." They are related to Eskimos in language and culture, but because they have lived on the islands a very long time their language has diverged from the Eskimo. In elements of their culture other than language, especially social elements, they share much with the peoples to the east, on the North Pacific Rim: the Pacific Eskimos of the Kodiak Island and Kenai Peninsula areas, and even the Athapaskans and the Tlingit Indians farther east. Before contact with Europeans, Aleuts had a well-developed social class system; concepts of wealth, property, and inheritance; and some religious beliefs and practices similar to those of the Tlingits.

After a prehistory of several thousand years, the Aleuts experienced in the historic period three major invasions. The first of these, of course, was by the Russians. The first fifty years of that foreign occupation—the second half of the 1700s—were the worst. Aleut sea otter hunters, and then fur seal hunters, were moved from one area to another to hunt by the ruthless Russian fur merchants. In the Pribilof Islands, for example, there were no human inhabitants until the Russians brought them there from the Chain. Groups of Aleuts also moved independently from one island to another. Around 1800 a group of Atkans led by a Russian moved to Attu Island to establish a settlement separate from the Attuans already living there. Between 1814 and 1816, some of these transplants and several Attuans moved with the Russians even farther west to a settlement in the Commander Islands, which still belong to the USSR today.

Russian seamen, traders, and fur hunters had to spend long periods on the islands and traveling between them, with the result that a mixed Russian-Aleut population segment, referred to in the historical literature as "Creoles," developed. By the early 1800s, when a degree of stability quieted the western and central islands, a probable 80 percent of the Aleut population had died from introduced diseases, mistreatment, and the effects of disruption of the social structure and the economy.

There was to be another half-century of Russian domination, although Americans were already active in the region by the time of the Civil War. A Russian chartered commercial company had established a degree of order, and with the coming of Russian priest-teachers in the 1820s and 1830s, a less chaotic life began to develop. A century of Russian influence accounts for the Russian names of most of the Aleut families whom Mrs. Oliver knew, for their continuing Orthodox religious tradition, and for the mixture of Alaskan and Siberian folk beliefs and practices prevalent in the region. In the early twentieth century, "bilingual" meant Russian- and Aleut-speaking for older Aleut people, and English- and Aleut-speaking for the young ones.

English speakers arrived in even greater numbers during the second half of the nineteenth century. This second invasion of the Chain was economically motivated and occurred with virtually no government control. Motley crews of New England whalers passed through the Chain en route to the Arctic, followed by crews of California fur seal hunters, then salmon packers from the Seattle area, and finally gold seekers from everywhere, heading for Nome. The eastern islands, especially Unalaska, were the most severely affected.

The worst period of this invasion had followed the purchase of Alaska by the United States in 1867. The Alaska Commercial Company (a federal lessee) and other hunters including Canadians overkilled the sea mammals, whose numbers had already been reduced by the Russians. This brought hardship among the Aleuts, and conditions improved little until about 1910, when the sea otter hunt was banned. The fur seal hunt was controlled by a 1911 international treaty, and most of the Chain became a wildlife refuge in 1913. With the establishment of American schools and with commercial companies extending the fox fur trade even to the westernmost islands, American administrative and economic domination was nearly complete, and it would continue until the third invasion, by the Japanese during World War II.

Since Mrs. Oliver's journal is a teacher's account, appealing to all readers but especially valuable for teachers, it is worthwhile to survey the history of teaching and schools in the Chain. Some Aleutian villages have had schools for nearly a century, Atka and Unalaska for much longer.

Under Russian domination, there seems to have been no regular local schooling until the installation of resident priests. Before that, however, there had been some efforts to build upon the accomplishments of the indigenous population. In the 1820s and 1830s, the impressive carving skills of the Aleuts, who had in pre-Christian times made masks and other religious forms such as small animal and human figures, were turned to the production of elaborate Orthodox religious objects and church decoration. With their remarkable navigation skills and their special knowledge of anatomy—which Simeon Oliver remarks upon in this memoir—some Aleuts were trained by the Russians as navigators and others as what we would today call paramedics. As one might expect, the Creole sons of Russians received preference in secular and religious training, especially in off-island schooling.

The Russian-American Company, a quasi-governmental as well as commercial institution, was supposed to provide schools. Whatever schools it had were placed under church jurisdiction after a remarkable priest, Ioann (John) Veniaminov, was assigned to Unalaska in 1824 and Yakov Netsvetov, of whom we read in this memoir, began his work at Atka in 1828. The Church of St. Nicholas was completed there in 1830. Netsvetov, son of the company's Atka business manager and an Aleut woman, was the first Orthodox priest of Aleut descent. After studying at the Irkutsk Seminary in Siberia, he returned to Atka, where he served until 1844. He founded and taught in the local school. Veniaminov had developed an alphabet for use in the Unalaska district, and Netsvetov revised it for the Atka branch of the Aleut language, so that Atkans too could have a written language. Other members of the Netsvetov family, including a ship commander and a ship builder, provided leadership on other islands.

Although for administrative and other purposes Atka was headquarters of the "Atka District," there were educational and other services on other islands, then occupied and later abandoned. The son of the chief taught school on Amlia, the island closest to Atka, and when more local men were trained, Lavrenty Salamatov in 1844 became priest on Atka, his home island. (Mrs. Oliver tells the story of the relocation of his grave.) Then children could be taught in Aleut and Russian.

Very little is known about Alaskan schools of the mid-1800s. In 1890, a Methodist mission including a coeducational school was established at Unalaska. Though it has been said that there was a Methodist school on Atka Island also, there is little evidence for it. Beginning at Unalaska in 1897, by presidential order small reserves of land were designated for schools. By 1913 all religious schools had been closed as the federal government had begun to provide village schools. These did not blossom everywhere at once, but by 1930 every community except the smallest settlements had an elementary school.

By the beginning of the twentieth century, Atkans evidently were living like coastal fishing folk in, for example, the Puget Sound (Seattle) area, or in old Russia—the latter still a basic (although declining) influence overlaid with modern American culture, especially its economic forms. Western education was inseparable from the commercialization of the culture and the creation of financial dependence upon the invaders. Thus, the modernizations of the twentieth century brought with them a new age of exploitation, business difficulties, and other woes of civilization.

Both Russians and Americans had introduced fox populations on the larger islands, but the trade had not boomed until the 1920s, when fur prices were high and outside commercial interests encouraging. Aleuts lived in a more modern fashion than most of the Eskimos north of them, and traders with small vessels brought food, coal for stoves, clothing, household goods, ammunition, and building materials—all to be paid for in furs. Atka men trapped not only on their own island but also on nearby Amlia and on Amchitka Island, some distance west. A trader would provide transportation out at the beginning of the trapping season and back at the end, and this too was to be paid for in furs, virtually assuring the traders of the entire catch. Other island communities had similar arrangements. The dominant trading companies from the Unalaska District westward were the old Alaska Commercial Company and the newer Kanaga Ranching Company. By the 1930s Atka was attached to both, despite complaints of the Kanaga Company's deceit and mishandling of Atka affairs, and the island was heavily in debt.

A community store had been organized in 1919. By the 1930s, the only Atka store belonged to the Kanaga Company, although the community had a contract with the Alaska Commercial Company (at least for 1933–34) guaranteeing the company the full catch of Amchitka furs in exchange for provisions and transportation. Fox skins from other islands could be sold to the store. Some trappers did not turn in all their furs, and records were sometimes incomplete. Finances became so confused that a representative of the Alaska Commercial Company, who was also a former Atka teacher, was given quarters and provisions in the village to try to straighten out its financial situation.

There were other, predictable effects of demoralization in the 1930s. Atka has fish, game birds, octopus, shellfish, sea lions, reindeer (introduced early in this century by the government), and edible plants, but morale was too low for the cooperation needed to gather each type of food at precisely the optimum time. There were personal conflicts and some child neglect; tuberculosis had long been a scourge. One thing the people did have: sourdough. No one has recorded exactly when Atkans learned to put yeast, potatoes, cornmeal, dried fruit, and anything else that would ferment in a keg and wait for the process to take its course, but a revenue cutter officer noted "alcohol abuse" already present in the late 1800s.

The Atkans themselves, in spite of their problems, were basically capable people. Their chief, William Dirks, Sr., who appears in Mrs. Oliver's memoir, was the son of a Netherlander who married a local woman. The community had some hard-working men and women who tried to act responsibly even in the generally depressed conditions preceding World War II, when U.S. military presence in the islands was increasing. In the summer of 1934, a Coast and Geodetic Survey vessel was based in Nazan Bay, where the village was and is located, to carry forward, despite the often unfavorable weather, the charting offshore and mapping on land as part of the first accurate mapping of the Aleutians by the United States. It was known by then that Japanese ships were scouting the islands. The U.S. Army and its Air Force were secretly becoming active.

When, responding to the Japanese invasion of Kiska and Attu Islands and to the bombing and strafing of those island villages not captured, the U.S. forces moved in with ships, planes, and shore units, there were more outsiders than ever before in this isolated region. Before the war, Atka and Attu would not see a trader's vessel or a Coast Guard cutter for about three months in the winter. As late as the early 1930s, without a short-wave radio there was no way to send out a message, no matter how great the need. Even in other seasons, communication of any kind west of Unalaska was rare since there was no government mail delivery and there were no airstrips for planes. The captain of any vessel, as a kind gesture, might bring the mail. Although they were remarkable navigators, the Aleuts, in their small boats, could not travel the distances between groups of islands in the often bad weather. The Chain, it must be remembered, is a thousand miles long.

The third major invasion of the Aleutian Islands occurred on June 7, 1942, when the Japanese landed at Attu and took all residents prisoner. This third invasion differed in several ways from the Russian and American invasions of the preceding centuries. It was a military action; it did not have immediate economic motivations; and it was even less welcome to the Aleuts because they feared the Japanese. They were already repeating tales of Japanese fishermen and hunters who had landed surreptitiously on the islands for poaching and to steal from residents' camps. The military invasion caused great material damage but little loss of civilian life, since the local people—except the poor Attuans— had been promptly evacuated. U.S. military personnel, however, did suffer injury and death.

In June 1942, two U.S. seaplane tenders were anchored in Nazan Bay. Because the planes were making bombing raids against the Japanese to the west, there was fear of retaliation. The villagers, encouraged by their resident Bureau of Indian Affairs advisers (the wife a teacher and the husband a maintenance man), moved out to their fishing camps for greater safety. In their absence Navy men, in order to discourage the Japanese, set fire to the village, destroying everything but two or three houses. The Atkans, returning to their village, saw the fire but were too late to save anything. The teachers and villagers had only a few minutes before boarding the ships for evacuation. As lawyers representing the Aleuts in a later reparations claim wrote, "The evacuation of Atka could not have been more chaotic."

The Atkans' three-year sojourn at Killisnoo in southeast Alaska, near the Tlingit Indian community of Angoon, was a test of their resourcefulness, skill, and patience. The BIA couple accompanied them and remained at Killisnoo for a year to teach and help with construction and communications. The evacuees were housed in the shedlike bunkhouses and mess hall of a disused fish-meal plant, built to be occupied only in the commercial fishing season and inadequate for year-round living in the damp forest climate. Tuberculosis and other diseases persisted even though the people were under federal care, and there were deaths among young and old. The people initially had to be supplied with all necessities—cooking utensils, food, blankets, fuel—and then gradually, after getting clothing and building materials, they improved the living quarters, fixed up a schoolroom, and built a church. They probably also assembled fishing equipment. Nevertheless, having come from a treeless region, they never felt at home in the great forests and heavy undergrowth of southeast Alaska.

At the end of World War II, the Atkans returned to Atka, which— along with other Aleutian villages—was being rebuilt by the American government. The Attuans, however—those who survived their captivity in Japan—were not allowed to return to their island, which was militarily strategic but much too isolated for civilian use. Few in number (only four men, four women, and seven children were well enough to return to the Aleutians), and needing modern services, the Attuans were taken to Atka, finally arriving, after a long circuitous journey, six months after the Atkans had returned there. Atkans and Attuans now faced a social test. In much earlier times they had been enemies, and they still spoke different dialects. (Long before the Attuan resettlement, and even before the nineteenth-century movement of Atka and Amlia people between their two islands, another whole community had been resettled. In 1790 the Russian trade-hunters, having already heavily hunted the sea otters around Amchitka, moved its residents to Atka to stop hunting for a while. Although the Amchitka people had returned home in 1812, one wonders whether Amchitka became an Atka fox island because of that long-ago association.)

When the Olivers arrived after the war, the military was still active in the Aleutians and there was even a small army unit on Atka itself. The Olivers went as government employees with the specific tasks of re-establishing the school and helping the Atkans with their postwar problems. Simeon was an official "liaison" between the village and the U.S. government, and Ethel was schoolteacher for the thirty-seven village children. Their actual duties, needless to say, were incredibly varied and challenging. In addition to the uncertainty of postwar recovery, there was another reason for discouragement. The captivity, the loss of homes, and the evacuation were the final blows in a period of depression: the Great Depression of the 1930s had ruined the market for the luxury silver fox and blue fox furs. Fortunately, the Olivers were unusually well qualified, full of energy, and eager to accept new challenges.

The U.S. government had been sending representatives to Atka for some decades before the Olivers arrived. Atka had been one of the communities to receive a school in the early years of federal school construction between 1912 and 1918, and in 1912–14 a teacher there had opposed the dominant trader because of his unfair practices. In the 1930s, the Alaska Native Service (Indian Bureau) school had only a single teacher, who could not handle all the problems presented by the community. In addition to the endemic tuberculosis, there were other respiratory illnesses, accidents, and especially infant deaths. The teacher, it must be recalled, had in her clinic only the prewar range of medicines, not the "wonder drugs" of the late forties and the fifties, and she was not a trained nurse. The only medical help came from a Coast Guard cutter ship's surgeon who might make a couple of one-day visits in the summer. There was a new hospital at Unalaska, but in the winter months there was no vessel or airplane to transport a patient to it.

About 1931 the old school, which was much weathered and out of date, was replaced with a larger one. In the second half of the 1930s, a couple instead of a single teacher was sent, and apparently communications also improved. The 1930s Atka structure, still a one-room school, also included a small "clinic" and three large rooms and bath for the teacher, all under one roof. Water was piped down from a spring on the hill behind the school. The Olivers in their 1945 structure had an improvement: a generator to provide electricity.

One of the hardest requirements has always been the maintenance of a schedule for classroom sessions. Before the addition of village health aides and community officers and workers with various responsibilities, the teachers were frequently interrupted to send an emergency radio message, help the visiting public health nurse, or guide and entertain Coast Guard officers or state or federal supervisors. Something was always interrupting classroom routine.

Two hundred years earlier, the Chain had been a geographic frontier; in the postwar period of the mid-1940s, it—like the rest of Alaska—was approaching a political frontier. The status of the whole territory would change: schools, social services, land use, economy, and the status of the Aleutian peoples. But in 1946 the Aleuts and their teachers were not thinking about statehood, state-run schools that would succeed the BIA nearly everywhere, oil revenues, or millions of dollars of reimbursement for lost lands: they were interested in re-establishing a familiar life. Yet, for adaptation to all the changes ahead, education was essential.

The Olivers had some advantages that many new teachers in Alaska do not have. They were somewhat older and more experienced; they considered Alaska their home and made their living by talking and writing about it. They therefore appreciated any new information—a good attitude anywhere, especially since some teachers tend to insist on imparting information instead of receiving it. There were village problems on Atka island, as we will see, but Mrs. Oliver seemed always optimistic that these could be managed. Long-term problems of the fur trade and the fish catch required wider attention and had to be faced later, after the year of this book. For health care and other assistance, both community and teachers benefited from the presence of the military, which continued on Adak Island (where the Olivers visited) after the Atka installation was closed. Not many village teachers have that kind of help. We must hope that outside help from some source continues to be still available, since Atka's frequent bad weather prevents bush planes from buzzing in and out, as they do for many interior Eskimo and Indian villages and for coastal communities closer to large centers.

Atka in 1946–47 was busy with new decisions, new activities. This was an important period of renewal and hope. After the generally optimistic year of Ethel Oliver's memoir, however, the local situation, at least the economy, became somewhat less hopeful. On mountainous Atka, as on most of the islands, it was difficult to travel far on land. Boats were essential not only for fishing and sea mammal hunting but also for coastal travel to bird rookeries and good places for shellfish, for landing to catch foxes, and for transporting goods to campsites. After the war, the community succeeded in getting a few boats by various means. The economy, however, could still not be adequately developed. Some islands, occupied by various government agencies, could not be trapped, or the foxes were in poor condition. In any case, long furs had become less popular than the short furs.

Though the marine resources were adequate for family subsistence, there were no big stocks of crab, salmon, and other marketable marine products that would bring needed cash income, at least not without factory ships. Kodiak Island, the Alaska Peninsula, and the Aleutian Islands westward to Unalaska, but not farther, did have commercial resources. Atka and Attu men therefore had to go to those locations for seasonal work. A few people moved even farther—to Anchorage, for example. Young women in the villages continued an old trend: they married white men. The result was an excess of single Aleut men. The Atka community, nevertheless, apparently remained strong.

By 1970–71, Atka had a population of 86 (93 in 1980) plus the two teachers. It was larger than several other villages but small compared with King Cove (252) and Sand Point (265), which also had white populations. Atka had a more traditional organization, authorized by the Indian Reorganization Act in the 1930s but actually continuing the chief's role, regardless of modern designation. In 1970–71 Atka had 22 housing units and 27 children in school, ranging from kindergarten to eighth grade. The number of households evidently had remained stable since 1947. The village was reported to have a boat dock but no airstrip.

Indian Bureau schools built in the 1950s and 1960s, particularly those in larger mainland villages, were impressive plants, with a guest room, quarters for two teacher-couples, utility room or building, kitchen for school lunch preparation, and other features. Along with the many improvements, there was, in the Natives' opinion, an important disadvantage. From the beginning of American education, school children were forbidden to use their own language. Teachers rarely tried to learn the language of their students and so were not able to translate and explain in the language of the children's homes; Mrs. Oliver was a good-natured exception. This situation improved in the 1970s, when several Aleuts were trained to teach in both English and Aleut, and Atka was one of the first schools to be involved in this change.

In 1970, the four grades of high school were taught only in the Unalaska school. Though there were four larger Aleut communities, Unalaska was so located that it was easy for students to come there from outlying villages. There was an alternative for high school students: the Mt. Edgecumbe School, which had been established at Sitka in southeast Alaska soon after World War II on the grounds of a U.S. Navy installation turned over to the Bureau of Indian Affairs. Young people from all over Alaska were brought by the BIA to the Mt. Edgecumbe High School; Mrs. Oliver sent some of her promising pupils there when they completed all the grades she could offer in her one-room schoolhouse. (After high school instruction was added to the elementary grades in many village schools in the late 1970s, Mt. Edgecumbe School was closed. It was reopened in the mid-1980s.)

Providing high school instruction in villages that desired to keep their youths at home was a somewhat controversial policy in a period of fast technological and social change that brought telephones and computers to the village schools. In 1985, Atka had a total enrollment of only twenty-one students for preschool through twelfth grade; this does at least indicate that high school instruction was being offered. There were two certified teachers with a "secondary education coordinator."

Alaska's change in political status from Territory to State in 1959 did not have as great an effect on the Native* villages as did passage of the

---

*It is proper now to use the word "Native" (always capitalized). The peoples of Alaska when they organized in the 1960s chose a common designation, and "Native," formerly a denigrating expression, became a prideful term, like "Black" instead of "Negro." Mrs. Oliver's journals, of course, were written before this convention was adopted.

Alaska Native Claims Settlement Act of 1971 (ANCSA). This act divided the state into ethnic/language regions, with an investment corporation to be formed in each region. The Aleut Corporation had a land entitlement of 1,250,000 subsurface acres and 52,000 surface acres—the difference evidently indicating recognition of the scattered island situation in an ocean domain—and a cash entitlement of $40 million. (According to another source, the actual amount was about $22 million.) Every person enrolled as a Native, as defined by the Act, became a shareholder in village and regional corporations. The money was to be divided among 3,249 people on the rolls in 14 villages. Villages could organize as profit or nonprofit corporations. While the regions were principal recipients of land and cash, the villages in a second step would select land and receive money and could disburse it to individuals.

In the course of implementing ANCSA provisions, even an isolated village like Atka learned much about modern business and politics. The learning experience did not, however, guarantee profits. Up to the mid-1980s, most of the village corporations were not income producing. And of course there were delays and complications. As late as 1972 Atka had only monthly boat service and weather might delay even that. By this time, however, all schools were supposed to have radio communication.

As part of a general movement in Alaska in the 1960s to form Native associations, the Aleut League had been organized in December 1967 and joined other regional associations in the Alaska Federation of Natives (AFN). Later the Alaska Native Foundation, formed by the AFN, received grants for research and various programs to help the Natives. The experience of all the Native peoples—north Alaska Eskimos (Inupiat), southwest Alaskan Eskimos (Yuit), Athapaskan Indians in the interior, southeast Alaskan Indians ("Northwest Coast"), and Aleuts—working together was good preparation for the campaign to get congressional action on the Native claims issue. Though none of the best-known Aleut leaders came from Atka, it participated like other communities in various new programs and elections.

In 1977, the nonprofit Aleut League, "devoted to development and delivery of social services to the Aleut people," merged with the Aleutian Planning Commission to form the Aleutian/Pribilof Islands Association, Inc. (A/PIA). To attend meetings of the A/PIA and other organizations is always a problem for the Atka and Attu people, however, because of uncertain transportation. The two communities on the Pribilof Islands, the famous "seal islands" in the Bering Sea north of the Chain, have similarly had a transportation problem.

To deal with the many federal, state, and private agencies now operating in Alaska, Aleut organizations had to come in from the sea: they do most of their work in Anchorage. In Mrs. Oliver's days in the Territory, Juneau, the capital in the "Southeast," was the source of instructions and funds, and for teachers it is still important. For Aleutian Natives the much closer Anchorage is the center of action. Patients are sent, if possible, to the Public Health Service Hospital there. Young people go there to high school and college. Aleut women give lessons in basket weaving, and artists work in Anchorage studios.

A/PIA action went beyond Alaska to Washington, D.C. A reparations claim was made for compensation for losses suffered when people were removed from their islands during World War II. In 1983 the Commission on Wartime Relocation and Internment of Civilians issued a favorable recommendation containing the provisions that Congress should:

1. Establish a fund of $5 million to be expended for community, educational, cultural, or historical rebuilding and for medical or social services;

2. Appropriate funds for payment of $5,000 to each of the "few hundred surviving Aleuts evacuated from the Aleutian or Pribilof Islands";

3. Appropriate funds and direct the relevant agency to rebuild and restore the churches damaged or destroyed, preference to be given to Aleuts in performance of the work;

4. Appropriate adequate funds through the public working budget for the Army Corps of Engineers to clear away the debris remaining from World War II in and around populated areas; and

5. Declare Attu to be Native land and be conveyed to the Aleuts through their corporation, provided that the Native corporation can negotiate an agreement with the Coast Guard that would allow it to continue its essential functions on the island.

The next step was to obtain action by Congress. An advisory committee of Aleut leaders was formed and met frequently to work with lawyers, consultants, and A/PIA staff. Nearly all were officeholders, such as the (for profit) Aleut Corporation president and (nonprofit) A/PIA chairman. The only woman member was an Aleut Corporation board member from Atka. (Her surname indicates that she probably had married a non-Aleut.)

Congress took no action in 1984. In 1985, Senate Bill 5222, cosponsored by Hawaii and Alaska senators, was reintroduced to implement the commission's recommendations. An identical bill, except that it related only to Aleuts, was introduced in the House.

Meanwhile, there was action on an old (1951) lawsuit initiated under the Indian Claims Commission Act, asking compensation from the Federal Government for not having dealt fairly with Aleuts. The Department of Justice proposed to pay $2.5 million to nine communities (of the "Aleut tribe"), excluding the two on the Pribilof Islands that had been under direct federal administration a long time for the internationally regulated fur seal hunt there. The nine villages had to agree to the settlement on this case, labeled Docket 369. By the fall of 1985, the offer had been unanimously accepted and Congress had appropriated the money. It was deposited in the Indian Trust Fund, earning interest, pending approval of a plan for distribution.

By law, at least 20 percent would go to tribal and/or community programs, and 80 percent could be distributed to individuals; but the entire amount could be given to communities—that is, distribution to individuals was permitted but not mandated. The Indian Bureau plan for distribution of the money became effective in October 1986. Since Atka's population included 88 persons legally defined as Natives, the island would receive 7.2 percent (estimated at $180,000) of the total fund. The money was expected to be used for a development project, education, or assistance to elderly and handicapped.

In addition to capturing a crucial year in the history of the Aleutian peoples and their region, Ethel Oliver's *Journal of an Aleutian Year* allows us to become acquainted with a remarkable couple. Simeon Oliver, son of an Eskimo mother and a Norwegian father, was born in a mainland village but spent much of his early life in Unalaska, in the eastern Aleutians, and was educated at a Methodist boarding school there. (In fact, he had grown up with some of the people he met in Atka after the war.) Because Unalaska had been a commercial and Orthodox Church center since Russian times, Simeon's life there was more varied than that of young people on outlying islands. After attending college, he became a concert pianist, lecturer, and writer, author of *Back to the Smoky Sea,* a book well known to older Alaskans.

Ethel was born in Valley, Washington, and grew up in Portland, Oregon. Her first husband, Ernest Ross, was a carpenter who worked on the building of the Alaska Railroad. Advised to do outdoor work as a result of a respiratory illness, he took Ethel and their three-year-old son and went trapping. For ten years they trapped along the old Iditarod mail trail in the Rainy Pass area of the Alaska Range, and Ethel claims that these "pioneering experiences" played an important part in her later career. On the trapline, she taught her young son, and after Ernest Ross's death of appendicitis in 1935, she took a degree in education and began her teaching career. (In the years that followed, she was to teach at many levels of education, from the first regular kindergarten in Anchorage to adult education courses at the University of Alaska, and in myriad capacities she has continued her advocacy of the Aleutian peoples.)

Ethel and Simeon Oliver were married in 1943. They were at home in Anchorage when they were not on tour, and they made their living by talking and writing about Alaska. When they went to Atka, not many stateside civilians had become residents of the Chain. They were an energetic couple, alert to new situations and open to new experiences. They had a wide range of interests, as the reader will see. In an isolated village, confinement to classroom and household can result in "cabin fever," something the Olivers certainly avoided, with their active interest in folklore, regional geography, traditional religion, infant care and child-rearing practices, birds, marine life, native foods and their preparation, and other aspects of the local culture and environment.

During her year on Atka, Ethel began the book that was later published as *Aleutian Boy.* She also collected and preserved samples of the local flora for the botanical collections of five American museums and institutions. Having received what they believed to be official permission, she and Simeon, together with the villagers, conducted excavations of several archaeological sites. (It was only later that they learned that such work requires specified institutional sponsorship.) The Olivers' enthusiasm for the folklife and archaeological heritage of the Aleuts seems not only to have brightened their own lives on Atka, but also to have awakened pride and enthusiasm among their Native students and friends. Ethel also kept the journals which later became this book, and which—though she often had to rely on secondhand information—have much to offer ethnologists.

The Olivers did more than simply accept the Atkans. They enjoyed doing things with them. Ethel's interest in learning and using her pupils' language—and her good cheer about her difficulty in pronouncing it—was ahead of its time and must have increased her pupils' eagerness to improve their English. (In her journals, as she makes clear, she transcribed Aleut terms as she heard them, without reference to linguistic authority.) And the Olivers understood the value of reciprocity in a small community, happily trading food from their own stock for gifts of fresh bread from their neighbors' ovens, or trading yarn and fishline for a duck or salmon.

In all communities, regardless of location, teachers are expected to be models and probably also leaders. It is interesting to observe how the Olivers met the continual challenges of their village, for in such intimate rural settings—where the families as well as the children are known—teachers must give more than in-class education; they must give personal help and realistic hope. Unfortunately, many of them tend to keep themselves aloof from their communities. All village teachers should read this journal. They can see that if they become part of a community and give a lot to it, they will receive much in return. The generous and enthusiastic performance of the Olivers on Atka Island provides a good model.

Margaret Lantis

Lexington, Kentucky
February 1987

Bibliographical Note

Regarding the geography, plants and animals, people, history, and almost all aspects of the Aleutian Islands, I recommend *Alaska Geographic* 7, no. 3 (1980), edited by Lael Morgan. The entire issue, entitled "The Aleutians," is devoted to the islands, and contains exceptional pictures. Another useful source is "Alaska's Native People," *Alaska Geographic* 6, no. 3 (1979), edited by Lael Morgan. It has an interesting and useful review of "Important Dates in Native History" in Alaska (pp. 285–98), with an account of each dated event or development.

There is also much of value in Volume 5 of the *Handbook of North American Indians* (1984), published by the Smithsonian Institution. It is devoted to the Arctic and includes two articles on the Aleuts.

Also helpful in preparing this introduction were Barbara S. Smith, *Russian Orthodoxy in Alaska* (Alaska Historical Commission, 1980); John C. Kirtland and David F. Coffin, Jr., *The Relocation and Internment of the Aleuts during World War II* (Aleutian/Pribilof Islands Association, 1981); and selected issues of *Aang Angagin, Aang Angaginas,* the newsletter of the Aleutian/Pribilof Islands Association and Aleutian Housing Authority, from 1983 to 1985.

✴JOURNAL OF AN ALEUTIAN YEAR

Simeon Oliver and Ethel Ross Oliver in 1946

❋ JUNE 1 TO JUNE 15, 1946

Along the Aleutian Chain to Atka

"The *North Star* will be in Kodiak for only a few hours on the eighth and we'll leave on the evening tide. You be on board then, because I won't wait for you!" Captain Salenjus sternly warned us as we left the *North Star* at Juneau, bound for a briefing by the officials of the Alaska Native Service, after which we would fly home to Anchorage to take care of personal business for the coming year.

The threat of missing the ship on its annual journey westward along the Aleutian Chain was a dire one. If our proposed Aleutian project in the year ahead was to be a success, it was vitally important that all of our last-minute preparations here and in Anchorage be completed, and that we be back aboard the *North Star* when it left Kodiak on the evening tide on June 8, three days from now. For the next seventy-two hours Captain Salenjus's warning was constantly on our minds as we strove to do all that had to be done: memorizing our instructions from the Alaska Native Service officials, arranging our personal affairs, and even contriving an unusual charter flight from Anchorage to Kodiak. We *had* to meet that deadline.

This project in which we were engaged was the culmination of months of planning. Actually the venture had had its beginning in 1942, when the Japanese had invaded the Aleutian Islands and captured the islands of Attu and Kiska. At that time the natives of Atka had been yanked from their homes, taken to southeastern Alaska, and placed in evacuation camps, to be almost forgotten while Uncle Sam sought to recapture the western Aleutian Islands and win the war in the Pacific. Now they were at last being returned to their island home, and we were to spend a year with them, helping them rebuild their village and resume their normal lives.

My husband, Simeon Oliver, although born and raised in the Aleutian Islands, was not an Aleut. His father, James Oliver, was a Norwegian fisherman and trapper who had married a young Eskimo woman. Simeon's mother had died in childbirth when Simeon, whose Eskimo name was *Nutchuk* (Little Seal), was two years old. His father, unable to care for him and his baby sister, placed him in the Jesse Lee Home, a Methodist mission at Unalaska; his sister was placed with the Baptist mission on Woody Island, near Kodiak. Simeon had therefore grown up with many of these native Aleuts; he had gone to school in Unalaska with some of the Atkans, and had worked with others in the fur-seal industry in the Pribilofs, in the whaling station at Akutan, and in the

Bristol Bay canneries and on the cod and halibut banks of the Bering Sea, before he had gone to college in "the States" and become a noted musician, author, and lecturer. He still loved the area and its people. Because of his knowledge of the region he served with Army G-2 in the Alaskan Theatre during the war, and had learned of the plight of the evacuees. After the Aleutian Campaign he had worked to help the Aleuts get permission to return to their homes.

In May of 1945 we were visited by Don C. Foster, the general superintendent of the Alaska Native Service, who told us that at last the Atkans were to be returned to their island. They would be assisted in the task of rebuilding their destroyed village by an A.N.S. construction engineer, but the man would be able to remain with them for only a limited time, since his services were also needed in other locations. Foster asked us if we would take his place the following year, when the rebuilding was largely completed. We eagerly accepted the invitation. For the remainder of 1945 and throughout the next spring most of our spare moments were devoted to planning and preparing for this adventure. In the spring of 1946 I took time off from our lecture tour in the States to order the groceries and other supplies which we would need in the coming year. When word of our plans spread among our friends and associates, I was asked to make collections of Atka plants and flowers for the University of Michigan, Iowa University, and the Smithsonian Institution.

We cut short our lecture tour in late spring and sailed from Seattle aboard the motor ship *North Star* on June 1. This vessel was the supply ship for the Alaska Native Service; it was specially designed for service in the polar regions, and under Captain Charlie Salenjus had operated in both the Arctic and the Antarctic before the war. It now carried supplies and A.N.S. personnel to remote communities along the entire Alaska coastline and the Aleutian Chain, and on this trip it even carried livestock for the Atkans: rabbits, chickens, and sheep.

When we left the *North Star* at Juneau we spent the remainder of the day, and most of the next morning, with Don Foster and with other officials of the A.N.S. Later we boarded a Pacific Northern airliner, with the Alaskan territorial flag painted on its nose, and set out for Anchorage. We couldn't see it as we crossed the Gulf of Alaska, but we knew that somewhere down below us the *North Star* was moving steadily toward Kodiak, and we resolved anew that we would make every possible effort to be aboard it when it sailed from that port on the eighth.

Although we managed to take care of everything else on our immediate schedule when we reached Anchorage, it appeared for a time that it would be impossible for us to reach Kodiak in time to rejoin the *North Star*. In growing desperation we went from airline to airline, but there simply were no flights to Kodiak scheduled until after the eighth. It was after midnight when we finally persuaded a friend at the Alaska Airlines office that it was absolutely imperative for us to reach Kodiak within the next forty hours. Even then he was unable to arrange a direct flight for us, but he could, and did, do the next best thing. There would be a charter flight to Naknek on the morning of the eighth, taking a planeload of commercial fishermen to their summer jobs, and the plane could return to Anchorage by way of Kodiak.

We spent the next day winding up our business arrangements for the coming year and packing items that we felt would be valuable, if not essential, to us in the months ahead, and finally we tumbled wearily into bed for a few hours of badly needed sleep. Early on the morning of the eighth we were at the airport with our overweight baggage, and soon we were on board the unfurnished DC-3 with the fishermen. After they disembarked at Naknek we were the only passengers on the plane during the side trip to Kodiak, flying over the Valley of Ten Thousand Smokes and the treacherous waters of Shelikof Strait, and finally over Kodiak's Women's Bay and the U.S. Navy installation. At the Navy docks we spotted our vessel, the *North Star*. "We've made it!" I cried joyously. "Captain Salenjus won't sail without us!"

Our plane set down at the Navy airfield, and as soon as our baggage was unloaded we engaged a convenient cab to take it, and us, to our ship. Our cabbie drove us right out onto the dock and deposited us and our belongings at the foot of the *North Star's* gangplank. The ship appeared deserted, but then Sig, the chief steward, made his appearance and welcomed us back aboard. "I see that you made it," he greeted us. "The captain and most of the crew are in town yet, but we'll be sailing before long."

We heaved sighs of relief. Simeon paid the cabdriver and Sig helped us aboard with our gear, most of which would have to be stowed under canvas and lashed down on the boat deck. We chatted with Sig for a few moments and then went to our stateroom, tired but happy that we had managed to meet Captain Salenjus's deadline. Just before we turned in we realized that we had forgotten our hip boots, which we would surely need; the islands are notoriously wet, and one spends a great deal of time on the beaches, gathering seafoods. "We'll pick some up along the way," Simeon promised, and then we went to bed and to sleep.

Sometime during the night a slight commotion on deck and on the dock half awakened us. The *North Star* was leaving Kodiak. We had slept right through two dinner calls and dinner itself. Unconcerned, we went back to sleep and awakened again only at the first call to breakfast, to find that we were somewhere well down Shelikof Strait, with the headlands of the western portion of the island off our port bow. The weather was still clear, and the vessel moved steadily on a quiet sea, save for a very slight ground swell. We took a swing around the decks before breakfast, refreshed after our long sleep. Odors of frying ham and bacon drifted up to us on the crisp morning air. The second call for breakfast found us already seated at the table.

At breakfast we learned that two ladies had joined the *North Star* at Juneau: Jeannette Stewart, daughter of B. D. Stewart, head of the Territorial Bureau of Mines, and Mildred "Buster" Keaton, who for many years had been a nurse in the Arctic. She would serve as ship's nurse on this voyage into the Arctic and would visit the various villages en route, checking on the health of the people and giving immunization shots. Jeannette, too, was making the round trip. She was a botanist, and she planned to gather specimens of the island and Arctic flora for the New York Botanical Gardens. I was delighted to learn this. Here was my chance to observe at first hand a trained botanist at work, if she would permit me to tag along. I broached the subject and received a warm invitation to join her when we reached Karluk later that morning.

Other fellow passengers greeted us. They told us that we had been lucky to miss the Gulf crossing, which had been pretty rough. Several of the native children who had been aboard had gotten off the ship at Kodiak, and others would be leaving us at Karluk. We asked Herman Turner, who was in charge of the animals, about the stock for Atka, and he reported that they were doing well. He told us that Mr. Holland, an A.N.S. school official from Juneau, was on board, too.

During breakfast that Sunday morning the *North Star* dropped anchor, about a mile offshore, at the village of Karluk, toward the western end of Kodiak Island. The vessel rose and fell on a heaving sea. Faintly in the distance we could hear the bells of the little Russian Orthodox church on a hill above the village, calling the people to worship. The village was spread along a gravel beach, facing the open sea. There was a slight indentation of the island at this point. Mountains rose on either side of the village, and heavy surf pounded at the foot of precipitous cliffs farther along the shore. Back of the little village green slopes reached far back into a valley and up to where the melting snows of the alpine meadows emptied cool waters into a large lake on the valley floor. From the lake a river meandered down the valley and emptied into the sea. The village nestled near its mouth.

We got our jackets and camera and stood at the rail, watching as a power dory raced out from the village and pulled in alongside the *North Star*. Happy children clambered down a rope ladder, bags and bundles were handed down, and moments later they were whisked away. In the meantime our launch was lowered over the side and loaded with supplies for the A.N.S. teachers. Jeannette, with a collecting box, Simeon, and I piled in also and went ashore with the crew. A tiny dock, sheltered from the heavy surf, lay just inside the mouth of the river. The launch pulled alongside it, and as the crew unloaded the supplies a young native offered to take us across the river in his skiff.

"Looks like a good fish year!" Simeon shouted over the roar of the skiff's outboard motor. The river was alive with salmon which were jumping or swimming in the waters beneath us. I had never seen so many. They were all on their way upriver to spawn in Karluk Lake.

"Strike on!" the boatman shouted back. "We only catch for ourselves. Cannery not working."

Once ashore, we walked up a path along the river bank, past the frame houses of the village, to a bridge suspended on cables. As we crossed the swaying bridge we looked down to see thousands of swimming salmon struggling to get up the stream. Some of the small village houses were on this side of the river, too. Above them on the hill stood the quaint little church. Its slowly tolling bell told us that church services were beginning. Up a well-worn winding pathway we walked with men, women, and children dressed in their Sunday best, on their way to the church. As we neared the church we could hear the singing of the priest and those villagers who had already assembled. We paused to listen as children from the ship looked from the doorway and, recognizing us, smiled. A well-dressed Aleut man came out and invited us to come in to watch the service or to worship with them. We hadn't long to be ashore and we did want to follow Jeannette, but we stepped inside to see the interior of the church and to listen for a few minutes to the chanting. The young man who had opened the door for us whispered softly, "Stay, or leave whenever you wish."

As we entered the main part of the church we smelled a strong odor of burning incense. There are no pews in these Russian churches. Everyone was standing, the women to the left of the center aisle and the men to the right. The singing was all in Russian; the women's high-pitched voices sang in unison with the lay priest, while the men's voices sang tenor, baritone, and bass parts. It was thrilling to hear. Wild flowers in great abundance decked the altar and we caught some of their fragrance through the odor of the burning incense. Simeon recalled that this was the holiday which the Russian churches in Alaska celebrate with the season's first flowers. We left quietly a few minutes later. The young man at the door smiled a quiet good-bye and invited us to come again.

Farther up the hill we spotted Jeannette, and we quickly joined her. She had already gathered several flowering specimens and carefully placed them, roots, leaves, and all, in her long aluminum box. I followed her around on the sunny hillside and received my first practical botany lesson since my college days. Jeannette showed me how she kept notes on the various specimens in a little notebook. All that she showed and told me was much the same as Dr. Bessie Kanause, the University of Michigan botanist, had given me back in Ann Arbor, but here it was in the field in actual practice. I was getting a taste of the pleasure which lay in store for me on Atka.

Not far from us on the hillside a yellow-crowned sparrow whistled its plaintive three notes. It was the first time that I had heard the bird that year. To me it has always said, "Oh, dear me!" John Burroughs, the great American naturalist, who as a member of the famed Harriman Expedition to Alaska knew this little songster on Kodiak, wrote of its song, "There were only three notes, but they were from the depths of the bird's soul. In them was all the burden of the mystery and pathos of life." This was not only the first time, but it was also the last morning that we were privileged to hear this appealing song for a year, for although the bird ranges as far west as the Shumagin Islands, we did not hear it again after we left Kodiak Island.

Simeon called my attention to another bird that was unfamiliar to me, the Aleutian longspur. The first one he pointed out to me sat on a nearby knoll, threw back its little head, and poured forth its liquid song.

He said that it brought back many happy memories of his boyhood summer days on Unalaska. Other little birds flew about us, chirping or singing snatches of song, and Simeon sat on the grassy hillside, enjoying them all and watching the scene below while Jeanette and I scurried about, hunting flowers.

A cooling, grass-bending breeze swept across the hill and brought with it the hailing voices of those down at the launch. Jeannette carefully tucked in her flowers and fastened the lid of the case. She slung the carrying strap over her shoulder, and the three of us trotted down the hill, past the little church, to the river bank where the young fisherman waited with his skiff to ferry us across the teeming river to the launch. Soon we were back aboard the *North Star,* well pleased with our lovely morning. We were not on board long before the launch was hoisted aboard and placed in its cradle on the forward well deck, and soon the ship was on its way to Chignik, on the Alaska Peninsula. The captain said that we were due there sometime that night. This was Simeon's birthplace, and we didn't want to miss it, so we decided that we would turn in soon after dinner.

After lunch I spent some time in Jeannette's cabin, watching as she placed her flower specimens between folded newspapers and copied onto the edge of the papers the data from her notebook. This, too, corresponded to the directions which Dr. Kanause had given me. My confidence bolstered, I joined Simeon at the rail and he pointed out the snow-capped peaks of the Alaska Peninsula in the distance. Off to the south we could see the Trinity Islands as they faded from view.

At three-thirty the next morning Simeon was up with his camera, shooting the dawn as we entered the harbor of Chignik. We were exploring the town by four o'clock. A little later we returned for coffee in the galley and to put on warmer clothes, for a cold wind blew down from the snowy hills. Soon we were off again, around the crescent of beach toward a pinnacle of rock on the shore a half-mile from the dock. Here we caught up with Jeannette, gathering flowers, and we helped her. Her delight was unbounded when, near a small seam of coal, I found some plant fossils of deciduous leaves and conifers. Then we searched among the layers of shale and found a rich store of fossil plant life. We returned to the ship laden with these and with several varieties of plants in Jeannette's specimen case.

On the dock one of our Eskimo crew members was fishing with a crab net. He brought up a pogy, the first that I had seen, though I had read about them. We could see two others in the clear waters below the dock, along with several sculpins, Dolly Varden trout, and a three-foot-long halibut..

We went aboard and had breakfast. Sig told us that we would not sail for an hour and a half, as there was still more freight to be unloaded, so we went ashore again. Jeannette and I headed for some low hills, in sight of the ship, to see if there were any new plants showing that high up. Simeon stopped to talk with a cluster of village boys who had gathered on the dock near the afterdeck of the *North Star*, watching the sheep which had thrust their heads up between the slats of their crates. They were keeping a wary eye on a dog on the dock. Later we saw Simeon sauntering along the beach, now and then stopping to pick up something, look at it briefly, and then toss it away. When it became evident that spring had not yet arrived on these hills I deserted Jeannette and joined him on the beach. Slowly we meandered along. Tiny gray wrens hopped among the boulders, a seal played a little way offshore, snipes and sandpipers ran along the water's edge, and harlequin ducks, pintails, and old squaws swam and dived in the bay waters a little distance out.

"Find anything?" I asked.

"Not yet, but as I walked along I was thinking of how much stuff the tides do bring in. I remember once out at Unalaska some Aleuts coming to the village from the adjacent island, Sedanka, told us that they had seen a 'small schooner' on the beach on the south side of the island. One Saturday, soon after that, some of us boys hiked fifteen miles across to the other side to investigate it. We found a Chinese or Japanese junk. We boarded it and rummaged through the funny little ship, covering it from top to bottom and from stem to stern. We came out with several coins with square holes in their centers and with chopsticks, some plain and others lacquered in bright yellows and reds. How that little vessel had drifted so far we, of course, could not tell. I can still almost smell the odor of waterlogged teak and bamboo. Under its small bunks we found some water-soaked garments, blankets, and raffia mats. The little ship had been badly battered and now it had come to rest, lodged securely high on the gravel beach. Its two masts were broken and its hull was half full of water. We could only wonder what had happened to its crew.

"Nothing so intriguing here," he added. "I'll bet that the islands today are strewn with debris from the war, though."

We pulled out of Chignik in the middle of the morning to head westward to the village of Perryville, not far down the Peninsula. It was a beautiful morning. The world of blue sea, green hills, and white, snow-capped mountains was bathed by the sun which at three-thirty that morning we had seen rise a fiery red. The breeze, however, was not warm on this bright June morning.

Chignik Bay is guarded on the west by a very unusual promontory. It juts out from a high mountain ridge and as it reaches out into the sea, where ceaseless pounding by the surf has eroded it, it takes on the appearance of a many-turreted castle. Early navigators named it Castle Cape. This is one of the most outstanding landmarks along the shores of the Alaska Peninsula. Not only do the peaks of this promontory rise several hundred feet, but the entire projection, from beach to top, is highly colored by mineralization. As we rounded it on our way south and west it was indescribably magnificent, rising above the vividly blue waters. We sailed close enough to have it tower above us and to see that thousands of murres, puffins, cormorants, kittiwakes, and auklets were nesting in its colorful cliffs.

Late in the afternoon we sailed between the coast and sheltering islands to drop anchor abreast the small frame houses which were scattered along the beach at the site of Perryville. In the background Veniaminof Volcano emitted a small puff of steam which rose whitely against the blue sky. This volcano is of such enormous size, even with its top blown off, that one views it in amazement and wonders at what devastation must have been wrought when that huge crater was formed. The highest rim of the crater is 8,400 feet high, and the mountain is snow-capped the year round.

The launch was put down and we climbed in, but we were unable to land and had to return to the ship. The next time the crew used a barge to take the cargo and us ashore. There was no sign of human life, but we were joyfully greeted by ten dogs. One of the crew members said that the villagers were all fishing above Chignik. They had left the dogs to fend for themselves. They appeared to be well fed. Simeon said that they could live on ground squirrels, which were abundant in the area, or forage as the foxes do along the beach. We built a bonfire on the beach and returned to it after collecting plants. While the crew finished unloading the cargo and putting it safely into a small warehouse we took a walk along the beach. Not far from the village we came across some very fresh bear tracks in the sandy dunes above the beach. They were so large that Simeon could put both feet in one print. The prospect of meeting one of these huge monsters face to face was enough to send us back down the beach to our fire.

Two curious seals, about a stone's throw out in the water, poked their heads up and looked at us with their large round eyes. They swam alongside us until we came abreast of the village, and then they dove and came up farther out. A cool breeze had sprung up. Until it was time to go, about midnight or one o'clock, we sat and watched the clouds drift across the face of the moon, whose reflection glimmered on the water. The dogs wanted to go with us when we left; we had to push them off the barge, and the last sound we heard as we reached the ship was their doleful malemute chorus coming forlornly over the water.

We headed to sea with a threat of "weather," for the wind had freshened and dark clouds were rolling in from the Pacific. We would not be in open water for long, however, for sometime during the night we would reach the shelter of the Shumagin Islands. We slept through breakfast call and all morning. The luncheon bell awakened us, and our day began at noon.

At 3:30 P.M. we put in at the Pacific American Fisheries dock at Squaw Harbor. Here an entire school was to be dismantled, packed up, and put aboard the *North Star* to be taken to Scammon Bay, a little Eskimo village near the mouth of the Yukon River. There was much grousing by the mate and captain about the time that we would lose. Mr. Holland took over and we found him sorting things when we went by the schoolhouse, on our way to the hills for flowers. Two young boys pointed out a hillside where Jeannette and I found, as they had predicted, a mass of brilliant wild flowers. Working daily with her, I was becoming more familiar with these beauties of the Aleutian Chain. Slowly we worked our way up until we reached the mossy, windswept heights. Here we found the fragrant pink *pedicularis* with its fuzzy gray hairs. Jeannette said its common name was lousewort. We also found three types of ground willow, violets, white and yellow cinquefoil, anemones, a white bell like a harebell, a daisy-like rock flower, and a brilliant yellow blossom; I found, and lost, the bud of a flower that promised to be blue.

The dinner bell brought us back to the ship, but later we walked down the beach and found a vein of red jasper in a low cliff and chipped off a few pieces. We also saw where an old lava flow had bubbled down the hill to the beach. Here we found some *pootchky* plants—wild cow parsnip. Simeon broke off several of the sprouting flower stalks, peeled them, and gave them to Jeannette and me to eat. He said that this was a favorite spring vegetable among the Aleuts. It must be carefully peeled before being eaten; otherwise a juice which exudes from the plant causes sores around the mouth. On the hill above us an Aleutian longspur whistled its cheery song. In the bay not far from us a sea lion fished. Low tide exposed a wide kelp-covered beach which we examined, looking for the various types of edible foods, but we found little. Figuring that we had exhausted the area, we headed toward the schoolhouse to see if we could help Mr. Holland. He put us all to work packing boxes of supplies. When he offered me the schoolroom curtains I gladly accepted them, thinking that we might need them in Atka.

The fisheries manager and his wife came aboard for coffee before the ship sailed. We found Nurse Keaton in the galley, drinking coffee with Sig. She told us that she had given a hundred and sixty-one vaccinations.

All morning on Wednesday, June 12, we traveled through fog too heavy to make walking on deck pleasant, so we spent the time in the galley, listening to Nurse Keaton tell stories of her years in the North. Some were dramatic, others were amusing, and all were extremely interesting.

"You should write a book," Simeon urged.

"There are too many books written about Alaska now, and many of them are a lot o' rot. Besides," she added, "I'm too busy doing my real job now."

High seas kept us from landing at Belkofski. A little purse seiner appeared out of the mist and came alongside the *North Star*. The man at its wheel lowered one of his windows and yelled to our mate, "She's pretty rough on the beach, but I think you can land with the barge."

"That's Father Hotovitzky!" Simeon exclaimed. "I knew him in Unalaska when I was a boy."

Father Hotovitzky came aboard. Everyone greeted him with hearty hand-shakes. He brought with him several large freshly caught king salmon and announced that they were just beginning to run in this vicinity. The King Cove cannery had canned its first run of 2,500 the day before.

He was delighted to see Simeon and boomed, "Seemyon Oliver!" He lingered on board long enough to have a cup of coffee, and we promised to see him in King Cove later. In the meantime our barge had been lowered and loaded with drums of gasoline and fuel oil. As he climbed aboard his little *Seattle* he smiled and waved, then headed inshore to stand by as the barge was unloaded. We stood on the upper deck and watched. From this distance Belkofski reminded me of a clump of rock flowers growing in a rocky niche, with its cluster of neat, well-painted houses, dominated by the white church, and all nestling amid very green grass against the foot of the brown mountain whose top was lost in the clouds overhead.

The barge returned safely and was hauled aboard. We were soon under way for King Cove, just a short run down the coast. We arrived there in the late afternoon. Father Hotovitzky's little one-masted purse seiner was already tied up, and he stood on the dock to greet us. He had evidently told some children about the animals, because several came aboard and raced for the afterdeck where Mr. Turner was getting ready to feed them. The captain said that we would only be there for an hour, so we hurried to the supply store of the big nine-line cannery and outfitted ourselves with slickers, sou'westers, hip boots, and several pairs of canvas work gloves. Father Hotovitzky went along with us and then insisted, "You must come up to the house and see Momma and have *chai*." Laden with our purchases, and accompanied by the superintendent of the cannery and his wife, Mr. and Mrs. Stenwick, we followed him down a plank walk to the neat little house he shared with his wife. Once inside, he began yelling, "Momma, Momma, *chai, chai!*" We heard an answer from an inner room and then his wife came into view—a small, gentle woman with silvery hair, big blue eyes, and a friendly smile. She called her husband "Poppa."

"Momma, you remember 'Seemyon' Oliver. This is Mrs. Seemyon. They're on their way to Atka." She greeted us and the Stenwicks warmly, then said something to Father Hotovitzky in Russian, excused herself, and left the room.

We wandered about the homey room, admiring the samovars, icons, pictures, and books. Father Hotovitzky took one particular book from the shelves to show us. It was titled *Account of Pedestrian Journeys in the Russian Possessions in America.* This was Mrs. Hotovitzky's translation of Lavrentii A. Zagoskin's memoirs of his travels in what is now Alaska.* She came in just then with tea and cake and shyly turned the conversation to Atka. They told us of the burning of Atka by the U.S. Navy and of the destruction of the church. He said that a sixteen-pound silver icon had melted in the terrific heat.

At that moment Captain Salenjus tooted his whistle for us. We were a bit uneasy; not so Father Hotovitzky. "Take your time. He'll wait for you." We were not so sure. The whistle sounded again, a long blast. We hastily swallowed the last of our tea, picked up our packages, said our thank-yous and good-byes, and left. From the *North Star's* bridge the captain and mate could see us as we hurried along the plank walk to the dock, where members of the crew were waiting to haul the gangplank aboard.

It was late in the afternoon when we left King Cove. The weather was cloudy, and as we headed westward after leaving the cove the wind began to rise. We would, however, be moving along in protected waters among many islands for several hours before we struck out into the open Pacific, along the south side of Unimak Island. After the usual good dinner we visited for a while with members of the crew and the other passengers, and then we went to our cabin where we wrote in our journals before turning in. Sometime toward early morning we were awakened by the heavy rolling of our ship, and we knew that we were in the open sea. I peeked out of the cabin window, but I saw only fog and rough water, so I turned over and went back to sleep.

When we got up we put on our new slickers and took a brisk walk around the wet deck before breakfast. A stiff wind was blowing and now and then a ghostlike "woolie" of whirling water would cut across our bow or hit the vessel. The wind screamed in the rigging, and huge waves crashed over the bow, sending spray up over the superstructure. The sturdy *North Star* was built to take it, however, and ploughed steadily along. Occasionally great flocks of whale-birds flew up from the seething waters ahead of us.

*Some years later these memoirs were published as *Lieutenant Zagoskin's Travels in Russian America, 1842–1844,* translated by Penelope Rainey. Mrs. Hotovitzky's translation was reprinted by the Borgo Press in 1986.

By 6:30 A.M. we were heading into Unimak Pass, next to the recently damaged lighthouse on Scotch Cap. A severe undersea earthquake in the depths of the Aleutian Trench on April 1 had triggered a *tsunami,* or tidal wave, a hundred feet high. Five men lost their lives. We were close enough, also, to see the Alaska Steamship Company's *McKinley,* piled up on the beach where it had run aground in a fog; this had happened on a return trip from the western Aleutians late in the war. For a stretch of several miles we were followed by a herd of playful fur seals which were headed for the Pribilof Islands. They swam alongside the vessel, came up for air with a puff and rose half out of the water to stare at us with bulging eyes for a moment, then disappeared again into the rough seas.

On this trip I had looked forward to seeing one of Alaska's—for that matter, one of the world's—most beautifully symmetrical active volcanoes, one which rivals Japan's Mt. Fuji. Eternally snow-capped Mt. Shishaldin rises almost ten thousand feet above the beaches of Unimak Island. Besides being spectacular, it is the highest peak in the Aleutian Islands, and one of the most active members of the great parade of active volcanoes along the Chain. There are other notable volcanoes on Unimak, including Isanotski and Pogromni, but that day low, fast-moving clouds obscured all of the mountains on this eighty-mile-long island.

Unimak Pass is about twenty miles wide, and very deep. It is the main entrance for shipping from the Pacific Ocean into the Bering Sea. Because of the woolies on this day the water appeared to be smoking. I could now understand why the Bering is sometimes called the Smoky Sea. Today these smoky waters were alive with sea life. We saw whales, sea lions, porpoises, and all manner of sea birds, and of course the migrating fur seals. We stayed on deck for hours, fascinated by this marvelous display.

When the *North Star* entered Akutan Harbor a good stiff wind was blowing the rain in horizontal sheets across our decks. It filled the sailors' pockets; one fellow got drenched twice. It was too rough to launch a boat or even a barge, so we rode at anchor and waited for the storm to subside, which it did before evening. Both the launch and the barge were then put overside and loaded with supplies, some of which were for Mrs. Benedict, the A.N.S. teacher. Jeannette, Simeon, and I went ashore to visit the people and to scour the damp hillside for flowers.

Akutan is a village of about sixty-five people. Its little white frame houses with their red roofs, with the school at one end of the village and the Russian Orthodox church at the other, are situated on a low short stretch of land at the base of abruptly rising hills. It is located on an indentation on the northeast side of the island and protected on all sides by land. Only on the eastern side is it open to the sea, and Akun Island, lying nine miles away in that direction, gives adequate protection from that quarter. Across the bay, just a mile away, lie the remains of a whaling station which ceased operation in the summer of 1939. During the war it served as a location where Lend-Lease Liberty ships were turned over to the Russians. While the whaling station was in operation the Akutan Aleuts had good summer employment near their homes, but after it closed down they had to go to Bristol Bay for the salmon fishing, or up to the Pribilof Islands to work in the annual fur-seal harvest.

The United States flag had been run up in greeting to us. Once we were ashore Simeon introduced me to many of his friends. Jeannette and I then took to the hills to look for flowers, promising to return to the school in a couple of hours. We left Simeon to visit with Hughie McGlashen, one of his boyhood friends. Jeannette and I climbed to the base of a rocky mountain peak where we made a good collection of flowers. The green was surely creeping higher and higher each day.

Later, back at the schoolhouse, Mrs. Benedict served tea, coffee, and cake, and while others danced Mrs. Benedict, Nurse Keaton, Simeon, and I sat and visited. Hughie McGlashen joined us after his store supplies had been unloaded. He told us that nearby Tigalda, Ugamak, Rootak, and Avatanak Islands had been stocked by the villagers with blue foxes. When Simeon asked about the effects of the recent tidal wave, he said that a peculiar thing had happened. The waters rose and fell about every twenty minutes all around the bay, rising higher than the highest tides normally did—almost up to the village houses at the top of the beach—then running out, exposing more beach than the lowest of low tides. This went on for nearly eight hours. He said that the villagers had not been alerted to what could have been a serious disaster. After they did finally learn what had caused the peculiar rising and falling of the tide they went to their fox islands to investigate the damage there. Ugamak, which had taken the brunt of the tidal wave, had been cut in two. The wave had swept completely over the island, carrying away their foxes, cabins, and everything. Their properties were a total loss. He noted, too, that there had been another interesting effect. Kitchen middens, ancient refuse heaps of earlier villages, had been completely exposed or washed away, leaving hundreds of artifacts of stone, bone, and ivory scattered over the hills and along the shores of the island. Mrs. Benedict showed us a fossilized whale eardrum which had been picked up there.

Fog closed down as we left Akutan, and the ship's whistle sounded intermittently throughout the night.

When morning came we went on deck to see how our animals were faring after nearly two weeks in confinement. The sheep seemed to be doing well enough, but we had lost several hens. From time to time Mr. Turner had taken to the galley fresh eggs from their coops. The rabbits were all alive and accounted for, and apparently had suffered no hardship due to the long journey.

The captain said that we would by-pass Unalaska and Umnak islands and the villages of Unalaska and Nikolski and head straight for Atka, which we should reach on the morning of the fifteenth. As we passed it Simeon pointed out Priest Rock, the three-hundred-foot-high pinnacle of rock which guards the entrance to Unalaska Bay and Dutch Harbor. He said that a family of bald eagles usually nested on top of that lofty head. We were both sorry that we were not going to visit the village, for Simeon had been raised in the little Methodist mission at Unalaska.

Through clouds and rain we sped along in the clear, cold waters of the Bering Sea, past the islands of Unalaska and Umnak. Dark clouds obscured their mountain peaks. I hoped fervently for a break in the weather so that I might at least glimpse Bogoslof, the famous "disappearing island." It lies slightly to the north of Umnak. It reportedly rose from the sea in an eruption on St. John's Day, May 18, 1796, and was accordingly named Joanna Bogoslova, or John the Theologian's Island. From time to time new eruptions have greatly changed its contours. At one time it was reported to have a castellated peak 360 feet high. For a time there were two separate islands, each with a high peak. In 1927 the men on the Coast Guard cutter *Northland* witnessed a volcanic eruption which united the two islands. They are now connected by a long sandspit where a large herd of sea lions basks on the warm sands. Thousands of birds make their home there, too. The weather did begin to clear at about the time we came abreast of Bogoslof. With binoculars I was able to see the northern cone and, dimly, a bit of the new part of the island.

By the time we reached the Islands of the Four Mountains the skies were clear and the snow-capped volcano on each island stood white against the blue sky. Porpoises played alongside the ship. We could look down into the clear waters and see them swimming, keeping pace with us. Albatross glided on motionless wings above our wake. At one time as many as six of these birds, with their four-foot wingspread, played in the air currents at our stern. At dinner, when we mentioned seeing albatross, Captain Salenjus stated emphatically, "Ain't no albatross north of the equator. They're gooneys." We didn't contradict him; nevertheless, numerous scientists report two species of albatross in these waters, the black-footed and the short-tailed.

Shortly after dinner we hurried to our stateroom and began packing the odds and ends which we had used during the two weeks aboard the ship, getting all in readiness for an early arrival at Atka in the morning.

View of Atka Village, from Nazan Bay. The church can be seen at far right.

❋ JUNE 1946

sadignam tugida

(month in which the wild creatures grow fat)

On the morning of June 15 we awoke early, filled with excitement and anticipation for what the day would bring. Quickly we dressed and went out on deck. Brilliant sunshine flooded the waters. To the north the skies were clear. To the south was long, narrow Amlia Island, its sharp mountain peaks jagged against a black, threatening sky beyond them and out over the Pacific. Atka Island loomed ahead over the port bow, and although the sun still shone warmly down on us, darkening clouds were building over the volcanoes of its northern end. The waters about us lay undisturbed except for the ground swell and our wake. Occasionally an excited fat puffin tried in vain to lift itself from the waters ahead of us. Porpoises no longer followed us, and the black-footed albatross deserted us as we headed in the direction of Nazan Bay. The storm came on quickly; wisps of fast-moving clouds moved across the sun and sharp little gusts of wind swept the water, ruffling and darkening the glassy surface of the Bering Sea.

Within an hour we would be in Nazan Harbor. On the shore ahead of us we could see that the green of early summer had begun to creep up the mountainsides from the surf-washed beaches. Then it suddenly grew cool. The ominous black clouds had blotted out the sunlight on the island slopes. We went below for our last breakfast on the *North Star*.

After breakfast we once more hurried up on deck. The storm had arrived. The waters were dark, and breaking under the full force of a driving wind. It whistled in the ship's rigging and sent spray flying across the decks. We were inside a bay, but no village was in sight. Instead we were headed for a large, well-built dock. It stood in the lee of a vast solidified flow of ancient volcanic lava, with a warehouse against the base of the perpendicular lava cliffs. There was no sign of human life on or near the dock. Deck hands, muffled in sheepskin coats and with wool caps pulled down over their ears, moved about on the decks fore and aft, getting ready to tie up.

Simeon and I stood leaning over the rail, watching this procedure or gazing with deep interest at the island landscape. Green hills sloped gently upward from a long beach of very black sand. In their gullies and ravines long fingers of snow pointed upward toward the higher eleva-tions which were now hidden in the wind-driven clouds. An eagle soared above the lava cliffs. Ravens squawked from their nests in the cliffs. Cormorants craned their long black necks as they sat on their

messy roosts, high on the rocks along the shore. Other sea birds sat on
shore or swam nearby, just beyond the breaking waves.

The *North Star* slid in close to the wharf, and with practiced skill the
crewmen soon made the ship fast and lowered the gangplank. Still no
sign of people. Impatiently the captain blew the ship's whistle, loud and
long. Everyone on deck scanned the beach for signs of life. In fifteen
minutes or so we saw a little Army jeep come bouncing along the road
that skirted the shore. It hurried out onto the dock and sped over the
rumbling planks, coming to a sudden stop at the end of the gangplank.
A young lieutenant jumped out and went at once to the bridge. After a
few minutes with the captain he returned and introduced himself to us
as Lieutenant Fegley. He said that he had come to take us to the village.

We loaded some of our duffle into the jeep, and Mr. Holland, the
A.N.S. field representative, climbed into the jeep with Simeon and me.
By this time the freight booms had been raised, the hatches unbattened,
and the crew was busily preparing to unload freight and our livestock.
With a wave of our hands to those on deck we took off, rattling across
the planks. The road led from the beach into sandy hills, past several
abandoned Quonset huts, and onto a rusting metal airstrip which had
been damaged by the wind and the Aleutian storms. Lieutenant Fegley
pointed out his own living quarters and the quarters of a ten-man
contingent of military personnel, explaining that they were stationed
here to maintain power for a radio beacon out on Kaduganax Point,
about ten miles beyond the wharf. The beacon served to guide air flights
into Adak, about 110 miles to the west. We stopped on the runway by
the men's quarters; the lieutenant ran in to wake his mechanics and put
them to work on the village truck so that it could be used to transfer
freight from the dock to the warehouse.

Shortly after leaving the runway the jeep skirted a beautiful crescent
of beach where green waves were breaking onto the black sand in a
smother of white foam. We passed many, many more deserted Quonset
huts where, during the war, seven or eight thousand men had been
stationed while the enemy occupied the islands of Attu, Agattu, and
Kiska. At last we entered the hills and followed the road round and
round and up and up, leaving the green below us, until we reached the
top of one of the many brown grass-covered hills. From this vantage
point we caught our first glimpse of the tiny village which was to be our

home for the next year. At the foot of the hill, near the shore, Atka Village nestled in the little green valley between two or three brown hills, and a high rocky and snow-streaked hill sheltered it from the rear. A rocky promontory and a large island hid this spot from the broad sweep of Nazan Bay and the open Bering Sea.

The unfinished church was the most impressive building in the community. It stood up the slope, isolated a bit from the rest of the buildings. Odd Russian crosses topped the two onion-shaped domes surmounting its roof. The houses clustered below it. Behind the church and still farther up the slope were some fenced graves, each with its own wooden Russian cross.

As we wound our way down the hill the lieutenant pointed out a huge crater where a Japanese bomb, aimed at the little village, had exploded on that other day in June, four years ago. We saw others on the way down; the hills immediately surrounding the village were pockmarked with them. Farther on he showed us the collapsed frame of a house. That had nothing to do with the bombings, though, he told us; the wind was responsible for this damage. It had blown the framework down a night or two earlier when it had been a little brisker than usual!

"That long tan building with all of the windows is the school," said our guide. Almost before he had finished speaking we drove up in front of it and stopped. Several little brown-eyed boys crowded around and greeted the lieutenant, and looked the rest of us over with interest. There must have been five or six of them. We said "Hello" to the group, and they all grinned and said "Hello." Standing on the porch of the schoolhouse was the construction engineer of whom Don Foster had spoken, Glenn Greene, a rugged-looking man of medium build. He greeted us warmly and led us into the building and to our new living quarters, which he and his wife, Lei Greene, were frantically attempting to vacate. The *North Star* had arrived three days earlier than anticipated, and Captain Salenjus had sent word that he wanted to leave that evening, as soon as he had unloaded. Our arrival, although expected for some time, had caught them unprepared to leave on such short notice. The small living room was a litter of partially-packed suitcases and boxes. People seemed to fill the room, and two or three young girls were busy in the kitchen. A couple of workmen were helping Mr. Greene install a radiator in the adjoining room.

We had been there only a few minutes when two of the girls came in from the kitchen with cups of fragrant hot coffee, cream, and sugar. Mrs. Greene introduced the girls, Sophie Dirks and Annie Golley. "The shy one in the kitchen is Nadesta Golley," she added. "I don't know what I would do without their help." The girls smiled at her praise and went back to the kitchen. It was evident that the people of Atka had won the hearts of both Mr. and Mrs. Greene in these months that they had spent with them, helping to rebuild their destroyed village.

"These are the swellest doggone people in the world," Glenn Greene told us. "You won't have a bit of trouble with 'em. They all know their jobs, and their young chief is a fine foreman. I've sent for him to come and meet you. He's Bill Dirks, Jr. Another fellow I've sent for is Bill Golley—Ruff. If you have any trouble with your furnace or the light plant, he's your man. He understands it all. His house is the one right outside this southeast window. Just open it, day or night, and call 'Ruff.' He'll come running."

Bill Dirks, Jr., and Ruff soon appeared. They were both in their early thirties. Solemnly they acknowledged the introductions with firm hand-clasps, but when Mr. Greene spoke a word of praise the young chief smiled a bit and the corners of Ruff's eyes crinkled. He had a most infectious smile. Both men listened intently while Mr. Greene told us of the progress of the construction work, where various materials were, how much time remained for the construction paid for by the government, the working hours agreed on by the men, and various other things pertinent to the building program. They said little, but nodded now and then. When either spoke it was straight to the point.

This conference lasted perhaps fifteen minutes, and all the time people were coming and going. The girls finished their work in the kitchen and began to scrub the hallway. I was conscious of their shy glances every now and then, and if I chanced to catch an eye on me my smile was always shyly returned.

The young lieutenant left to round up some of the men and boys and take them down to the ship to help on the dock. Mr. Greene took Simeon to his tiny office to show him how to do the payroll and the reports for the Juneau office. Then he took him to the basement and explained the workings of the small electric plant there and the operation of the oil-burning furnace, and pointed out the storerooms for school supplies and for our own. Next they went up to the dam, above the village, to see the progress made in laying the water main. Simeon said later that Glenn Greene had all the details of the village construction at his fingertips, and all the time that they were out he was pouring a flood of data into Simeon's ears.

In the meantime Mrs. Greene was showing me the schoolhouse. Just off the living quarters was a small office. There was room in it for only a desk, a chair, and two filing cabinets. A row of potted plants stood on the narrow window sill. My heart almost failed me when she opened the filing cabinets and showed me the records to be kept. Among other things, she showed me a most formidable book which she told me was the "bible" of the Office of Indian Affairs: the manual of instructions and procedures. Mrs. Greene also gave credit to the Army and the Navy for providing many of the things which she pointed out to me here and in other parts of the building. When we reached the clinic at the other end of the hall I had ample evidence of the generosity of the military. Mrs. Greene opened cabinet after cabinet and proudly displayed the contents of the well-equipped dispensary.

"Here are your vitamin pills, cod-liver oil, plasters, bandages, gauze, and cotton. Here are rubber gloves, hot-water bottles, ice bags, and sterilizer. In this drawer you will find thermometers, forceps, eyecups, eyedroppers, etc., etc." This array of medical supplies was both reassuring and frightening. The dispensary certainly looked well enough equipped to take care of anything from a scratch to a major operation, but I knew that I was not!

Adjoining the clinic was the schoolroom. This was to be my winter workshop, so I looked over it with interest. It was a long room, relatively speaking, and would accommodate thirty children without too much crowding. Mrs. Greene said that there would probably be more than that this year, though. A row of double windows along the east wall gave light and a fine view of green slopes. Fresh white curtains lent a homey air to the room. The most striking thing, however, was the great number of books. Three-foot-high bookcases, filled with books, lined three walls. These, too, were gifts from the Army and Navy to the village.

"Twice a week, on Tuesday and Thursday, two of the older girls conduct the library, and the people come here to exchange their books," said Mrs. Greene. "Everyone enjoys the library very much." There was little at the moment to indicate that this was the schoolroom, except for the area of blackboard across the front wall. A few small table desks were pushed against that wall, and chairs of varying sizes took up much of the floor space. The usual classroom atmosphere was totally lacking.

While we were inspecting this room Nurse Keaton and Jeannette joined us. Nurse Keaton wanted to see anyone in need of medical attention. Jeannette wanted to ask the children the Aleut names of some of the flowers that she had already gathered, and to find out where she could obtain some of the lovely brilliantly yellow cowslip that she had seen in the living room. She was soon off with several willing little guides.

I accompanied the nurse and Mrs. Greene to see one of the women who was very ill with TB. We walked down the road to one of the new white houses. All of the village houses were painted white, with either red or green roofs. Only the school struck a rather drab note, with its buff color. When Mrs. Greene knocked, a girl in her late teens, in a freshly ironed shirt and blue jeans, opened the door for us. Mrs. Greene introduced her as Clara Snigaroff, and told her that we had come to see her mother. Smilingly she took us into a small southern room, overlooking the bay. On a single bed by the window lay one of the tiniest women I had ever seen. Her small, thin hand was hot when I took it in mine, and two red spots flared in her cheeks. When Nurse Keaton asked her how she felt, her brow furrowed as she placed her hand over her heart.

"Pain all the time here," she said.

We lingered only a few minutes, then left. As we walked back toward the school Nurse Keaton turned to me and said, "She is in a bad way. She probably won't last the month out."

I was shocked. All at once the job that lay ahead seemed much too big for me.

"What can I do for her?" I asked.

"There isn't anything you can do. She is in the last stages now. You've a supply of sodium bromide, and when the pain is too intense you can give her some to quiet it a little. I'll give you the directions. I don't believe in just letting them suffer if there is anything to relieve their pain." Certainly I agreed with her.

"Now, about these expectant mothers," the nurse went on. "You will probably have to officiate, I guess. You see to it that everything is clean and sterilized, and you put the drops in the babies' eyes yourself." I could see that this teaching position was going to bring with it a lot of learning, too.

Mrs. Greene smiled at the expression on my face and said reassuringly, "There are only four or five of them now."

When we returned to the living quarters of the schoolhouse Mr. Greene was packing boxes and talking to Simeon, who was taking notes. Mrs. Greene began filling and closing suitcases. As soon as a case or box was packed Mr. Greene closed and bound it, and it was grabbed by a husky little native boy who piled it outside, to be picked up by the incoming loaded truck. All of the Greene's things were not yet out when ours began to arrive in an endless stream.

While we had been out, one of the native women had come in to fix lunch for Mrs. Greene. Sophie Dirks and Annie Golley returned and set the table in the living room, and soon six or seven of us gathered around it. Everything was delicious, from the big slices of homemade bread to the berry pie. The item that brought the most praise, though, was roast reindeer. A heaping platterful melted away under our warm appreciation.

The entire day sped by on wings. Even so, we all tried to speed up a little bit more when the captain sent word that he wanted to pull out by seven sharp. I didn't see how the Greenes could possibly make it, but when six-thirty rolled around and the jeep appeared at the door, Mrs. Greene put a leash on her little dog and put on her coat. Mr. Greene fastened the last suitcase strap, locked a tool kit, and was ready. The entire village, I think, climbed aboard the two trucks, and Simeon and I joined the Greenes in the jeep. Off we all went to the dock to bid the Greenes bon voyage.

We bade our former shipmates good-bye and wished them well. Some of the crew of the *North Star* expressed sympathy with us for "having to remain here on this godforsaken, windswept piece of nowhere," but we just smiled, for we had no regrets that they were sailing without us. Nurse Keaton gave me an envelope: "Read it later," she said. The Greenes went aboard with some reluctance, and tears were in their eyes and in their voices as they bade their friends good-bye. It was wonderful to see the way they gripped brown hands, extended from all sides, and to hear the friendly last-minute reminders. Then the *North Star* swung away from the dock, turned its bow out toward the Bering Sea, and moved slowly out of Nazan Bay into the dusk of a windy, stormy night. We watched it until the figures on its stern deck were very small; then once more we climbed aboard the trucks and hurtled back over the sandy roads to the village and home.

For a long time that night, after we had gone to bed, we lay and talked of our first day in Atka and of the many things we had been told—all of the little details and the tremendous responsibilities. We remembered that Glenn Green had said in comforting tones, "It seems like an impossible thing, I know, but as time goes on the answers, and all that we've told you, will come to you. Besides, the people themselves will be your greatest help."

We spoke, too, of the many things that we wanted to do for the village. Alas, we knew that so much would remain undone when the *North Star* came for us at the end of our one short year.

The next day was Sunday, and breakfast was scarcely over before our neighbors, men whom Simeon had known as a boy at Unalaska, began dropping in with friendly offers of help in getting us settled. Among the first to come was the real chief of the village, William Dirks, Sr., a tall, impressive man in his mid-sixties. We had met his son, young Bill, the acting chief and foreman of construction, the day before. Mr. Dirks and Simeon spoke of mutual friends and smoked a cigarette or two together. His visit was followed by another, and another. Toward one in the afternoon a stocky man of about thirty, with a warm friendly smile, came to ask if we would like to take a boat ride out in the bay and get some clams. He told us that his name was Mike Lokanin and that he had been a prisoner of war in Japan. We told him that we would be delighted to go with him. In a few minutes we were off in the sunshine. One of the schoolboys, Moses Prokopeuff, and Pari, Mike's wife, went with us. While the men leaned over the side of the little skiff and scooped up cockle clams from their beds with their hands, Pari and I began to get acquainted.

She told me that her real name was Parascovia, Pari for short. She was not much more than a girl, about ten years younger than her husband, I judged, slender and frail, with a shy sweet smile. "Some time I tell you about how we are Japs' war prisoners for three years," she offered.

The whole warm sunny afternoon was filled with indelible impressions. I knew that I should long remember the boat ride out to and around the island which forms a protective barrier against the storms that sweep into Nazan Bay. Equally unforgettable were the clear whistle and the startling appearance of the black oyster-catchers, with their stout red bills and white feet, nesting near the clam bed; the fragrance and enormous size of the beautiful violets that carpeted the ground on the slopes up from the beach; and the sight of the "drowned" engine and broken wings of the big Navy plane in the depths of the cool green waters, with cod swimming over it and flat flounders sliding like shadows across the pale surface of its wings. Moses told us of the five Navy fliers who had crashed in this ship, coming back from a mission over Kiska,and we hovered in the water over it as he pointed out the bullet holes which riddled it.

Two little boys met us at the village dock and carried our pail of clams up to the house for us. Pari showed me how to clean and cook them, and then all seven of us ate them for dinner. I had almost forgotten how hollow eight- and nine-year-old youngsters are, but as I watched hot biscuits and jam disappear I remembered. These little boys were the same as my own little boy had been at that age. As soon as they had filled up they brought out wooden pistols and a game of "cowboys and rustlers" took them out of doors to their stick horses.

The other three left shortly afterward, and a few minutes later two of the village women came for a short visit—Vasha Zaochney and Mattie Dirks. Vasha and Simeon had known one another in Unalaska years ago, when they had both attended the village school there. Vasha's family had moved back to Atka, their original home. Now she was a widow with four children. Mattie, a very pretty younger woman, was the young chief's wife. She told us that she had two boys who would be in the second grade in the fall. We visited briefly over a cup of tea, and then they left.

It was then that I remembered the letter Nurse Keaton had given me the night before at the dock. I retrieved it from the dresser where I had placed it and read it aloud to Simeon.

Dear Mrs. Oliver:

    Enclosed are a few notes on the usual type of cases Teachers have to deal with which I hope will be of some benefit to you.

    I feel that I will only add to the confusion by returning to the village as you have so much to talk over with the construction engineer and Mr. Holland that you will be pressed for time, so I believe by writing these things up for you, it will be best. Then you can have them for reference later on.

I suggest Sodium Bromide for the woman with advanced TB, as you have plenty of it and it takes too much of your meager supply of Morphine.

In case I do not have the opportunity of seeing you to talk to you again before we leave, I want you to know that it has been a pleasure having met you both, and I feel certain you are going to enjoy your year here and the natives are going to gain much by having you.

Do not worry too much or feel unequal to the health problems when one comes up, seems one always finds a way to do something about them and I'm sure this will be your reaction. We will look forward to your next book, Mr. Oliver, and perhaps some day I may get the urge to do a bit of writing but I doubt it. You see it is difficult for me to explain it, but I love the country and people as I know them and both are so horribly misrepresented by so many writers it has made me cold to the thought. Perhaps you will not understand me, the Irish are difficult that way. I guess we feel things so strongly.

I should love hearing from you this winter, am anxious to know how life is going for you.

My sincerest wishes for a good winter for you both.

Sincerely,

Mildred H. Keaton

"She's a fine woman!" Simeon said as I finished. I immediately took the letter and notes into the clinic where I could refer to them when I needed to.

Monday morning brought us our first sense of the intense interest the people had in rebuilding their beloved village. All of the men and the boys eleven and older met at 8:00 A.M. in front of the school and Bill Dirks, Jr., their foreman, assigned the day's work. Then the men went off to their various jobs. Simeon and I watched from our kitchen window as they moved off briskly in little groups. The young chief and Mike Lokanin, our boatman of yesterday, then climbed into the old Army truck and headed up over the hills, on the road back to the base. After breakfast Simeon left to look around the village and to see how construction was coming along. I tackled the job of unpacking and of

finding a place for my plant specimens. Out in the hall I found a stair-
case that led up to a fairly large attic. It had been used as a storeroom by
the Greenes, and some of our dry staples had been placed there by the
Aleut boys when the trucks were unloaded. I moved things around and
arranged a space large enough to accommodate the drying plants.

Work stopped in the village at lunchtime, and Simeon came home
excited about all that he had observed. After lunch he went down to
confer with Mr. Dirks, Sr., the Old Chief, and I went back upstairs to
continue unpacking and checking the huge grocery order. Quite a number of items had either not been shipped or had been greatly reduced in
quantity. Beside some items on the list were the words "To be shipped
later." I wondered when, since I had been told that supplies came in
only once a year.

When I went downstairs to start dinner I noted that the workday was
over. I watched a group of older boys climbing a deeply trodden trail up
over the hills. Later I learned that there was a small lake back in the hills
where they went to swim after work.

Simeon joined me at the kitchen window shortly after five, when we
thought that the village workday was over, and there we learned differently. The regular life of the village took place from then until after
darkness fell. Men and women came from their homes, carrying pails
and fishing gear. Dories were launched, and the hills soon echoed the
purr of "Johnsons" (outboard motors) as boat after boat left the village
dock for the cod and halibut banks far out in Nazan Bay. A couple of
the men and some of the boys climbed into the truck and went to
salvage coal near the Army base, where it had been abandoned after the
war. They had already gathered up the garbage, which they would leave
at the dump en route to the base.

About eight that evening, while we were going over the events of the
day, we heard a timid knock. Simeon went to the door, and there stood
a young man, grasping his right wrist with his left hand. Beads of sweat
clung to his forehead. He nodded at his upheld hand, and we saw a big,
wicked-looking hook imbedded in his thumb; suspended from it was a
ragged length of chalk line.

"I can't get it out. You try, eh?"

Simeon drew the trembling man into the room and on into the
kitchen, where he sat him astride a chair with his hand supported on its

high back. Turning to me he said, "Go to the clinic and get whatever antiseptic you can find while I get a shot of whiskey for . . . ?"

He hesitated, and the man replied, "Innokinty Golodoff."

I seized the clinic key and ran down the hall. In the clinic I found a bottle of carbolic acid and another of hydrogen peroxide. I locked the door and ran back to the kitchen with them. Simeon took the bottles, glanced at them, and said, "Now will you get me a new razor blade?" He had rolled up his sleeves and he prepared to scrub his hands in a pan of hot water as I left for the bedroom. When I returned he unwrapped the single-edged safety-razor blade and dropped it into a hot carbolic acid solution.

He folded a terry-cloth hand towel and used it to cushion the hand resting on the chair back. Taking up the razor blade and handing the now empty wash pan to me to hold in readiness, he said to Innokinty, "This is going to hurt like the devil. I'll get it out, but it will take a while. If you feel like yelling, yell. First, I have to find out how hard it's stuck. OK?"

Innokinty nodded, and Simeon took hold of the huge halibut hook with his sensitive thumb and forefinger and tried to move it. It remained firmly imbedded. "It's in there tight, but we'll get it. Ready?" Again Innokinty nodded, and he braced himself for the ordeal. Simeon gently washed the small brown hand, then started cutting around the hook, holding Innokinty's thumb in a firm grasp.

I suppose that it was no more than five minutes later that Simeon held up the huge halibut hook, with its bloody barb, but to each of us it seemed ages.

Innokinty heaved a great sigh, the only sound that he had made during the operation, and leaned his white face for a moment on the chair back. Simeon took the bottle of peroxide and poured quantities of the antiseptic over his patient's thumb.

Innokinty looked up at Simeon and a broad smile spread across his face. "Thank you! I think maybe I have to wear that hook all my life!"

After his hand was dressed and another shot of whiskey had brought some color back to his face he told us what had happened. He had gone alone to a halibut bank about four miles out. His line had snarled, and he gave it a quick jerk to loosen it. The hook flew back and imbedded itself in his thumb. The hook itself was fastened securely with heavy chalk line to a carved wooden piece. He cut this loose and tried to remove the hook. When he found that he was unable to, he started his engine and came back to the village to seek help.

This was only the first of several medical emergencies that we would have this year. The very next day twelve-year-old Billy Golley jumped from a painting scaffold and ran a nail into his foot. A day or so later Sergeant Wallace came from the base to the village for first aid. He had torn off a fingernail while moving oil drums.

When I went to see Billy Golley the day after his accident I met his mother, Annie Golley, for the first time. She told me that she was a widow with four children, Billy being the youngest. She called her younger daughter from the kitchen, and I recognized young Annie as one of the girls who had been helping Mrs. Greene when we arrived. Her older boy, Dimitri, eighteen, worked with the men. Her daughter, Elizabeth Snigaroff, was the mother of the baby which was sleeping with Billy on the sofa; she was helping one of the other women this afternoon. Annie and I visited in whispers for a bit, and when I left I knew that I had found a delightful new neighbor and friend.

Later that same afternoon I climbed up on the hillside above the village, ostensibly to collect flowers, but really to get better acquainted with my new home and to think about my new neighbors.

I sat on the sunny hillside among the heather and gazed down at the unfinished village below me. Out beyond lay the clear waters of Nazan Bay, reflecting the blue of the sky above. It was a peaceful scene, but not a silent one. Down there small groups of men were working together on various houses, their voices raised above the ring of hammers and the hum of saws. Children fished off the old sunken barge which served as the village dock, and hunted shells along the beach. Their higher voices joined the symphony of sounds, as did the songs of the little birds nearby and the racous "adak, edonk" of the many curious ravens that soared overhead.

Before the war, Simeon had told me, there were no roads in Atka. Broad paths led from the beach to the different homes and to the church, school, and store, with short paths between neighboring houses. These paths were renewed each year with fresh layers of gravel and white clam shells carried up from the beach. Paths still crisscrossed the village, but in addition a road now led from the dock where the *North Star* had tied up when we landed four days ago, past the military base, and on over the hills and down into the village and so to the beach, ending at the village dock.

Glenn Greene had told us that there were twenty-two houses. Three of the original houses had not been totally destroyed, but they needed extensive repairs. The houses for the Atka people I could easily recognize, for most had been completed and were painted white. When the Attu people had arrived six months ago they were taken in by friends and relatives. As their homes were framed sufficiently, families moved into them and construction continued around them.

Most of the houses were neat one-story homes. From where I sat I could see only two two-story houses. Two small boys played with a large black-and-white dog near the one farthest up the road toward the base—young Bill Dirks's home. The other I recognized as the house where Mrs. Greene had taken Nurse Keaton and me to visit Mary Snigaroff, the tiny woman with TB.

From my pocket I took a paper on which I had written the village family names. I wanted to learn to pronounce them all correctly. I would have no trouble with *Dirks* and *Gardner,* but the unfamiliar Russian names required a little practice. Glenn Greene had said that *Golley* was pronounced "Gooley." Alex *Prossoff* said "Proosoff." Then there were *Golodoff, Hodikoff, Lokanin, Nevzoroff, Prokopeuff, Prokopioff, Snigaroff, Zaochney*—all pronounced a bit differently from what I would have expected.

Construction for the day ceased; I gathered a small bouquet of lovely rosy lousewort and headed home, like the workers.

During the rest of June we took every opportunity to learn more about our environment and our neighbors. The children, noting my interest in the wild flowers, brought me bouquets and told me where they found the blossoms. They would stay for a few minutes to visit, and then run out happily with a cookie or a piece of fruit. Ten-year-old Larry Nevzoroff was a frequent visitor and my welcome tutor. He was a happy boy, with unusually large eyes for an Aleut, and an engaging grin. Because of his eyes he was nicknamed "Owl Eyes."

Larry was present one afternon when one of the men brought us a fresh halibut.

"Are you going to raw it?" he asked.

I told him that I was going to cook this one, but I'd try "rawing" one some day soon.

It was Larry, too, who taught me to eat my first raw "sea eggs," as the Aleuts call the spiny sea urchins which abound in the clear shallow waters.

The second Sunday we were there, almost the entire village went by truck across the island to a small stream which emptied into another bay: Korovin, named for an early Russian explorer. Here, every year just before the red salmon run in late June, the men build a fish trap. One truckload of men and boys had gone over to the site before the others came and asked us to go. When we reached the stream the men and boys were already hard at work. Some were driving planks of wood at an upright slant, side by side, clear across the creek in two long rows about forty feet apart. Others were carrying heavy stones and piling them against the plank dams to keep them from being washed away. One of the older men, Cedar Snigaroff, sat on the grassy bank, whittling small slats which he tied together into a funnel which would be fitted into an opening in the downstream dam, the idea being that the salmon would swim in through the large end of the funnel and into the enclosed pool and remain there, unable to go up the stream to spawn or to find the small funnel opening leading back downstream again. Later the trapped salmon would be gaffed out and hauled to the village to be distributed and dried for winter consumption.

We watched until the trap was nearly completed, took a few pictures, and then, escorted by several small boys, went down to the beach where the women and girls were. The little boys deserted us to play in the sand, except for Larry Nevzoroff, who followed us out to the kelp rocks where some of the women were fishing for pogy. Several of these color-ful foot-long fish lay on the rocks near Mattie Dirks, the young chief's wife. Ann Dirks, her sister-in-law, picked one up to clean it as we approached. Its olive-green body was splotched with brilliant orange and red. When Ann cut into it, the flesh was a vivid green. Simeon told me that the flesh would turn pure white when it was cooked, and its delicate flavor makes it easily the Aleuts' favorite fish. Ann and Mattie smiled and nodded in agreement. Simeon added that pogy was known to science as Steller's Green-fish. It is a shallow-water fish indigenous to the waters of the Alaskan Peninsula and the Aleutian Islands.

Larry, in the meantime, had been poking around in some of the shallow pools, digging out sea urchins. He called me over, and I watched him place one on its side and tap it smartly with a rock. It broke open, exposing the egg-cluster, a rich orange-colored bit in the center, which he scooped up on the back of his thumb and swallowed. He looked at me and grinned. "Try it, Mrs. Olivie!" he invited.

"Mrs. Olivie" did, and found it surprisingly good with its rich and slightly salty flavor. Simeon joined us and the three of us spent some time scrambling into the little pools in search of sea eggs and cracking them open to eat the egg-clusters. Later the wind sprang up as the tide turned, and we all gathered at the mouth of the stream for hot Russian tea and wonderful homemade bread before crowding aboard the truck for the ride home.

Each day the new spring green crept further up the hills, and although both of us could find plenty to do at the schoolhouse (there were always stacks of paper work), the lure of the deeply trodden trails leading up over the green hills often proved irresistible. We left our paper work and the cleaning and sorting, and with camera, knapsack, and knife for gathering flowers we followed the tempting trails. Sometimes we climbed up the flower-clad slopes clear to the bare, rocky, windswept mountaintops. Not totally bare, to be sure, for the tiniest of flowers clung to the rocks everywhere, along with beautiful lichens. Here they were all very short; violets with stems only long enough to put the blossoms above ground, dwarf lupine, dainty short-stemmed rosy primula, a miniature bluebell, and ever so many more. In fact, most of the flowers which we found growing so beautifully large in the lower meadows we also found on the mountains, clinging close to the ground, for the winds really blow across the heights.

Tramping along the beach held as much fascination for us as climbing the hills. Here again the multitude of flowers proved a constant delight. Right at the top of the beach grew some types that we found nowhere else. Every crack in the great gray stone outcroppings was brilliant with shiny yellow blossoms of cinquefoil. Tucked in little pockets at the top of the beach we found a number of plants which we gathered for salad greens. The one most popular with the villagers and, as Simeon had said, with all of the Aleuts, was *pootchky,* the flower stalk of the cow parsnip just before it comes into bloom. The stalk is peeled and eaten like celery. Great armloads of this are gathered and added to the diet. The stalk must always be peeled in order to prevent bad burns from the plant juice. Fannie Prokopeuff, one of the little girls, peeled some with her teeth, and she had great burns around her mouth.

Two other events of interest occurred before the end of June. One day the barge came into Atka with supplies and mail for the soldiers at the base. It was supposed to come from Adak every two weeks, but weather and the situation at Adak often interfered with the schedule. With the base supplies some village mail came, too. Even we received a few letters. The coming of the barge was an excuse for a dance. The schoolroom was put in order—it was the only place in the village, outside of the church, which was large enough for such functions. Chairs were pushed back against the wall, and an area was left for the musicians. By eight or nine o'clock the entrance was filled with soldiers and our village boys. The girls and women began to come, with the little children and babies. The musicians, with guitars and accordions, played several numbers before shyness left the group sufficiently to allow couples to get out on the floor. The young commanding officer at the base, Lieutenant Jack Miller, about twenty-five years old, went right down the line and danced with every female, young or old, pregnant or not. Most of the Aleuts were very good dancers. The musicians played old country dance tunes—"Darktown Strutter's Ball," "Roll Out the Barrel," "You Are My Sunshine," and others. One very popular tune was unfamiliar to me. They played it several times during the evening, and every time they all sang. At last I asked what it was. They laughed and said, "It's a Japs song!" The Attuans had learned it while they were imprisoned in Japan, and they had brought it back to play at times like this, when they were happy.

The second major event was the coming of the Fish and Wildlife motor ship *Brown Bear*. It dropped anchor in Nazan Bay, and we went out in the skiff. Dr. Ira Gabrielson, Director of Fish and Wildlife Service in Washington, D.C., was on the rear deck, skinning a Pallas murre. His wife, daughter, and sister-in-law, and other fish and game men were traveling with him. Later they all came ashore to visit for a while.

A Council meeting was called to discuss the coming fox-trapping season with Mr. Gray, the Alaska Fish and Wildlife man. Mr. Gray reassured Alex Prossoff, who spoke for the Attuans, concerning their right to trap Attu, Agattu, and Kiska. Because of the growing herd of sea otter which lived in the Amchitka waters, Mr. Gray also wanted Amchitka cleared of foxes. The village men were told that the *North Star* would take them and their equipment out to their fox islands in November on its way down out of the Arctic.

A number of years before several islands along the Aleutian Chain were stocked with blue foxes; they thrived along the beaches, and their numbers multiplied. Certain islands were alloted to the different villages, and each winter, before the war, men left home for two or three months to trap the foxes. This was the real source of the villagers' income, so news that they would be able to resume their trapping was most welcome. From now on the "coffee-cup conferences" held at our kitchen table when the men came in to discuss building plans and programs included some discussion of blue-fox trapping plans as well.

By the end of June I was sufficiently familiar with the people of Atka to sort them into their family groups and to place each individual in one of the twenty-two houses in the village. Here is the list I made:

1. Dirks, William H., Sr. (over 60, the Old Chief)
     Sophie (daughter)
     Ann (daughter)
     Lydia (daughter-in-law)

2. Dirks, William H., Jr. (Bill, the Young Chief)
     Mattie (wife)
     George (son)
     Henry (adopted son)

3. Gardner, Matrona
     Johnny (son)
     Stepanita (adopted daughter)

4. Gardner, Teresa (Matrona's daughter-in-law)

5. Golley, Annie (widow)
     Dimitri (son)
     Annie, Jr. (daughter)
     Billy (son)
   Snigaroff, Elizabeth (daughter)
     Nicky (Elizabeth's son)
   Golodoff, Innokinty* (brother)

6. Golley, Sergius (over 60, owns private store)
     Jenny (wife)
     Theodore (son)
     Nadesta (daughter)

*Asterisks indicate Attuans who had been prisoners of war in Japan.

 7. Golley, William "Ruff" (bachelor)

 8. Golodoff, Olean* (widow)
        Nicholas* (son)
        Gregory* (son)
        Elizabeth* (daughter)

 9. Lokanin, Mike*
        Parascovia* (wife)

10. Nevzoroff, Danny (village storekeeper, church reader)

11. Nevzoroff, John
        Ann Lillian (wife)
        Nicky (son)
        Joseph (son)
    Creveden, Titiana (foster daughter)

12. Nevzoroff, Periscovia (nearly 70, oldest person in Atka, mother of
    all the Nevzoroff men except Philip)
        Max (son)

13. Nevzoroff, Peter
        Annie (wife)
        Vasha (daughter)

14. Nevzoroff, Philip
        Mary (wife)
        George (son)
        Larry (son)
        Vera (daughter)
        baby (son)

15. Prokopeuff, George
        Lucy (wife)
        Fannie (daughter)
        George (adopted son)
        Anna Bell (adopted daughter)

16. Prokopeuff, Mary (widow, about 60)
        Danny (son)
        John (son)
        Moses (son)
        Peter (son)
        Ralph (relative)

Kudrin, Titiana
    George (Titiana's son)

17. Prokopioff, Alfred*
    Hodikoff, Stephen* (adopted son)

18. Prossoff, Alexei*
    Elizabeth* (wife)
    Fekla* (Elizabeth's daughter)
    Agnes* (Alexei's sister)
  Prokopioff, Alfred Jr.* (Elizabeth's brother's son; the only surviving Attu baby born in Japanese prison camp)

19. Snigaroff, Andrew (about 60)
    Mary (wife)
    Clara (daughter)
    Michael (son)
    Oleana (daughter)
    Affia (daughter)
    Annie (daughter)
    Angelina (daughter)
    Anfusia (granddaughter)
  Golodoff, Julia* (relative)

20. Snigaroff, Cedar (about 60)
    Poda (son)
    Vera (daughter)

21. Zaochney, Vasha (widow; daughter of Mrs. Nevzoroff)
    Spiridon (son)
    David (son)
    Clara (daughter)
    Mary (daughter)

22. One of the houses was reserved for the use of an ordained priest of the Russian Orthodox Church, should one visit the village. On occasion it was also available to house other guests in the village.

Hot springs on Korovin Volcano

✳ JULY 1946

cagalilam tugida

(month when young amphibians flourish)

July proved to be a month of much activity. The building program went on. Work was now concentrated on getting the six houses for the Attu families in shape so that they could at last move into their own homes and ease the crowded conditions throughout the village.

The government had promised to replace all items lost by both villages as a result of the war. This included hunting and trapping equipment as well as clothing and household effects. Some of the Atkan replacement orders had arrived, but not all were complete, so reorders were necessary. Some requisitions had been made for the Attuans before we arrived, but much had remained for us to do. Simeon and I spent long hours consulting with the people and typing out orders to send to the purchasing agent at the Juneau office.

Late one afternoon in early July, while I was busy at the typewriter, I saw my neighbor, Annie Golley, come slowly down the road from the top of the hill. I knew by the way she walked that she was very tired. A few minutes later I saw her older daughter, Elizabeth, go up the hill and disappear.

Half an hour later Annie came to the door. She carried her baby grandson, Nicky, in one arm and in the other a warm, fragrant loaf of freshly baked bread, wrapped in a snowy towel. As always I was delighted to see her.

"Come in, Annie, and have a cup of coffee with me," I invited.

"Sounds good to me," replied Annie. She heaved a sigh as she sat down. "I'm tired."

"What have you been doing?" I asked as I poured each of us a cup of coffee. "I saw you coming down the hill a while ago." We sat at the little table in the breakfast nook. I pushed Simeon's cigarettes over to her and gave Nicky a graham cracker to munch while we talked.

"I pick grass since one o'clock," Annie answered, and smiled, for she knew how pleased I would be.

"Oh, Annie, did you!" I exclaimed.

"When I come home I send my Elizabeth to spread it out. I too tired to walk those hills. I come home and finish baking bread."

"When may I go with you to pick grass?" I asked.

"You want to know how to weave basket? I show you. You tell me when you want to pick grass. I'll go," Annie graciously offered.

"Tomorrow?" I asked eagerly.

She smiled, nodded, and repeated, "You tell me when you want to go." She added, "I pick little grass last year. I work on basket after supper when my Annie wash dishes."

"How many women make baskets now?"

"Mary Snigaroff before she get sick makes very good baskets. We make baskets when we in Killisnoo for Juneau Museum. Jenny Golley, too. Mostly Attu women. Maybe Olean Golodoff, Elizabeth Prossoff, Julia Golodoff, Parascovia Lokanin make baskets this year. They got no grass now."

Simeon came in then and joined us. He told Annie of our arrangement with the Juneau office to hire a woman in the village to teach basket weaving in school.

"Good thing!" agreed Annie. She said that Mattie Dirks, the young chief's wife, wanted to learn. She was going with Annie the next afternoon to gather grass, and I was welcome to come, too. She left soon after, carrying Nicky and a fresh pack of cigarettes, to get supper for her family.

Shortly after lunch the following day Annie, Mattie, and I headed up the road over the hill. We walked slowly, because several years ago Annie had fallen and broken her leg. It had been improperly set, and it still troubled her. We lingered for a moment on the hilltop and looked back at the village before starting down the winding road to the beach.

The road skirted a swampy alpine meadow, brilliant with a multitude of flowers and crisscrossed by paths, shortcuts down the slope to the road along the beach. Because of Annie's leg we kept to the road, which wound down the hill. Ten minutes later we reached the sandy shores of Nazan Bay. Annie led us to the stand of grass where she had worked the day before.

"All right," she laughed. "You pick grass now. I guess this is plenty grass for your basket."

I was sure that it was. The tall, broad-bladed grass stood waist and shoulder high all about us along the top of the beach, lush and green. Mattie and I didn't have the faintest idea of what to do first.

"You show us what to do, Annie. We don't know what grass to take," I said.

Annie stooped over, bending at the waist only, grasped a stalk of grass at its base, and with a deft motion of her strong brown hand pulled it from the sand. The stalk was as thick as one of my fingers. With its white end it resembled a leek. She stripped off all of the outer blades and very carefully exposed the tender curl of a new blade in the center. This she lifted out. It was limp and pale green, fifteen inches or so in length, and about the size of the lead in a pencil. She held it out for us to see, then tossed it away.

"This good grass," she said, and reached for another stalk. Mattie and I watched her deftly pull it, and another and another, from their sandy bed.

Then I gripped a stalk of the grass at its base and pulled. Nothing happened. I jerked harder and it reluctantly came free.

"No, no!" Annie cautioned me. "That way you bend them. I spoil plenty that way when I first pick grass. You and Mattie better cut him, down deep under sand like this." She showed us how to cut down through the sand and slice off the stalk on a slant. Mattie had a short heavy-bladed knife and I had my hunting knife. Annie watched for a moment to see that we cut the stalk properly and laid it straight, and the next and the next. Then she resumed her picking. We harvested grass until we each had a big armload, and then Annie led the way to the lee of a tiny grass-grown knoll.

Annie dropped to the ground and stretched her legs out in front of her. She placed her bundle of grass on her left and motioned for us to follow her example. When we were seated she lifted a long stalk of her grass. First she cut off the root end and examined it critically for a moment, and then she stripped off all the blades but four. That reduced stalk she carefully placed to her right.

Mattie and I watched while she treated the next few in the same manner. Then she turned to us, saying, "You do same way."

I took up a stalk, cut off the root, and stripped off all but the four inner blades. When I laid it down Annie took it up. She looked at the end and pinched it between her thumb and forefinger. A tiny bit of green popped out. It was the start of a new shoot.

"Have to get this out or it spoils the grass," Annie told me.

All afternoon we gathered grass from the sandy dunes along the beach. Then we stripped it in the lee of the knoll, while overhead the ravens soared after coming to investigate our activities.

In the quiet time of sitting and working together Annie talked of the days before the war when the women and girls of the village walked over the hills to pick grass where the matting of the Army airstrip was now laid.

"That was best basket grass on whole island," she said, sadly shaking her head. "Army bulldoze it all away." Her face brightened as she continued, "But those other days, all us women and girls hike over there in the morning and pick grass all day. We make tea and have picnic and pick more grass. Sunset time men bring dories from village. One boat take whole load of grass, piled high in dory, back to village. It was pretty, white and green. Everybody go in other dory. We sing songs all the way home to village. Oh, we have lots of fun!" She smiled at the memory.

We each had a great armload of cleaned grass, and the afternoon was nearly spent. A breeze sprang up with the change of tide, so we gathered up our bundles of grass and started back up the road toward home. Halfway up the hill Annie pointed to the slope on our left.

"That's a good place to spread grass. Wind still here." We carried our grass up the slope to the spot she indicated and carefully spread it out fanwise on the slope, to cure in mists, sun, and fog—three beautiful white and green fans.

"We leave it here one week. Then we come back and turn it over. That way we cure it," Annie told us as slowly and wearily we continued on up the road and over the hill to the village. It had been a wonderful afternoon.

A day or so later we went again to gather grass. This time others joined us, and in a few days all of the older girls and several women went nearly every afternoon to pick grass for two or three hours. Word was out that there would be a weaving class.

We had good times, for after we reached the beach and chose the grassy place to work we all pulled great armloads of the five-foot grass, then sat down in a group to visit while we stripped off the outer blades and cut off the root joints. It was during these periods that they bantered good-naturedly, telling me little tales on each other. One day Mattie told me how they teased Annie all one winter at Killisnoo because they overheard her exclaim when she saw a shipment of Kool brand cigarettes in the commissary, "Oh, boy! Colds!" Annie countered with a story of Mattie cooking seal and being watched by a bunch of officers when they were living at the base area, shortly after they first returned to Atka. The women are very shy when it comes to cooking or serving their own foods around strangers, although they are fine cooks, and their food is interesting, and good by any standard.

After our armloads of grass were cleaned we took the resulting smaller bundles up on the shorter grassy slopes and fanned them out to cure. Every few days the grass was turned so that all parts were exposed to the elements. After two weeks we carried the bundles home. Now all of the outer blades were removed, leaving only the innermost one, called *anaq* (the mother), and the curl of grass that is its heart, *khla* (the boy). Both are a pale ivory when they have been properly cured.

When we brought our first bundles home, for two or three nights we spent hours on the floor of the living room in the litter of sweet-smelling grass, separating the "mother" and "boy." Then Annie showed me how to split each of these with the fingernail or thumbnail and discard the hard center vein. Curing was still not completed. With fine chalk line the tips of the "mothers" were woven in a long strand, and the tips of the "boys" in another. These were hung out of doors each morning and brought in each night, carefully wrapped in a clean dish towel, and put under the bed to keep them clean and flat. I smiled each time I saw these strands of grass blowing in the breeze, for they looked like giant blond wigs hanging from nearly every house.

The villagers were not the only ones in Atka who were busy. The rats were equally active. We knew from our study of Alaskan history that the island group which included Amchitka and Kiska was called the Rat Islands. Rats were believed to have been introduced in the early years of Russian exploration and exploitation when rat-infested ships were wrecked in these treacherous waters.

My first encounter with rats on Atka came soon after we had arrived. One morning when I answered a timid knock at the door I found two of the Snigaroff girls there—Annie, ten, and Affia, twelve. Affia asked, "You got juice?"

"Yes, I have some juice," I replied.

Now Annie said, "My mother like to drink juice. None in store."

"The juice is in the basement," I told them. "Come, I'll get you a can for your mother."

Together we went downstairs to the storage area where our canned goods were stored. As I reached for a can of juice a rat darted out from behind some cases and, dragging his snakelike tail, made for a corner. I jerked my hand back, and although I suppressed the scream that rose in my throat, I could not suppress the shudder of revulsion that followed.

"Rat!" the two girls chorused. Affia continued, "Atka got lots of rats.

Some get in store and warehouse. Eat holes in lots of things." I gave them the juice and told them to come back when their mother wanted more.

When I told Simeon about the rat he said that we would send to Adak for some traps. Glenn Greene had mentioned that they had put a cat upstairs as protection for the dry supplies there.

The little girls came every day or so for juice for their mother, but now I kept a supply for them upstairs. It was late July before a barge brought us six rattraps, which Simeon immediately set. In the meantime Danny Nevzoroff, the storekeeper, enlarged on what the girls had told me of the annual destruction and loss caused by the rats in the store and in the warehouse over at the dock. He added that rats were the reason that they planted their gardens over on Amlia Island, which was relatively free of the rodents.

Two or three times each week I visited for a few minutes with Mary Snigaroff, the little woman Nurse Keaton had feared would not last through June. Each time she appeared stronger. Her daughter Clara told me that the hens we had brought on the *North Star* had begun to lay, and the first eggs had been given to Mrs. Snigaroff. She had also eaten a little of the fresh greens gathered by her girls and Mr. Dirks, Sr. The fruit and tomato juice had helped, too, and she did enjoy the sunshine and flowers. She spoke almost no English and I no Aleut, but we smiled at one another and communicated through Clara. One day we went for a very short walk in the sunshine together.

After our first dance we averaged one a week. We found that the people not only worked with vigor, but they played with vigor, too. The shyness that had held them back at first was soon gone. Almost as soon as the musicians had their instruments tuned and struck the first notes of a lively dance tune, couples were on the floor. The broom dance was a particular favorite. It brought much kidding and laughter, and though it was hard on my broom, seeing their joy was worth the price of a new one.

Sometimes there were dances and movies at the base, and when they were over we all piled into the trucks and came home singing and laughing. The movies were shown through the courtesy of the men at the Army base. They received the films from Adak whenever the mail came or a barge came in. The young men of the village and those of the base had organized baseball games, held on a sandy area near the camp.

Often in the evening after work many of us would walk over for a game. Simeon usually served as umpire. The contests stirred up much enthusiasm and good-natured ribbing. Often after a game the crowd went over to the mess hall to see a movie. Later we found that the older men and women in the village felt left out, so arrangements were made to show the movies in the schoolroom, where everyone could enjoy them. One evening we were all delighted when Mary Snigaroff came with her beaming family.

Atka was and is a flower lover's paradise. To anyone with an appreciation of nature it is a beautiful island. By mid-July the green, which begins in early spring at the shoreline, had crept to the hilltops and flowers were everywhere. Violets of immense size and delicate fragrance, which were just beginning to bloom when we arrived, later carpeted all of the slopes and valley floors. With the violets were great clumps of large ivory-white anemones, yellow buttercups, a red-brown lily, purple lupine, and orchids. The orchids came in a variety of colors, ranging from white and pale green through shades of pink, rose, and lavender to almost violet. There were a myriad of other flowers, too. I never had to go far from the village to continue my flower collecting. By the end of July I was drying five sets of fifty-four varieties.

One evening when the Old Chief was visiting us I expressed my wonder at the wealth and beauty of the flowers of Atka. He smiled and said that when they were down in southeastern Alaska during the war, he went walking one day and came to where a woman was working in her yard, planting flowers. The woman, recognizing him as one of the evacuees from Atka, asked him if he planted flowers in his village. He told her, "No."

"Oh! Don't you have flowers in Atka?" she asked.

"Yes, we have many," he answered.

"Well, then, who plants them and takes care of them?"

"God does," he told her. "We just enjoy them."

The most impressive display of wild flowers I have ever seen came the last weekend in July. That Friday evening, following a movie, several people came to our quarters to visit for a bit. The subject of the hot springs on the island came up, and on the spur of the moment it was decided that now was a good time for a trip to them. The Old Chief told us the same thing that we had read about these springs. He said, "Long ago these hot springs on the side of Korovin Volcano were very famous.

The Russians brought sick people from faraway Russia and carried them up to them. They were left in the springs for a week and then they were able to walk by themselves down to the beach." I wanted very much to go on this trip, not only to see the famous springs, but also to learn what flowers, if any, grew in their vicinity.

Accordingly, early the next morning young Annie Golley and I joined the eight men and boys in the truck for the drive to Korovin Bay. We stopped at the base to pick up Lieutenant Jack Miller. We made a second stop at the fish trap where George Prokopeuff, a man in his forties, got down into the trap and gaffed out seven red salmon. He threw them out onto the bank where the young men killed them and put them in flour sacks, and then into their packs.

Our driver took us along the bay to Milk River. We had been told that this was the westernmost glacial stream on our continent, and the glacier from which it rises on the north slope of Korovin Volcano the last glacier. Simeon questioned that surmise, having seen the mountains on Attu as a young man, and after questioning some of the Attu men. He had written, expressing the belief that there were glaciers on Attu, to a friend, Dr. Robert Coates of the United States Geological Survey, who was studying vulcanology in the Aleutians in 1946 and 1947.

We crossed the milky waters in the truck, sometimes almost afloat. On the far side we shouldered our packs, took our two shovels, and started our climb. It grew warmer and warmer as we climbed, and everyone shed as much clothing as possible. Often we stopped to rest as we angled up the mountainside. Then we looked back down upon the beautiful full moon of Korovin Bay, across the rolling green hills to the big lake which fed our fish-trap stream, and on over to the landing strip at the base. The village itself was hidden in a fold in the hills. When we looked up Milk River we could see not only the glacier, but also jets of steam rising from hot springs nearby. Those were not the springs we were headed for.

"Too dangerous! Too hot!" said Bill Dirks, Jr., the young chief, who was guiding us.

We stopped once to drink at a big snow patch, and here I found the earliest spring flowers just peeping through the still brown vegetation of last year. When we got up on top of the hills we truly stepped into a world of beauty. For miles around, as far as eye could see, lay clouds of flowers—blue, yellow, and white. The mountainsides were misty with them, the air heady with their perfume. It was a glorious experience for a flower lover. Everything belied the old cry of the military men stationed here during and after the war—"The godforsaken, windswept, rockbound Aleutians!"

We hiked for three and a half hours before we topped a rise, up near the peaks of a mountain range, and came upon a valley in the crater of the volcano where hot springs bubbled out of the red earth. Great beds of a beautiful brilliant yellow snapdragon-like flower, called monkey flower, with rich green foliage, fringed the warm pools and nestled in the hollows. We dropped our packs on a tiny knoll above the largest pool, and here we lunched.

Annie and I were then asked to make ourselves scarce while the menfolk got out of their clothes and into the water. We obliged, and went digging *sarana*, the bulbs of the red-brown lily, to cook over one of the boiling fumaroles with the salmon we had brought from the trap.

Shouts and laughter drew us back to the pool, where the fellows were playing with a little duck they found swimming in the warm water. They tried to make it fly away, but it was reluctant to leave and kept paddling around just out of their reach. They, too, were reluctant to leave, and they spent most of the afternoon in the pool. It had been several years since any of them had been to the springs.

Annie and I found a smaller pool on the other side of the knoll, where we went wading, and when Simeon finished his swim he brought cups, and by dipping them into an adjoining boiling spring he made afternoon tea for us. Later we went on up the side of the volcano to the rim, where we surprised a ptarmigan. When we came back to the spring the others were just polishing off a huge feed of salmon and *sarana*. George cooked the fish by hanging it in a flour sack in a bubbling hot spring.

This type of cooking was a delight that I had never before experienced. Seated on the warm earth amid the flowers below the snowy mountain top, we found the simple fare was a source of pure joy. Many of the younger ones went back into the pool after supper, but the rest of us were content to crawl into our sleeping bags and let the Aleutian longspurs which nested in these heights sing us to sleep.

A gentle rain fell during the night, but it bothered no one. Next morning, after a hearty breakfast and another period of fun in the pool, we saw a real rainstorm gathering. We packed up and headed back down the mountain. Before we left I saw most of the others fill quart fruit jars from the hot springs and carefully stow them in their bedrolls. I was fascinated by the colorful mineral clays deposited by the belching hot fumaroles—even more so when George Prokopeuff told us that this was where the Aleuts used to come to dig the clays for paint. He said that they had ground it and mixed it with fish oil to paint their homes and church when they lived in the old abandoned village at the foot of the mountain, Old Harbor. Simeon took a shovel and dug some out for me to take home to dry, and to learn what more the Old Chief could tell me about it.

Coming back down the mountain was much easier than going up. When we reached a steep slope we all sat down and took turns sliding on the dead grass to the next level place. Milk River had risen considerably since the heat of the day before, so five of us did not attempt to wade it. Simeon, Lieutenant Miller, and I kept Annie Golley and Peter Zaochney with us while the other six men went back to the village for the truck and a dory to take us safely across.

When we got back to the village, we found that Andrew Snigaroff had taken his family to their summer camp. I was surprised to learn that he had taken his wife Mary, who was so ill with TB, as well as the little girls.

Elizabeth and Gregory Golodoff. These Attuan children, former war prisoners, came to Atka from Japan in December 1945.

✳AUGUST 1946

uxnam tugida

(month when the grass begins to wither and animals grow thin)

The success of our trip to the Korovin hot springs sparked the desire of many more of the villagers to go there on the first weekend of August. This time they planned to take scrap lumber and build a shelter there.

In the meantime the regular work went on in the village. The men and older boys appeared each morning for their work assignments. I missed Mike Lokanin, and Simeon told me that he now looked after the sheep. The schoolchildren and older girls worked with me, cleaning up around the houses, getting ready for the Army bulldozers to do some grading. One day we cleaned up around our lovely little church. Two men were painting the window trim and corner boards red to match the roof. The children worked around them, running to me every now and then when they found chunks of melted brass from the lovely old Russian bells. Every villager, from the oldest to the youngest, grieved over their loss. The five bells had been cast in Russia, and they had varied in size from one foot to three feet in diameter. We knew that they had been the gift of Czar Nicholas I of Russia and were a hundred years old. He and the church had borne the same name, and he had equipped it with beautiful and priceless treasures—all lost now. We put the chunks aside so that each family might have a bit.

Since the people had returned, at church time the warden tolled a small bell whose dull clang could not be heard through the village, and the people spoke nostalgically of the days when they could hear the chiming of their great bell even on Amlia's far shore, many miles away across the waters. These people are deeply religious, and much of their lives centers around their church. A hundred years ago, when this village was established by uniting the villagers from Old Harbor on Korovin Bay with those from the village on Amlia, the island which separates Atka from the full sweep of the Pacific Ocean, the people took up the body of the beloved first priest, Father Lavrenty Salamatov, and brought it here for reburial. Here his grave was always carefully and devoutly tended. After four years of neglect the tiny house over it would have to be rebuilt, a new fence erected about it, and the grave properly marked.

As the week wore on excitement mounted for the coming trip to the hot springs. One evening Mr. Dirks, Sr., came in and Simeon and I asked him about Old Harbor, the old village site at the foot of Mt. Korovin. He told us that he understood that the site was very old and had been occupied long before the Russians came, so on this trip we elected to stay down on the beach to explore and do some digging at the old village site. (This was one of the things which the officials in Juneau had given us permission to do in connection with our research work. It was not until the end of our year in Atka that we learned that the Alaska Native Service did not have the authority to give us permission to dig in the middens. Any archaeological work must be approved by a museum or college.)

That weekend most of the able-bodied villagers went by truck over to Korovin Bay, taking with them five boats, and several soldiers from the post went along in addition to Simeon and me. We crossed the bay and they put us and our duffle off at the old village site, and the others continued on up the long lagoon to a spot directly below the springs. Here they unloaded, pitched camp, and started straight up a high bluff with the scrap lumber which they had precut at the village to use in building the hut at the springs.

Old Harbor was on a spit of land between Korovin Bay and the long lagoon. Our bags and shovels were dumped on the beach along the spit, a short distance inside the lagoon. We left them there, climbed up on the knoll above the beach, and walked through heavy stands of grass and *pootchky* to the end of the spit. Here we came down to the beach again and walked back to where our things lay. On the way we found the remains of what must have been an old fish trap. It consisted of a circle, ten or twelve feet in diameter, constructed of large stones, with a small gap in one side where a funnel might have been placed. We decided to make our camp above this on the knoll. The entire knoll appeared to be an old midden, so anywhere we worked should bring to light a few artifacts. While I made sandwiches Simeon sharpened the side of one of the shovels with a piece of pumice he had picked up on the beach. That done, he swung the shovel like a scythe, and cleared a small area of the nearly head-high vegetation. This was to be our initial work site.

After lunch we set to work to remove the topsoil and pile it well back from the area. We were working at the edge of the midden, just above the beach, and we found nothing but earth to a depth of one foot. Between one and two feet down the earth was mixed with clam and blue mussel shells. In this we found pieces of glass, a carved bone, a sperm whale tooth, two blue beads, and one white one. Next was a two-inch layer of volcanic ash and cinders. Below this was a foot-thick layer of clam and echini (sea urchin) shells. Here we found evidence of rotted wood, bones of sea mammals, bits of chipped stone, one arrowhead, a bone spearhead, broken women's knives, two bone wedges, and a round stone sinker, drilled through the middle. At the three-foot level, in the same mixture of clam and echini shells, we found a group of several round stones. Six inches lower was a large wooden labret. Four inches below that was a broken stone lamp. At the four-foot level we struck a heavy layer, two feet thick, of echini shell. We searched every shovelful meticulously before tossing it back on a refuse heap, as we had been doing all along, but not one artifact did we find in that entire layer. When we cleared that layer we struck a layer of cod, duck, and seal bones, and we decided to call it a day. We had now cleared a work space about two feet by five feet, and six feet deep.

"Oh, my aching back!" sighed Simeon as he put aside his shovel. I echoed him. Wearily we gathered our duffle bags and carried them up on the small knoll, where we spread out our sleeping bags. After a very meager bite to eat we turned in. Stars shone overhead; a soft breeze blew, rustling the tall grass, and to that sound and the lapping of nearby waves we fell asleep.

One of the things we hoped to find was a sadiron-shaped stone lamp such as we had seen illustrated in Dr. Jochelson's books. Next morning, while Simeon still slept, I dressed and went back to the diggings to resume my search for one. I had worked for only half an hour when my shovel struck stone. I dropped to my knees on the damp ground and with a piece of driftwood I carefully scraped away the debris. Slowly I uncovered a flat stone, roughly triangular in shape. My heart was beating in wild anticipation as I worked to free it. There was no visible hollow in which oil had been burned. I could only hope that when I had it out of the surrounding material and turned it over I would find that it really was my lamp. At last it was clear, and my eager fingers found the hollow before my eyes did. Jumping to my feet, I ran back up onto the knoll, shouting, "I found it! I found it!"

Simeon was sitting up in his sleeping bag when I dropped down beside him and showed him the sadiron-shaped lamp. He was almost as excited as I. After a hearty hot breakfast we went back to work. Almost at once Simeon spotted a large, thin stone blade protruding from the pit wall at a flat angle. He carefully removed it. It, too, was just below the six-foot level. We came to a thick layer of clam and blue mussel shells. These layers in which no sea-mammal bones appeared caused us to wonder if the villagers had for a time used this site only as a summer camp. In this layer Simeon uncovered a large stone which weighed about twenty-five pounds. It also was triangular in shape, and my first thought was that it was another lamp. However, it proved to be a mortar in which clay or stone was ground for paint. Faint red color stained the hollow in the center. The stone measured twenty inches along the base, with sixteen-inch sides, and was six and a half inches deep. Only one other artifact was found in this same level; it was an oval stone about seven inches long with a natural hollow in the center in which oil had been burned, leaving a crust. Simeon made note of the fact that despite dampness at every level, cod bones were well preserved, while larger bones were quite badly decayed. When we reached the level of the beach rocks we decided to dig no more. We hoped to come back later and work on the pit wall that we had uncovered. We worked on notes, cleaned artifacts, and went to bed early in preparation for an early return to the village. We were well pleased with our trip to Old Harbor.

True to their word, the men and dories came down the lagoon early in the morning. Our gear was on the beach and was soon stowed away. We climbed into a dory and were off across Korovin Bay. By midmorning we were back in the village and the normal schedule of daily life was resumed.

Soon after our return Annie Golley came over. As usual she was bearing gifts: fresh bread and six eggs. She stayed only long enough for a cup of coffee and her usual cigarette.

"We go pick grass after men come for lunch?" she asked. "Soon too late for good grass. Need much grass for even little basket. I like to make four, five baskets. Maybe sell at Adak. We have no money for long time."

"I'll be ready right after lunch. Send Annie over when you're ready to go," I said as I took her to the door.

Alex Prossoff, the Attu second chief, came in just as I was clearing the table. Simeon took his coffee and went into the living room with Alex. I poured a cup of coffee for Alex, and the two men were looking over a list of materials needed for the Attu houses when young Annie came for me.

A stiff breeze was blowing as seven of us set out over the hill for the long beach. We had all had sufficient practice in selecting and picking grass that each chose her stand of tall grass and set right to work. Two of the Attu women were with us today, Parascovia Lokanin and Elizabeth Prossoff. I wondered about Elizabeth's baby, year-old Alfred, and suspected that he had been left with Olean Golodoff, her neighbor.

Annie Golley stopped her work every now and then to examine the grass that the other women and girls had picked. They were being very careful, and she smiled and nodded her approval.

A misty rain was blowing down the hills when we finished our work on the beach and headed home. A real rain meant a day in the classroom with the smaller children and older girls. This was good, for it gave me the opportunity to get closer to the individual child. I set tasks for the older ones, who would have a full school day. They worked quietly in the back of the room, alone or helping one another, while I had the little ones up front. While in Anchorage we had learned that our own piano, which we meant to give to the village, had been picked up (and presumably shipped), but it had not yet arrived at Atka. The little piano in the classroom, which had seen better days at the base and which had been donated to the village earlier, was moved into our quarters. Simeon had set up a schedule for its use, and a large number of both boys and girls were eager for him to teach them to play. From time to time one child would quietly leave the classroom and return, beaming, half an hour later to resume work while another took his or her turn.

Meanwhile, up in the front of the room where the chalkboard was, the little ones and I sat on a blanket on the floor and played games and carried on a prekindergarten program in English and both Atkan and Attuan dialects. There were only eight of these shy little ones; their ages ranged from four to seven. None had gone to school before. They all spoke their native dialects at home, chanted in Russian in church, and were to learn English in school. To complicate matters even more, the four little Attuans, who had been forced to speak Japanese while in Japan, now also had to learn the Atkan dialect, which was quite different from their own.

When I first realized the task facing these children I went to the Old Chief, Mr. Dirks, Sr., and asked him to teach me Aleut.

"Why?" he asked.

"Because I want to help the little ones in school when they are learning to speak English. If I can use the Aleut term and tell them the English equivalent, I think it will be easier for them. So, please, will you teach me?" I really wanted to learn some common, everyday Aleut, too, for there were some of the older people who spoke no English or were reluctant to use it. I wanted to be able to do more than smile and say "*Ang!*" in greeting them.

"No," he answered bluntly. "You teach them English. You will be here a year. What good is Aleut to you? You don't need it where you go. These children need to learn good English for all the rest of their lives. You teach them good English." He smiled down at me, but the subject was definitely closed. His philosophy was essentially the same as that of the Juneau office. There I had been told that English was to be used at all times in the classroom. However, the *Manual for the Indian School Service* stated, "As language expression is essential for the development of thought, the use of native languages by Indian children may not be forbidden or discouraged."

In any event, the children taught me Aleut words as I taught them English words. Much was accomplished with pictures and familiar objects and games. These children, like their parents, were intellectually keen and sensitive. The Aleut language has many back-of-the-throat sounds which I found difficult to reproduce accurately. It did not bother me that the children should see and hear me struggle to pronounce their language, which tripped so easily from their tongues. They were pleased that they could do something better than Teacher could. Often they had difficulty in trying to control their amusement. We would all laugh together and try again. Because I tried their language, they tried mine. Rainy mornings in the classroom passed happily.

There were many rainy days in early August, so school was pretty regular. Normally school is not held during the summer months in the village. It is an age-old practice for the families to go to their summer camps to put up fish, gather grass and berries, and enjoy themselves on the beaches. This had not been possible for the past two summers because of the building program. Occasionally a family would go for a few days, but for the most part everyone remained in the village to speed the work before the trapping season arrived.

Often in the late afternoon, when classroom work was over, Simeon and I donned our rain gear and hiked over to Korovin Bay and gazed longingly across the dark waters toward Old Harbor and our digging site. Prospecting around one day, we came across a promising site near the outlet of a small stream. Here the beach was littered with razor clam shells. We had not seen this shell anywhere else on the island. Rank grass and vegetation assured us that this had at least been a campsite. We decided that in the near future we would bring shovels and see if we were right. In the meantime we would ask the Old Chief what he could tell us of this place.

The biweekly barge, bringing military supplies from Adak for the eleven men at the base, came in very early on August 13. One of the soldiers brought over a small bag of mail for the village and told us that the barge would go back early the next morning and would take mail if we would send it over.

There were two official letters and a personal letter or two, but nothing else. One letter was from Frances Wingfield, U.S. commissioner at Unalaska. It was the formal appointment of election judges for the October 8, 1946, Alaska territorial election. Simeon, Bill Dirks, Jr., and Bill Golley were the appointees.

The other official letter was from the Juneau A.N.S. office, confirming the appointment of Annie Golley as teacher of basketry for the school at twenty dollars per month. She would be happy about that. Simeon and I spent the entire day working on correspondence and requisitions to go back on the barge. After supper a couple of the big fellows who had worked all day came for the mail. We saw quite a group hike over the hill to the base.

After a day at the desk and typewriter Simeon and I were happy to go up on the hills, back of the village, for flowers and to see if the crowberries (*Empetrum negrum*) were nearly ripe. We found some wild strawberry blossoms for the collections. The crowberries would be ready to pick within a week.

In our diary the next day I wrote that Simeon had caught our twentieth rat. The traps had almost cleared the rats from upstairs and from the basement storerooms, although it proved impossible to completely eliminate them.

On Friday of that week, after school, Simeon and I went back up the mountain for flowers. The gnarled, twisted ground willow intrigued me. It barely lifted its leaves above the rocky earth to which it clung, growing along the ground for many feet. Heavy clouds were massing on the far horizon when we started back down the mountain, but we stopped long enough to pick a pint of crowberries for dinner. By the time we reached the village the wind had risen and the rain was blowing in. Sophie Dirks had brought us six fresh eggs. I pressed the flowers before fixing dinner. Over sixty varieties were now drying in my makeshift presses upstairs.

Rain falls frequently during July and August. The weather seemed to change with the tide, alternating between sun and wind and misty rain nearly every day. Ordinarily no one paid particular attention; all went about their work as usual. That mid-August rain storm was different. The rain fell in sheets and with force. People didn't go outdoors unless it was necessary. However, Mike Lokanin braved the storm and came down to the schoolhouse. I made a batch of doughnuts, and over these and coffee we visited. Since Mike had become the shepherd we did not see him nearly as often as we would have liked. When he left he took some paper and a pencil, and promised to write down the story of his life for us.

Rain fell gently the next day. The Old Chief came in the afternoon to see the artifacts from Old Harbor. He identified several for us. We asked him about the presumed midden by the stream where we had found the razor clam shells on Korovin Bay.

Chief Dirks said he thought that storms brought the razor clam shells in from farther out in the bay.

"You want to dig some more?" he asked. "You go try Tutusax. That old-timers' lookout camp. It not far from Atka Village. Davy Zaochney show you when you want to go."

Although the next day was Monday there was no school. It was the holiday commemorating the Sermon on the Mount, and everyone attended church. After church several of us piled into the truck and went over to the lake. The villagers wanted to get the salmon from the trap and split them for smoking, and Simeon and I wanted to investigate our earlier find at Korovin Bay. When we reached the lake we found that the heavy rain of Saturday had flooded it, washed out the road, and wrecked the trap. Salmon spawned in the lake. We decided to go on to the beach where we women gathered grass. The men built a driftwood fire and "boiled the kettle" for our picnic lunch. Out in the bay a sei whale played and sighed. The men had a short net in the truck, and later in the afternoon they did some seining with it. They caught several crabs, much to the delight of everyone. We bumped and bounced home about seven that evening. At our makeshift baseball diamond we stopped for a three-inning ball game. Darkness, at nine o'clock, brought it to a close. It had been a good day.

After school the next day Simeon and I found our way over the hills to Tutusax; the word means ear, we learned. We stumbled into the grass-grown depressions of a small barabara (half-underground hut) or two and then cleared an area on the bank in front of one where we thought it was logical to sit and watch for sea animals, or toss kitchen refuse. We worked in misty sunshine, and both ends of a rainbow touched the shore near us. I constantly marveled at the beauty of this island.

An Army boat coming in from Adak cut short our archaeological work, but not before we had found some lovely things, among them two long stone points which had been lying side by side just under the turf. Reluctantly we hurried back across the hills to take care of village business.

In the evening a couple of soldiers brought over a film to show for the villagers. After the show a Council meeting was held, and Bill Dirks, Jr., Mattie Dirks, and Annie Golley stayed on. For a time we discussed the lost church properties. Simeon then showed them the artifacts that we had found at "the ear." It was after 1:00 A.M. when we reread our personal letters and went to bed.

For the following couple of days the rain fell heavily. The Army boat remained at the dock, and the people were clamoring for a dance the night before it was to leave. Somewhat reluctantly, the Council and Simeon agreed; it meant the disruption of the schoolroom—the only place large enough for a dance—and the Council was worried about the possibility of liquor being brought into the village. Lieutenant Jack Miller gave his word that his men would not bring any liquor, and said he would also speak to the captain of the boat.

Jack's tour of duty was nearly over. He had received official word that his replacement would arrive within a few days. We would be sorry to see him go, for he was a great favorite in the village, and was most cooperative. He had joined Simeon's piano class and was brushing up on his early training. His goal was to surprise his wife by playing "Clair de Lune" when he reached home.

On the evening that the decision was made about the dance Jack and the two Annie Golleys came for a visit. Mike Lokanin came, too, for a short time. The store was out of cigarettes, and Pari missed them. Mike said that he had bought her a cigar, but he doubted that she would smoke it. He left with a pack of Simeon's cigarettes for her. Simeon was sketching artifacts, Jack was at the piano working on "Clair de Lune," Annie was knitting and keeping one eye on me as I worked at splitting grass, and young Annie played solitaire. Later, after coffee and dough-nuts, Simeon played the piano for us. Schumann sounded good, even on that little piano.

After the schoolroom was cleared for the dance, the next afternoon, Simeon and I hurried over to Tutusax for an hour's digging. In the next foot we found two bone otter spears, sea-otter bones, a small green arrow tip, and a red jasper flenser. Then we struck a foot-thick layer of volcanic ashes and soil above the cliff rock.

Back home we found that Nadesta Golley had brought us some *baleek* (dried salmon), our first, and very good. Sophie Dirks came in with half a dozen eggs. The young chief came to tell us that there would be no dance—the boat had pulled out. Some of the village women had gone on board, and the men resented this. Jack was sending over an-other movie for the village tonight, and we could have a farewell dance for him the next night.

Preparations for Jack's dance took the place of regular classroom work next day. The older girls were in the kitchen making cookies for most of the afternoon. Pari Lokanin came to see me after they had gone. She said, "I got no blouse. You give me blouse and toose-brush?" Of course I would give her a blouse; that was no problem. The toothbrush was something else, since I had only the two that I used daily. I offered to sterilize one and give it to her, and that is what I did. She went home happily with my best silk blouse and a toothbrush under her coat.

The dance was a huge success. Jack danced with all of the women and girls. The musicians were exceptionally lively. Several villagers called on George Prokopeuff and his wife, Lucy, to do an old Aleut dance.

The floor was cleared. George and Lucy went out onto the floor. Each danced alone, Lucy doing a quiet dance step, demurely holding her skirts, and George shuffling about her, hands clasped behind his back. It was evidently a courtship dance, with Lucy pretending indifference, yet coyly leading George on. For some time he pursued and she retreated; then he grabbed her and they danced a mad sort of two-step together. This brought cheers and clapping from the onlookers. George and Lucy smiled broadly as they resumed their seats. The dance continued until after midnight.

Although we had brought home several bundles of grass that had been partially cured on the hillsides, we continued to gather more at every opportunity. One evening, while Annie Golley and I were getting some strands ready for me to start a basket, Alex Prossoff came in to visit. Annie told us a little tale on her brother, Innokinty Golodoff, the young Attu man who had had the halibut hook in his thumb.

One day when Annie was preparing lunch for her menfolk she found that she had no potatoes to go with the sealion meat. The store was closed, so in place of potatoes she cooked a big pan of rice. She set the table in the dining room for the boys and put the bread and butter, meat, and rice on the table. Innokinty, who lived with his sister, was the first one in for lunch. He sat down to eat. Dimitri came in, and then Alfred Prokopioff and Billy. Annie was busy in the kitchen.

"Hey, Mom, where are the potatoes?" yelled Dimitri.

"You'll have to eat that rice. We're out of potatoes, and the store is closed," replied Annie, coming to the doorway.

"What rice?" asked Dimitri, looking over the table.

Annie came into the room and looked, too. She was positive that she had put the rice on the table. She went back to the kitchen to see if she was mistaken. No rice. Puzzled, she returned to the dining room. Innokinty was busily and silently eating. The others had started.

"Wasn't the rice on the table when you came in?" asked Annie. Dimitri and Alfred shook their heads. Innokinty suppressed a smile but said nothing. The others laughingly accused him of eating it all so they couldn't have any of his favorite food. He finished his lunch, and as he left the table he said, "If you guys want rice, it's in the bathroom. That's the best place for it!"

Alex laughed with the rest of us. "Rice is all we get to eat in Japan. We pretty tired of it." Then he went on, "I can remember enough Japs yet to tell any I meet in his own language, 'I don't like Japs!' " He then told us of the terrific wind that swept down from the mountains, while they were still on Attu, and destroyed the first Japanese encampment.

On the Sunday following Jack Miller's dance we hiked over to the base to see him off. The plane came in for him as scheduled, but a cross wind prevented it from landing. Jack invited us back to the mess hall for fresh melon and coffee. On the way home the group stopped at our baseball ground for a game or two. I walked on home to get in some work.

After school the next day Simeon went with Annie Golley, Mattie

Dirks, and me to take movies of us picking grass. It was clear and bright and quite warm. He wandered along the beach while we worked, and after a bit he came hurrying back. He had found a large skate or ray and he took me back to see it.

Simeon interrupted school the following morning to have me come and take notes on a meeting being held in our quarters. A serious situation had arisen, partly due to Mike Lokanin's desire to really celebrate August 27, his first birthday since leaving the Japanese prison camp. He had made a keg of sourdough liquor from yeast, sugar, and fruit, and perhaps still other ingredients, and kept it in his house, busily fermenting. This was technically illegal, but it was a fairly common practice; the liquor was strictly for home consumption and not for sale, and so a moderate amount of homebrew was tolerated. Unfortunately, three of the older boys had broken into his house and made off with his sourdough keg, scaring Pari half to death.

Mike complained to the Old Chief. He in turn called a Council meeting and came to Simeon, who after a fashion represented the law. That is, he could wire the U.S. commissioner in Unalaska if a case warranted it. Part of Mike's concern was because Pari was six months pregnant, and her health after their prison stay was very poor. They had lost two babies in Japan, and they wanted this one very much.

The guilty three were lectured and warned. The base was put off limits for the village for the time being; beer and other liquor was much too easily obtainable there. The boys were silent but scowling when they left. After the Council and Mike had left, Simeon called the three boys back in. They came reluctantly. They told us that they questioned the sincerity of our interest in them and their people. They knew that Simeon had written a book, and they accused him of planning a book about Atka which would belittle them, like "that woman who called herself storekeeper's wife." They were referring to Helen Wheaton, who published her book *Prekaska's Wife* in 1945. "Called us damn Aleuts, mixed up people's names," complained the boys. "We don't like that. A lot of lies, too."

Simeon answered them straightforwardly. "We came here because we are interested in helping you resettle. We do like you, and we want to learn more about the old-timers. Did you know that you Aleuts are considered to be some of the most skillful boatmen in the world? That your women do the world's most beautiful grass weaving? Your ancestors probably knew about the circulation of the blood before the English scientists did, because old-time Aleuts mummified their dead. They had names for all the body parts, even to the tiny capillaries under the finger nail! You fellows have a lot to be proud of. You don't need to take a back seat to those fellows over at the base, or to anyone!"

The boys broke down then and told us that while they were in southeastern Alaska they had met discrimination for the first time. Strangely enough, it was from the Indians with whom they came in contact.

We got out the reference books we had brought with us and showed them what scientists like William Dall and Henry Elliott of the Smithsonian Institution, Aleš Hrdlička, and Waldemar Jochelson had to say about their people. We showed them pictures of their island that they recognized, and familiar names. We told them that we hoped to go down the island to dig where Dr. Jochelson had dug at the old village site of Atxalax in 1910. We showed them the artifacts we had found at Old Harbor and invited them to go with us when we went to Atxalax next month. Last of all Simeon assured them that if we ever did write a book about Atka we would certainly never call them "damn Aleuts." When the boys left they smiled as they said good-bye.

Pari Lokanin came down later and told me of her fright. We went into the kitchen and each of us baked a cake. Hers was Mike's birthday cake, and mine was to serve when Jack Miller came after dinner. Pari went home happy and reassured, bearing her birthday cake for Mike. A sad situation safely resolved, we hoped.

Jack had just arrived and I was cutting the cake when Navy Commander Cole flew in from Adak with Jack's replacement. Commander Cole came over to the village, bringing two other officers and a crate of oranges and a bottle of burgundy. A little later Bill Dirks, Jr., and Mattie Dirks joined us, bringing Lieutenant Marvin Barker, Jack's replacement. The electric light would not work, so Simeon lit the Aladdin gas lamp, and we had coffee and cake. Again we told Jack good-bye and promised to visit him in Wisconsin when we made our next lecture tour. The others stayed on until after 1:00 A.M. When Simeon got up next morning he surprised Moses Prokopeuff coming from the basement. Nothing was said, but at nightfall Simeon started the generator without any trouble.

Our first snow fell on the night of August 28—not in the village, but up on Korovin Volcano. Bill Dirks, Jr., said, "The peak looks moldy with that new snowfall," and so it did.

A plane buzzed the village later that morning. Soon a truckload of men came in, executive personnel from Adak: Colonel Johnson, Major Spaetz, Major Mann, Lieutenant Agler, Civilian Engineer Wood, and Lieutenant Barker. After a short discussion with Simeon a meeting was called and the children were dismissed so that the classroom could be used. The following list was on the chalkboard at the end of the meeting:

1. Transportation to trap islands assured
2. Eventually a boat to be released for Atka
3. Adak Special Services to help Atka youth center
4. No one to go aboard boats without the Chief's and Simeon Oliver's permission
5. Supplies to come in for village construction
6. Bulldozers and trucks to be available when road finished to the range
7. Troublemakers warned

After the meeting the officers were taken to inspect the work in the village, and the dam. While they were gone I learned that the older boys, and some of the younger ones, too, had gone over the hills on a reindeer hunt. I also learned that Stephen Hodikoff had come home on the plane. In mid-July he had broken his arm while working with the men. It was a serious fracture, and the bone protruded from the flesh. Simeon gave the frail sixteen-year-old a shot of morphine to ease the pain and immobilized the arm. A call was put in for a doctor from Adak. Captain Henry Thode arrived as quickly as a plane could bring him.

"This boy needs hospitalization. He's one of the prisoners from Japan, isn't he? Who is his guardian? Is his father or mother here?" asked Dr. Thode.

Both of Stephen's parents had died in Japan. Alfred Prokopioff had adopted the boy. He agreed to let the doctor take Stephen to the hospital in Adak.

"He'll get good treatment. We'll fatten him up a bit for you, too," the doctor assured Alfred.

Now he was back in the village, six weeks later, in a GI jacket and a beaked cap. He had obviously been well treated, although he did not appear much fatter. It was good to have him home.

The assurance that they would be taken to their trap grounds in mid-November made the men eager to lay in a supply of meat for their families. They needed reindeer, seal, and sea-lion meat to dry and salt down. The village supply of fish had been curtailed when the fish trap was destroyed by the recent heavy rainstorm.

Danny Nevzoroff, the storekeeper, warned that there was shortage of salt for brine in the store. The *North Star* had failed to bring the complete order in June. Much of the meat would have to be dried, and it was none too early to begin. All agreed.

We heard dories taking off very early next morning, heading for the south side of the island. I took the schoolchildren up on the hills to gather crowberries. These appeared to be the only berries on Atka that matured, although I had collected both blueberry and strawberry blossoms. The children told me they planned to "jam their berries if they got plenty."

At sundown the hunters came racing their boats in, using oars as well as engines in their efforts to be first to reach the dock. They brought back no deer, but the boats were loaded with the meat from ten seals and a huge sea lion. The sea lion's head was as large as the head of a Kodiak bear, and looked not unlike one, save for its heavy, stiff whiskers. Annie Golley, bless her heart, sent over a big chunk of sea-lion meat. Alex Prossoff came up that evening and told us details of the hunt.

August came to an end with the hunt. How quickly the summer had gone. Snow was already creeping down the flanks of the mountains at the north end of the island. Tomorrow would be September 1, and exciting plans were made to usher in the new month.

Construction of St. Nicholas Church, Atka Village

❈ SEPTEMBER 1946

cngulim tugida

(month when animals shed fur)

The main highlight of early September was the camping trip we took with the older boys and girls to the old village site a few miles down Nazan Bay.

Atxalax, long abandoned, was occupied before the coming of the Russians in the mid-eighteenth century. In 1909–10 a scientific expedition was sent out to the Aleutian Islands under the auspices of the Imperial Russian Geographic Society. Its leader, Dr. Waldemar Jochelson, carried on some archaeological work while in the islands. Atxalax was one of the places he investigated. He also took several bodies from the burial caves in the adjoining cliff. We had brought with us to Atka copies of his two books, *Archaeological Investigations in the Aleutian Islands* and *History, Ethnology and Anthropology of the Aleut,* published in 1925 and 1933. These were two of the books we had used to convince some of the young men that they had a heritage of which they should be proud, one which had attracted scientists from across the world.

The older members of the community had been gravely concerned about the attitude of those young people who had been old enough to be adversely affected by the discrimination they had met in southeastern Alaska and, since their return, by Helen Wheaton's book. They were pleased with what appeared to be a new pride and interest in their backgrounds.

From the first the schoolchildren had been interested in the artifacts we brought back from Old Harbor. They asked many questions about them and their use. We told them that if their parents gave them permission we would take them with us when we went to Atxalax in September. With any artifacts that they found they could set up a small display in the schoolroom, and add to it from time to time. They would also be welcome to come to our quarters and use our books to identify their finds and to learn more about their early ancestors.

Permission was readily granted, and tents and equipment were offered. Boats would be made available for transportation. The first weekend in September was the date set for our trip.

The day before the whole party was to go, Simeon got the boys started down to the site to put up the tents—a large one for the nine girls, Annie Golley, and me, and two smaller ones for the ten boys and Simeon.

A strong wind sprang up that night, and a misty rain fell. White waves curled in on our beach at Atka, and farther down toward Atxalax and the waterfall we could see the waves dashing high against the rocks. Simeon and I debated exposing the young people to these conditions. However, each family sent a representative to us, and each one said, "My father says it will be safe to go if we stay in the shelter of the protecting island, then scoot across."

With this assurance, and with complete confidence in our boatmen, we took off, although the wind still blew and the waves ran high. All of the girls, Annie Golley, and I climbed into George Prokopeuff's power dory. The boys and Simeon took off in two skiffs with outboard engines, and we headed for the lee of the long island. We rocked and rolled, little Annie Golley got seasick and her mother worried about the boys, but we all landed safely on the beach at Atxalax. Again I had seen that strikingly beautiful waterfall on the way. From a narrow opening high on the cliff the white water fell in a broadening stream to the black beach rocks many feet below—a truly lovely bridal-veil fall, worth getting wet to see.

Simeon told me later that his boat had a narrow squeak as they came across. A huge green curler stood the skiff on end, throwing all of them from their seats, but Dimitri Golley got the boat under control before the next wave could strike it. "Good boatmen, these Aleuts!" he added.

With all of us safely on the beach and our gear unloaded, George took off for Atka and home. The skiffs were drawn up high on the rocks and our duffle was carried to the tents. The drizzle prevented us from starting work on the huge midden nearby. We sat around in the tents, eating and singing to the music of the guitar that Spiridon Zaochney skillfully played.

The change of tide brought a change in the weather. The drizzle ceased and the wind abated a trifle, so Simeon got out his shovel and started clearing a place for the next day's operations. Some of us explored along the beach. Here I found my first Bering Sea bluebells, tiny bells of pink and blue, surrounded by a mat of blue-green foliage which spread out in a circle from a central root cluster over the wave-washed gray stones. I left them to be gathered later for the collection.

On the way back to camp we gathered driftwood for a bonfire. Some of the youngsters went for water to a small creek about a quarter of a mile away, although we found at a lesser distance a little fresh-water lake where ducks had nested.

With a cheery fire going, everyone gathered for cake and coffee. Later Spiridon, known familiarly as Spike, played his guitar again and we all joined in singing song after song. The favorite song of the evening was "Dry Bones." When Davy Zaochney sang out, "The hip bone connected to the neck bone," the songfest ended in laughter. That was the prelude to a good night's sleep, even though our beds were pretty lumpy.

Camp was stirring about 6:00 A.M. The morning was fresh and clear, but quite windy. We had the promise of a fine day ahead of us, plus an eager group of young people to work with and a fascinating place in which to work. After a hearty breakfast I followed Simeon and a small group of boys to the south side of the mound to lay out the pits. This midden was huge, approximately two hundred feet long, one hundred and fifty feet wide, and twenty feet high, sloping down on all sides. The entire mound was covered with a rank and colorful growth of shoulder-high clumps of redtop grass, the white umbrella-shaped heads of *pootchky* (cow parsnip), and the tall huge-blossomed dark blue monks-hood. From the latter plant the early Aleuts made the aconite poison that they smeared on their stone lance blades when they hunted whales.

The chosen spot was about a third of the way along the mound at its lower edge, very near the still visible excavation made by Dr. Jochelson nearly forty years before. Four small areas had been cleared of vegetation. Sites were allotted to the three groups of boys. Each had a chosen leader who had charge of the work and who was to do the recording. The fourth site Simeon and I planned to work personally.

Simeon suggested to me that we put off our own digging until after lunch. He would in the meantime explain the procedure to the boys and get each team started, and then they would all come in for lunch.

I thrust my shovel into the topsoil of our site and headed back toward camp. I noticed that the top of the mound was pockmarked with old barabara depressions, and so were the adjacent knolls. This seemed to be a good time to get an overview of this ancient village site, so I turned and climbed one of the knolls, sat down among the heather, and looked toward the water.

Atxalax appeared to have been ideally situated by its early inhabitants for life in those times. It was located on a low, narrow stretch of land at the base of a high rocky promontory that jutted out into Nazan Bay. The low neck of land lay between two smaller bays; one opened into Nazan Bay, the other into the open Pacific. The promontory would have served as a lookout point for spotting sea animals or enemies. Warning given for either, the small skin boats, or bidarki (Aleut kayaks), could be easily carried across the neck of land as need dictated.

Water for the village would have come from the creek where we got ours for the camp, or from the little fresh-water lake, which was even closer. The boys had told us that cod and halibut swam in the deep water around the end of the promontory. When we were walking along the beach the evening before they had pointed out the reef rocks where we would find great pockets of sea urchins. Annie Golley would probably fish for pogy among the waving fronds of the kelp beds. Driftwood for the gathering lay in windrows along the beach, and stands of beach grass for weaving grew at the tide line. On the hill back of where I sat the knolls and slopes were dark with crowberry heather.

For a long time I sat there, thinking about the many generations of people who had lived and died here at Atxalax, and whose refuse had built up the huge mound before me that we would be digging into and sifting through in the next few days. I hoped that Simeon would bring the group to this vantage point and show them a different view of this familiar area. When I saw the boys and Simeon heading for camp and lunch I followed.

While we were gone the girls had done the camp chores, gathered grass to soften our beds, and brought up beach gravel mixed with bits of shell to strew on the tent floor, just as their ancestors used to cover the floors of their half-underground barabaras.

Annie found that we were low on meat, so after lunch she sent a couple of boys back to Atka for more seal and sea-lion meat, and Dimitri asked them to bring back more gasoline for the outboard engines. Most of the girls planned to go after berries back on the hills. The rest of us hurried back to the diggings.

The area marked off for each team was about the size of the one we had worked at Old Harbor, approximately two feet by five feet. A little over a foot of soil and decayed vegetation covered the mound. Although we did not expect to find anything in that, each shovelful was carefully examined before it was thrown back out of the way. Once below the topsoil we found layer after layer of blue mussel shells, the green spines of sea urchins, ivory clam shells, brown codfish bones, and an occasional layer of volcanic ash marking the eruption of a volcano on this island or another. At the very bottom we found a layer of dirt or sand,

and then the beach gravel. Distributed through the various layers we found bone, stone, and ivory artifacts, the tools and weapons which the early people had used in their everyday lives. Someone was always finding something; this kept us all at a fever pitch, yet the leaders maintained strict observance of the rule for careful examination of everything. Every bone and every stone was checked for signs of manmade marks before it was discarded. Several times I looked up, while examining a stone, to find Simeon watching me with a grin on his face and saying, as I started to speak, "It just fits your hand, doesn't it?" So many did, too—a woman's stone knife or a grindstone that filled the hand. The artisan who manufactured the tool had chipped away little flakes at just the right places so that one's fingers could get a good grip on the tool.

We worked in the pits until dusk, then went back to the camp where Annie fed us a fine supper of boiled seal. After that we followed the others over a deeply trodden trail to the other beach, where under a huge overhanging cliff they had built a fire. We sat around it and ate crowberries and cream and sang as we watched all the stars come out and put the new moon to rest behind the dark mountains.

A brisk wind still blew, and the surf ran high along the beach when we started back to camp and to bed, Annie, Simeon, and I bringing up the rear. Suddenly Annie darted out into the surf and started kicking at something. The next thing we knew, flopping fish lay on the beach.

"The wind is bringing in cod," cried Annie. Simeon and I dashed into the water and began kicking out fish, too. The fish caught on shore were wriggling and flopping vigorously, trying desperately to regain the water. Annie grabbed one and called Simeon to hold his flashlight so she could see to clean it, while I ran after the others, bringing the flopping fish back from the waves. When we had as many as we could carry we went on to camp and showed them to the surprised young people.

We had fried codfish for breakfast, after a fine night's sleep on our improved beds. It was another glorious sunny and windblown day for working. White water dashing across the reef all day kept the girls from gathering sea eggs, so again they went up on the slopes for berries. The boys and Simeon and I went back to our digging. Interest remained keen, and everyone found objects to exclaim over and compare with others.

"Old-timers sure eat plenty blue mussels and sea eggs!" marveled Davy Zaochney as he looked at the various layers they were uncovering.

That night Annie fried sea-lion steaks for us, and Clara Snigaroff made *takusaq* for us. They had asked me at breakfast if I had ever eaten it and I said, "No. Will you make some?"

Clara agreed to do so. She boiled some of the codfish and flaked it, mixed it with some crowberries and seal oil, and whipped it all together. I found it very good, and so did all the others.

We were in the middle of the *takusaq* when Bill Dirks, Jr., came to tell us that the barge was in with mail and was leaving at four o'clock the next morning. We dropped everything, grabbed our slickers, and stumbled through the gathering darkness to the boats. We pushed the two skiffs into the breakers, the boys clambered aboard, and the rest of us tumbled into Bill's dory. These people know their waters well. Although it was dark and the wind was howling above the noise of the engines, they kept in contact with each other by intermittently blinking their flashlights. In spite of the fact that spray drenched us we were enthralled with this night boat ride.

At Chuniksax, just as the moon slid behind the dark bulk of the high mountain, we saw the tiny lighted tent at its base and we knew that Nadesta Golley and her mother, Jenny Golley, were tending their drying salmon at the fish camp.

The whole male population of the village was down on the dock, ready to help pull our boats high above the greedy reach of the waves. Wet but happy, we hurried home to get the mail sorted for our eager neighbors. Annie Golley knew that our place had had no heat for three days, and it took our oil stove a long time to heat up, so she sent Billy to tell us that she had hot coffee ready for us. By then we had sorted out the mail for the waiting villagers. After we returned home we kept our "post office" open for the village until after 1:00 A.M., when a jeep came from the base for the outgoing mail.

Among our personal mail was a letter from Superintendent Don Foster, telling us that he intended to visit us when the *North Star* made an unscheduled trip to Atka to bring the balance of the village store order and the rest of our supplies. The orders had been loaded on the ship in Seattle in August and would be dropped off on its second trip to the Arctic. Don expected to see us by the end of September.

Next morning after Bill Dirks, Jr., assigned the day's work for the crews he came in. He and Simeon were busy going over village matters and the trappers' needs when I went into the classroom. Simeon was still whipping out telegrams and letters when George Prokopeuff came to take Annie Golley and me back to Atxalax, late in the afternoon.

At the camp site we found that the wind had blown down one of the tents. George set it up again while Annie washed the dishes and put things to rights. I went after the Bering Sea bluebells and artifacts. On the way home George ran the dory in to Chuniksax where several of the men were seining salmon. While we were there they drew in about two hundred humpies and reds, and a few silvers. They gave me a humpy and a silver. The new civilian engineer for the base, Larry Pagnac, had arrived and was conferring with Bill and Simeon when I came in, arms laden with fish and flowers.

A stretch of four days of clear, sunny weather was unusual, and ours came to an end with rain the next day. During the day it was back to the classroom for me, and more correspondence and paper work for Simeon.

After supper our quarters filled with people. Youngsters sprawled on the floor, poring over our reference books and comparing their artifacts with Dr. Jochelson's illustrations. They made no attempt to read the text. Annie Golley came in with the socks that she was knitting for Dimitri, and from time to time other adults came in for business or to visit. When Danny Nevzoroff came in to borrow something from Simeon, Annie asked him about yarn for socks and mittens. He told her that there was none at the store.

"What the trappers going to do? I rip out old sweater to make these socks for Dimitri. Is all I have," Annie said, holding out her knitting to illustrate her problem.

"When *North Star* come end of month we have plenty socks and mittens, plenty yarn, too," Danny assured her.

"Mr. Oliver," Davy Zaochney asked, "can we go down to Atxalax Friday night instead of waiting until Saturday morning? We are going back to dig this weekend, aren't we?"

"I hope so, Davy," Simeon answered. "It all depends on the weather, and if George is free to take the girls, Annie Golley, and Mrs. Oliver. You still have two days of school before then."

I made hot cocoa for the youngsters and coffee for the rest of us, and

soon everyone gathered their belongings and left, happy at the prospect
of another camping trip if weather permitted.

During the night the first fog of the season drifted down from the hills
and lay like a gray blanket on the water. When the children came to
school their chief concern was our weekend at Atxalax. We had no idea
when the fog would lift; we could only say that we must wait and see
what would happen.

"Maybe wind come when tide changes, blow it all away," one of the
boys said hopefully.

By noon it was raining and a light wind started to blow. The fog
drifted away. Finally, around five o'clock, the rain stopped and we
could see a sundog over the ancient village. Word was sent to eat a
quick supper, pack, and then we would be off. Once we were at the site
we dug until dark. Then we joined the group gathered on the beach for
cake and coffee by the bonfire. We stayed there until nearly midnight,
singing to the accompaniment of Spike's guitar and watching the stars
and the moon through the drifting clouds.

We awakened to a clear sunny day. When Annie Golley and I started to
get breakfast the coffee was slow to boil. Annie plucked a handful of dead
grass, deftly twisted and ignited it, and held it under the hanging kettle.

"This is what I do," she said. "When I was a girl I used to spend
whole day picking white grass. I wonder what I going to do with it. One
morning I find out. Old woman who adopt me say, 'Boil the kettle.' I
know there is nothing for fire so I say, 'How I going to boil kettle?' She
tell me to take that grass I pick and make it into bundles and burn little
bit at time. I hold it under kettle like this."

As soon as one handful burned she made another twist, and soon our
coffee boiled. Annie said that most of the families kept a supply of dead
grass on hand for a quick fire. Driftwood was often scarce and grass and
heather were used to save seal or whale oil.

As soon as breakfast was over the digging teams went back to the
mound. Annie said that she and some of the girls were going to go fishing
when the camp work was finished. We dug until midmorning, and everyone found several interesting artifacts. I found a human jaw full of teeth,
most of them still firmly embedded. Worn places in the front teeth near
the gum line showed that a labret had customarily been worn.

Shortly after this Simeon and I decided to take time out and join the fishermen. The others were down on the rocks by the kelp beds. Simeon rigged lines for us. The pogy stole my bait every time, but Simeon caught four. I left him and went to where Annie was attaching a new hook to her line. Her stout chalk line would not go through the eye of a fishhook, which had to be small because the pogy has a little mouth. The line, which was a hand line, was stout for two reasons. First, pogy live among the rocks in the kelp beds and every rock is covered with barnacles, which sever a line quickly. Second, all fishlines on Atka are hand lines, and a thin line would be hard to grasp (or to untangle). I watched Annie pluck a blade of beach grass, embed the shank of the fishhook in it, bring part of the grass blade down close to the barb, and with a raveling of her line wrap the grass and shank tightly together. Around this larger shank she used the same hitch they all used on the eyeless cod and halibut hooks. She lifted the hook and sniffed at it, then extended it for me to sniff. "Pogy will like this," she said. They did, too. She caught twenty of them that morning, out on the rocks among the swirling kelp fronds. We all had fried pogy for lunch.

Bill Dirks, Jr., brought a boatload of folks down from the village to fish, and after lunch they came over to inspect the excavation. Most of them wanted to do a bit of digging, too. The Old Chief squatted beside the pile of artifacts and talked to the boys about their use. He picked up a sea-lion flipper bone from our pile and turned it about in his hand, a smile on his face.

"This old-timers' game bone," he said.

He placed the big bone upright on the ground near where he squatted, and we all crowded around to watch him. He flipped it as though he were playing mumbletypeg with a jackknife. He continued to flip the bone until it fell on its side.

"Now other man's turn," he said.

He also told us of a game of skill between two old men which consisted of flipping a small carved fish into the air in such a way that it fell head first through a small bone or wooden ring held close to the body. The game was called *unghida*. The penalty for missing was a rap on the knuckles with the sea-lion flipper bone. The Old Chief laughed as he indicated how the loser's hand would swell after the knuckle rapping. And no wonder, for that bone was a foot long, five inches wide, and five inches high, and weighed over two pounds. The game could go on indefinitely.

After our visitors reluctantly headed back to the village we dug until dusk. Again, after a hearty supper, we enjoyed an evening by the fire, singing and telling stories. That night Annie, Simeon, and I slept out under the stars. The songs of the little birds swinging on the tall beach grass woke us next morning.

Clouds were gathering when some of the group went to gather sea eggs and the rest of us hurried to the pits. We had been at work for only a short time when George Prokopeuff came for us. A PBY had brought mail, so we picked up the artifacts and our gear and hustled home in a rising storm. Halfway home George ran out of gas. We investigated two drums along the beach—no gas. The skiffs had gone on ahead, so we couldn't borrow gas from them. George rowed with a stick, and Simeon with a broken oar. We were missed, and Mike Lokanin and Johnny Gardner came to our rescue and towed us in.

We learned that our friend, Navy Commander Cole, had flown the PBY that brought in the mail. He had also brought us the new *Fall and Winter Sears Roebuck Catalogue*. From the time that it made its appearance on our three-legged coffee table next morning it was in great demand. I was amused when I saw the two little Zaochney girls, aged six and seven, sitting with it on their laps. As they turned the colorful pages they would point at something, turn and say a soft Aleut word, and smile at each other. Later I asked the little girls what they liked best. They chorused, "All the little girls!"

Bill Dirks, Jr., heard them, and when they left he told us that a few years ago an Attu man had decided that instead of coming to Atka for a wife he would order one, and he was quite surprised and disappointed when he got a dress instead of a woman!

Morning brought another clear day. I spent the morning in the schoolroom with my little ones. Nearly every afternoon after school the little boys climbed the steep hill behind the church to slide on the dead grass. They sat on pieces of scrap plywood or heavy cardboard. They never coasted far, for any hump or dip tumbled them off. They took turns, and after every tumble each scrambled to get his "sled" and himself out of the way of the next coaster. Hour after hour they climbed back up for another turn, boosting their ungainly makeshift sleds in front of them, for another turn on the slope.

Sometimes the older schoolboys joined them. They, however, stood upright on their pieces of plywood and with their agile young bodies often maneuvered their sleds to the bottom of the hill. They attained a terrific speed, and when the sled stopped their momentum carried them several strides farther. I never saw one fall.

Annie Golley took the older girls down on the beach to pick grass and to bring back what was ready to come home for the next stripping. Bill Dirks, Sr., spent the morning with Simeon, discussing the geology of Atka Island. Simeon had had a letter from Dr. Robert Coates, of the United States Geological Survey, in which he made some inquiries. Dr. Coates was spending 1946–47 in the Aleutians, studying the volcanoes and glaciers of the Chain. Simeon was answering Dr. Coates's letter when a boy burst in to say that reindeer had been sighted and the boys were going after them.

Back in 1914 the Coast Guard had brought twenty pairs of reindeer from Unalaska and turned them loose on Atka to augment the diet of the people. The deer had found the mild winters, good forage, and lack of predators—except man—much to their liking. They multiplied rapidly, and thirty years later several small herds roamed over the sixty-mile island.

The boys returned late in the afternoon with four deer which were divided among all of the households, ours included.

A roast was in the oven, spreading its tempting aroma through the apartment, when Alex Prossoff came in. He asked me to help him make out an order from the Sears Roebuck catalogue. He wanted to get some new clothes for Elizabeth, his wife. Often when he visited he told us little incidents of his life on Attu or of the Japanese prison days. The odor of the roasting meat reminded him of the hungry days in Japan.

"That was very bad time that winter of 1944. I nearly starve to death. Some peoples did. That was time we eat two dogs. The men eat the dogs. The girls don't. We give them our rice. Dog was good. I can work hard that day because my stomach is full."

We asked him to share our supper with us, but he smiled and said, "My wife cook reindeer, too, so I go home. No dog tonight."

A few evenings later Mike Lokanin dropped in for a visit. Simeon asked him who the earliest Attu chiefs were that he remembered.

"Filaret Prokopioff was earliest I remember," said Mike. "That was when I was very small boy back in 1910. I don't know who was chief before him. He was Alfred Prokopioff's uncle. Then there was Mike Prossoff. He was Alex Prossoff's father. Next, John Artumonoff was chief. These three men all dead when Japs came in 1942. Mike Hodikoff was the chief then. He was captured when we were and taken to Japan. He died eating poisoned food in January, 1945. Now Alfred Prokopioff is Attu chief. Alex Prossoff is second chief."

Mike paused and sat silently for a few moments, drinking coffee and smoking. Then with a serious expression on his usually happy face he said, "I tell you something. I don't think Filaret died a natural death. In 1910 he, Stepan Prokopioff, and Eliazar Prokopioff went in a three-hatched bidarka to trap foxes around the island of Attu. George Hodikoff, Mike's father, and another man I don't remember went along in a two-hatched bidarka. They were gone all season and didn't come back when trapping season was over. Two younger men, Steven Golodoff and Mitrofan Golodoff, went out in their bidarka to look for them. They went all around the island and when they reached a bay we call Namux Bay, on northwest side of the island, they went in a barabara there. It looked like a big fight had happened. Everything was upset. The stove was knocked over and the grass from the bunk was scattered all over the floor. They found the crucifix, usually up in a corner near the roof, in the grass on the floor. They went outside and looked all around. On the beach above high water mark they found tracks leading to the barabara, strangers' tracks made with shoes. Attu men wore mukluks. Along the beach they saw long running tracks, then about one hundred fifty yards away they found Filaret's overalls and suspenders. The overalls were ripped. That's all they found. We never know what happened to the men. All of them were missing. We never saw them again."

Mike drank his coffee and lit another cigarette. He sat musing, as though debating adding to his story. Simeon asked, "Did you ever hear about any chief before Filaret?"

Mike said, "Yes, but let me tell you this. That summer Attu people received a letter from Bill Dirks, Sr., addressed to Chief Filaret Prokopioff. In that letter Bill said he had boarded a big Jap ship that came to Atka. On board he saw many blue and white fox skins. He said he saw five native *kamleikas* [seal-gut raincoats] and several Attu native bidarka paddles. The Attu natives made theirs different from other natives, you know. Bill's father had a trading store there in Attu, and he was afraid our people had sold fox skins and these things to Japs. We think the Japs took these skins and other things and kill our men."

The account ended there and Mike got around to the second question Simeon had asked. His face brightened.

"In Russian times Attu had big chief once. He was the biggest Aleut we ever had. His name was Laurenty Golodoff. The king of Russia gave him lots of fine robes. They sent him two fine big chairs, a long narrow carpet with Russian eagle seal on it, and a big sword. There were lots of other things, too. He was the biggest chief we ever had."

Old Chief Dirks had spoken of the Japanese ships that had come close to Atka from time to time before the war. "They always say they need to take on water. One summer ten or twelve years ago big ship anchored in Nazan Bay and stayed many days. One man go back on hills while boat takes water. Native peoples don't trust the Japs. Chief Mike Hodikoff try to tell the government about Japs coming to many Aleutian islands. He thinks they want to find good harbors. Government don't believe him." Old Bill shook his head sadly.

The next time the barge arrived with the mail, it came earlier than expected. The soldier who brought our mail over by jeep told us that the barge would leave on the morning tide. This meant keeping the "post office" open late and helping to write out orders for Sears Roebuck, orders that would not be delivered until the spring trip of the *North Star*.

When Annie Golley came in the next evening to work with me on basket grass she said, "I got voting papers, too." She laughed and added, "One, he send me pencil, even. He must know I have hard time to find pencil in Atka when I want to write letter."

With the coming of fall my flower collecting ceased. Five sets of eighty varieties were upstairs, dried and carefully packed. They had turned out very well, and it seemed a pity that their beauty was destined to be hidden in musty files.

Archaeological work, too, came to a halt until we caught up on accumulated paper work and the youngsters got their pieces numbered, identified, and mounted for display. Their interest remained keen.

Simeon and I had a thrilling expeience one Sunday in connection with archaeology. It was late in September. Everyone had been working very hard, preparing for the expected visit of Don Foster on the *North Star*. The cleanup was finished around the buildings and the village was ready for the bulldozer to do its work. The warehouse was cleaned and repaired, ready for the supplies, and the truck was again in running order

when word came that the creek at Korovin was full of trout. When the
sun came out from behind the clouds a truckload of us, armed with
gaffs and poles, drove over. We found large schools of trout—more
than I had seen in years. They shot up and down the creek as though
playing follow-the-leader, and nobody caught a single one. There was
good reason for that, though. The stream was filled with spawning
salmon, and masses of salmon eggs drifted in the water. The little boys
had fun running along the creek bank with gaffs, jerking out of the
water red salmon that were still searching for spawning beds.

When we saw the trout fishing was futile Simeon and I decided to go
exploring. For some time we had been intrigued by a certain spot where
a mound had been cut through by the road builders. Scattered about
were several boulders, and white bits that appeared to be shell frag-
ments. Whenever we had gone with the group to Korovin we had sped
by this spot, bent on getting somewhere else. We decided that now was
our chance to investigate it, when everyone was busy for the afternoon
and the mound was within a half-hour's walk.

We approached the place hopefully, and in a few minutes our hopes
were realized: I found a beautiful little gray arrowhead. It was exciting
to find a midden on our own. The bulldozers had cut through several
old barabara depressions on an old summer campsite on a sand dune
overlooking Korovin Lake. The lake was to the south and Korovin Bay
to the north. We found some beautifully worked artifacts, much paint,
and the mortars and pestles used for grinding the paint. The truck came
back almost too soon, and everyone climbed out to dig with us. None of
them had known of this old site, and they were amazed that we had
found it. Everyone found something in the exposed eight- or nine-foot-
high roadside banks. We left with reluctance when darkness fell.

The previous week Annie Golley and the girls had gathered the last of
the available grass and spread it on the hillside to cure. Late one afternoon we went to bring it home for further stripping. Going down the
hill into the village, arms laden with sheaves of grass, one of the girls
found a gray-green caterpillar about an inch and a half long. She
brought it to the schoolroom and put it in a box with some green leaves
to feed on. It lived only two days, and then a strange thing happened. It
turned on its back before death, and from its leg sections, close to the
body, tiny white worms or larvae crawled forth. It took some hours for
each to crawl out of the large caterpillar. Shortly after emerging, each

spun for itself a tiny silk cocoon and went to sleep. This was a marked departure from the usual moth-egg-larva-cocoon cycle. We were eager to learn what would eventually come forth. Alas, we were never to know, for the box was inadvertently put in the trash and taken to the dump before it was missed.

The caterpillar episode, however, did make me aware of how few insects there were on Atka. Shortly after our arrival I had noted with pleasure the absence of mosquitos. True, there were the ever-present big blowflies wherever raw meat and fish hung. I had wondered how the flowers were pollinized, for only rarely did I see the huge slow bumblebees around a flower. There seemed to be no butterflies, and even tiny moths were rare. Could the constant winds and gentle breezes be the pollinizers? Would the lack of insects be the reason that the blueberry and cranberry shrubs blossomed but did not produce fruit? Now and then we saw a bronzy beetle that looked like a walking jewel, and when we went beachcombing we often saw great masses of a small insect clustered on the rocks around high water line, but on the whole there appeared to be few species of insects on Atka.

On the last Thursday in September the barge brought the election material, movies, and mail. The village had had no movies since Jack Miller's departure, so the prospect of a show on Friday night was welcomed by all. After school the next day the classroom was cleaned and the chairs set up for the movie. The people gathered early, so Davy Zaochney had a good audience when he came to the door with the film equipment and shouted, "Open in the name of the Lord!"

Simeon and the editorial staff had worked all week on the first issue of the school paper, *Aleutian Islander*. He was running it off on the mimeograph and I was tying grass to hang out when a plane flew in. It buzzed the village on its way to the airstrip, so we knew that we would have a visitor soon. I gathered up my grass and put it away and went to put the coffeepot on. From the kitchen window I saw several of the men sauntering toward the schoolhouse to greet Don Foster when he arrived.

A jeep came hurtling over the hill and down into the village to stop at the schoolhouse porch. The smiling man who jumped out was not Don, however. Instead it was Glenn Greene, but he was equally welcome. Everyone was delighted to see him.

Glenn handed me a letter from Jeannette Stewart, and a flat package of big blotters which she had sent for drying flowers in the spring.

Sometime during that busy day of "open house," amid much coming
and going, Glenn told us why Don had not come. Captain Salenjus had
had to change his plans and head directly for the Arctic instead of
coming to Atka first. Weather is the dictator in the Arctic and the Bering
Sea. Don sent his regrets, along with his assurance that the *North Star*
would return to Atka in time to take the trappers to their islands.

Jeannette's letter, dated September 27, told us that the *North Star* had
been in Adak several days, with crews working night and day loading
fresh supplies brought up from Seattle by Liberty ship. The *North Star*
was due to leave for the Arctic that night; the captain hoped to be in
Atka in six weeks. Glen Greene had literally dropped out of the skies the
night before. He had come out to Adak by plane to see what surplus
materials he could find there for the new TB hospital and school at
Sitka.

The men took Glenn around to show him what progress had been
made in the construction and what remained to be done. They were out
all day, coming in only for coffee or meals. Alex Prossoff and Alfred
Prokopioff met with Glenn and Simeon to discuss shortages of materials
for the Attu houses. In the evening several of the women dropped in for
little visits. It was after eleven o'clock when the last visitor left. Then the
three of us sat up until six in the morning, talking.

Atka's problems and prospects got a real airing that night and during
the next week. I attended some of the evening discussions, but school
went on as usual, and so did the preparation of the monthly reports for
Juneau. The discussions centered around various suggestions relating to
the ultimate independence of this village. Some of the immediate aims
were the perpetuation of ancient arts and crafts, the revival of the
custom of the Christmas Star, the building of a youth center and a
Brotherhood Hall, and the encouragement of interest in higher education among the older pupils.

One afternoon after school we took Glenn to our Korovin Road
midden. He had been most interested in the youngsters' artifact display
and their account of our trips to Atxalax. The Greenes had had no
opportunity for such outings while they had been in Atka. We took GI
shovels and each of us dug a foxhole at the site. Glenn found the digging
as intriguing as we did, and we shouted to each other over every find.

A brisk shower forced us to stop, but before leaving Korovin we went
to look at the berries and onions we had brought up in June. Only two

or three of the raspberry shrubs and a few of the strawberry plants had survived. The long boat trip was too hard on them.

One of Glenn's most pleasant surprises was learning that Mary Snigaroff was still with us and had even gone with her family to summer camp. "How pleased Lei will be when I tell her that I've had a visit with Mary," he said after he had seen her.

The end of September held two highlights for us: Glenn Greene's visit, and Mike Lokanin's autobiography. True to his earlier promise, he brought it in one evening and gave it to me, saying, "Here is my lifetime's story."

Mike's story was copied as soon as possible and as accurately as possible from the many scraps and pieces of paper on which he had written it in longhand. His ability to remember details and to relate vividly this obscure bit of vital Alaskan and American history impressed us greatly. We knew that as an orphan raised on the remote Aleutian island of Attu Mike had had almost no formal education, yet even when he was writing in what was for him a foreign language his meaning was always clear. We felt that his account would lose something if we endeavored to edit any part of it, so it remains totally Mike's story. The entire story, as he wrote it, is on page 219.

Reindeer hunt. The man on the right is Bill Dirks, Jr., the young chief.

✳ OCTOBER 1946

saqudakinan tugida

(month of autumn)

Glenn Greene remained in Atka through the first week of October. He was an ideal houseguest. He took our shortages in stride and ate with us whatever fortune provided. With Glenn we had an opportunity to discuss the wonderful potential of Atka and its people. Discussions went on twenty hours out of the twenty-four concerning ways and means of achieving a better way of life on the island. These included plans for developing hydroelectric power from the swift mountain streams, maintaining a cold-storage plant for reindeer meat, building a cannery at Korovin, exploring the coal possibilities, and acquiring a boat for inter-island transportation. The men of the village were party to most of the talks. They came and went as they found time from other work. The coffeepot was always on, and they smoked up the last cigarettes in the village.

Disappointment had been keen when it was learned that the *North Star* had headed for the Arctic before bringing needed supplies to Atka. One evening Annie Golley spoke again of her worry concerning warm socks and mittens for the trappers. She held up the socks that she was knitting for Dimitri, her son. "I make from old sweater yarn," she said. "Could use plenty old sweaters now *North Star* not come."

Later, after Annie had gone, Glenn said, "You know, I think there's a duffle bag of rat-chewed sweaters that the Navy gave us last year, when we first came, in one of the storerooms downstairs. Unless you threw them out they should still be there. You think that they could be used?"

Since my encounter with the rat, shortly after our arrival, I never went to the basement except when it was necessary, and I never lingered. Now, however, all three of us hurried down, and Glenn led the way to a storeroom that contained odds and ends of plumbing equipment and pipes. Back in a corner we found the duffle bag. It was stuffed with dark blue and gray sweaters, some hand-knit and others machine-knit, which would provide a great quantity of yarn.

Next day they were turned over to a delighted Annie. When they were washed she put the older girls to work raveling them and rolling balls of yarn.

"Some womans got knitting needles, but not enough," she mourned.

In Seattle I had purchased two boxes of jackstraws, thinking that they might be a welcome form of entertainment for the young people. Now, remembering the resemblance of the slender wooden sticks to knitting needles, I showed them to Annie. "How would these do?" I asked.

She was delighted. "Is enough for all the school girls to have knitting class!" Basketry was immediately put aside while Annie taught the girls to knit socks and mittens to outfit the trappers.

Before Glenn left the people gave him a dance which he said he would long remember. Everyone turned out to honor him. It was, in truth, a wonderful party. George and Lucy Prokopeuff did their Aleut dance again for a laughing and clapping audience. When the dance was over, around 2:00 A.M., and the last happy guest had gone, Glenn limped into the living room, dropped into a chair, and took off his shoes.

"It was wonderful," he sighed. "I sure hope I danced with everyone. I tried not to miss a single girl or woman."

A telegram the next day recalled him to Adak. Simeon went, too, to try to get some immediate supplies for the village and to put into operation some of the new plans. When the barge was ready to leave on Monday morning, although it was stormy and a gale was blowing, the entire village climbed into the truck and went to wish Glenn and Simeon Godspeed.

The general Alaska territorial election was held on the second Tuesday in October, the day after Simeon left for Adak. Bill Dirks, Jr., and "Ruff" Golley, the other election judges, took over. They came early and set up the voting booths in the schoolroom. Political material had flooded the village for a month, and we had heard some lively discussions. The people of this isolated village took their voting privilege seriously: on election day, every eligible voter came early to vote. The only exceptions were Mary Snigaroff, who was again bedridden, and Periscovia Nevzoroff, in her seventies, who did not speak, read, or write English.

Some discussion took place as the people gathered on the schoolhouse porch that crisp sunny morning, but when the door opened at 8:00 A.M. they filed in quietly. They signed for and received their ballots, entered the booths, and voted. Then they went about their daily work.

Ruff said with a grin, "I 'sewed up' the election." It had been his job to collect the ballot numbers and fasten them together, using needle and thread. By 3:00 P.M. the polls were closed, the votes tabulated, the books in order, and the telegrams stating the returns dispatched. Thirty-eight people voted. One of the important issues of this election was the territory-wide referendum to ascertain the will of the people concerning statehood. Seven people on Atka voted against it.

Bill Dirks, Sr., came to see me one noon when the children went home for lunch. He wanted me to try to make arrangements for his fifteen-year-old daughter, Ann, to go to Adak for a medical checkup. He was very worried, since he thought that she was underweight.

Before the war, teachers in outposts such as Adak were provided with radio communication equipment. Atka's equipment had not yet been replaced. Through the kindness of the men at the base a line had recently been strung and a telephone installed in our quarters, connecting us with the base. This made it easier to send emergency messages there for transmission to Adak. Previously all messages had to be hand delivered.

Immediately after Mr. Dirks left I called the base and sent a message to Dr. Henry Thode. Before I returned to the classroom he had replied. Ann would be picked up by the plane which was due in Atka that afternoon. One of the little boys ran down with a note to Mr. Dirks, so Ann was ready to go, a couple of hours later, on the plane that brought Simeon home.

School was still in session when we saw the loaded jeep top the hill and come careening down the road into the village. The children were dismissed, and we all hurried out to join the welcoming committee which was gathering on the porch.

It was obvious from the smile on Simeon's face, and from the boxes and bundles being carried in out of the rain, that his trip had been at least partially successful. Most of these things had been purchased for the Church Brotherhood Canteen, little things that had been out of stock for a very long time: bobby pins, lipstick, Kleenex, lighter fluid, shampoo, razor blades, gum, candy, and cigarettes. The village had been out of cigarettes for weeks, except for those Simeon had given them, and these Larry Pagnac, the base engineer, had sold to him. We were saving our cigarette "crumbs," as Annie Golley called the butts, and the person getting these salvaged the tobacco and rerolled it. Tobacco meant a lot to these people. The Russians introduced smoking and "snoose" chewing about two hundred years ago. Old and young indulged. I recall my dismay when I found one of my small boys chewing tobacco in school. Simeon told Bill Dirks, Sr., and the old man laughed at me and said, "That's nothing. He chewed four years ago and sucked gasoline, too."

Newly made friends in Adak had sent a number of gifts for us, too: a big ham, frozen vegetables, fresh lettuce and tomatoes, and two cases of beer. We divided it all as far as it would go, trying to see that every family got someting. We invited the bachelors to dinner with us. One day and it was all gone, but we all enjoyed it while it lasted.

Simeon had had a wonderful time. He had given two lectures, had played the piano for the hospital patients, had taken care of a lot of business, had been wined and dined, and had made several valuable contacts for the village. Among the latter was Major Schleuder, of the Adak Post Exchange, who arranged the sale of goods for the Brotherhood Canteen. Most important to me, he had seen my son, Ernest Ross, who was working as a civilian carpenter on Adak following his discharge from the Army. Ernest had been included in some of the evening entertainments. Simeon said that much interest was expressed in the courageous people on Atka. The Red Cross group was gathering materials for the youth center and appropriate clothing for children and adults. Simeon had spent the last evening with Major Schleuder, Mr. Groves, and Glenn Greene, and they had talked all night.

October is traditionally the month for hunting on the island, and in spite of the constant wind and rain the men were out every day. Late one afternoon someone sighted a herd of reindeer over the mountain to the south, and immediately a hunt was planned for the following day. Many of the men and boys started out early; Simeon was among them with his camera, hoping to get some good pictures in spite of the weather.

They had just left when Annie Golley came in to say that Vasha Zaochney's baby had been born during the night. I got Annie some breakfast, then gathered some things together for Vasha. Annie went home to rest, and I went to do what I could for Vasha and to put silver nitrate drops in the baby's eyes. I came back to get the scales to weigh the baby and to fix some breakfast for Vasha.

This baby's birth would be recorded under her father's name, although Vasha and Innokinty Golodoff were not yet legally married. This pointed up one of the inconveniences of living in this remote area. The lay priest (or reader) of Atka, Danny Nevzaroff, had no authority to perform marriages; only a regular priest had that authority. A couple wishing to marry went before their neighbors and declared their intentions, and then began living together as man and wife while they waited for a priest to visit the island. No one knew when that would be.

The summer of 1946 there were two couples in the village awaiting the visit of a Russian Orthodox priest to solemnize their marriages: Vasha Zaochney and Innokinty Golodoff, and Olean Golodoff and Ralph Prokopeuff. Olean and Innokinty were former Japanese prisoners from Attu. When they came to Atka the previous December to start over each had found someone to make a new life with and for. With the birth of this baby the happiest man in the village that October day was the new father, Innokinty.

The barge came in, but it did not bring much mail. It was mostly magazines for Clara Snigaroff to sell. She was taking them home when the hunters returned and came ashore. They quickly took their guns and headed for their homes to eat and get warm before dividing the meat. Simeon brought a reindeer heart, liver, and tongue when he came in. Then he handed me an unhatched ptarmigan egg—a lovely little thing, brown and white like the bird that had laid it last spring. He said that gusty snow squalls had kept him from getting many pictures. Later that evening we went over to Annie Golley's to hear Alfred Prokopioff play his accordion.

Friday night the weekly dance was held at the base because I was suffering from a migraine headache. I heard the group come back later, and I knew that Annie Golley had gone to Vasha Zaochney's.

Sunday our second baby arrived. Ann Lillian Nevzoroff had a baby girl. Annie Golley came for me to put the drops in the baby's eyes and weigh the little one. Titiana Creveden, who lived with John and Ann Lillian Nevzoroff, whispered to me that she would not be at school for a few days, since she would be needed at home.

Next day at school a batch of obscene pictures was being passed around. When I was called out of the room to get something from the clinic for Annie Golley some youngster copied one on the blackboard. One of the little girls thrust them at me, unsolicited. I erased the blackboard and put some work on it for some of them to do, very aware of the eyes on me. School continued as usual. After school Larry Pagnac moved the Brotherhood Hall over from the base and put it up on the hill by Danny Nevzoroff's house. He let the little boys take turns driving the bulldozer.

I showed the drawings to Simeon and asked what I should do about them. At his suggestion we consulted Mattie and Bill Dirks, Jr. Had it been only the big boys involved, probably nothing would have been called for, but they were getting fun out of shocking the little girls. Bill, in his capacity as young chief, decided to call a Council meeting the next afternoon.

The Old Chief, Bill Dirks, Sr., knocked at our door about four o'clock the next afternoon while the councilmen were gathering in the schoolroom. When he stepped in he said, "I want to say something." Then, beaming proudly from ear to ear, he announced, "I am a grandfather! Lydia's baby came about three-thirty." We congratulated him and gave him some cigars, and he told us Lydia was fine and so was her baby girl.

Young Bill called us to the meeting. Both he and his father addressed the group. They spoke in Aleut. George Prokopeuff had his say; so did the fathers of some of the girls. One word used often was familiar to me: *ochetla* (teacher). At last the drawings were taken around by the Old Chief, and they were greeted with frowns, tongue clickings, surreptitious smiles and, again, with serious concern. Young Bill spoke again. I asked to be excused, and I went to the clinic for medical things for Lydia Dirks and the new baby.

One of the outcomes of that episode was a request that I talk to the girls and answer the questions they were too shy to ask their mothers— if they had mothers, as some did not. The request came from the girls themselves. This I did, to the best of my ability.

Earlier in the month, after Simeon and Glenn went to Adak, telephones were installed for Bill Dirks, Jr., and Mike Lokanin, and connected to our line. The marvel of being able to call someone on the phone brought much joy. The tiniest incident was ample excuse to ring the school or the house next door. Our phone rang late one evening and I answered it. Mike said, "That you, Mattie? Pari is coming over to visit you in a few minutes."

One Friday, the night the dance was held at the base, the phone rang madly. Simeon answered it and so did someone else. Simeon waited, and at last Mike said, "Mattie, let me speak to Pari."

When Pari came to the phone, Mike asked, "Where are the towels, Pari?" Pari did not answer right away so Mike asked again, "Where are the towels? I'm taking a bath and I can't find the towels." Pari laughed into the phone and said something in Aleut. A moment later Mike laughed, too, and said, "Oh, thank you. Good-bye."

The telephone was used for serious purposes, too. Ann Lillian Nevzoroff's baby was just three days old when Annie Golley came to tell me that Ann Lillian was running a temperature. I checked and found it to be 102 degrees. She had a pain in her side and a headache. I went home and telephoned the base to send a wire to Dr. Thode, asking him to come.

That morning fresh snow covered the ground lightly. Lieutenant Barker called on the phone to invite Simeon and Bill Dirks, Jr., to go after reindeer in the "weasel," the post's small amphibious vehicle. At noon he came by for them and found his party enlarged. Mike Lokanin had heard the invitation on the phone and he and Dimitri Golley decided to go, too. They got two deer, and Simeon got a few camera shots. With such a load it was no wonder the weasel broke down as it was coming back over the hills.

That night Mike came down, at my request. Pari's baby was due in early November, and we had talked before about sending her to Adak for her delivery. She was very frail and had gained neither weight nor strength since coming to Atka, as most of the other Attuans had. I suggested that he might want to send Pari to Adak the next day when Dr. Thode came to see Ann Lillian. Weather would be uncertain from now on through the winter, too, Mike added. "If Dr. Thode will take her Pari will go to Adak on the plane tomorrow," he decided, and went home to tell her.

The next day dawned clear and calm. The plane came in about 11:00 A.M., bringing Dr. Thode, Captain Blizzard, and Major Foley. Simeon entertained the latter two officers and I took the doctor to see Ann Lillian. He found her too ill to be moved and immediately started penicillin treatments which were to be given every three hours, day and night. He looked in on several other patients, including Mary Snigaroff and the other new mothers. Then I took him up to Mike's house to see Pari. He too thought it best that he take her to Adak on the return trip. Mike went to the base to see her off and returned to the village relieved and happy, but already lonesome.

The wind came up as the evening tide came in, and by dark it was a gale. The houses shuddered with every blast. The John Nevzoroff home was only about a hundred and fifty feet from the school, but bucking the wind every three hours made it seem farther. Ann Lillian was very ill. Annie Golley stayed with her. At midnight when we went over with the penicillin we took Annie sandwiches and hot coffee.

For the next three days the wind blew with constantly increasing force. Great gusts picked lumber off the piles and hurled it about like matchsticks. Through the island channels williwaws boiled and blew. Spume and white water often obscured the island beyond. The village paths were deserted except when it was necessary for someone to be out.

The treatments every three hours continued, too. On the second day a message came that Lydia Dirks was running a temperature. When I left the Nevzoroffs' I battled a stiff wind all the way along the path down the hill to the Dirks's home on the beach. I literally blew in. Lydia's temperature was due to exhaustion. There were too many visitors and too many bright lights; she needed rest and quiet. She fell asleep immediately when her visitors left and her room was darkened. As I turned to leave the Old Chief thanked me and said, "Be careful. The wind is strong. You'd better go back around by the road—safer."

"I will," I replied. "Anyway, it won't be so bad going back."

"That's right," he laughed. "You've a fair wind home."

In spite of the wind a plane made a quick trip to Atka next day. The jeep came for Simeon when the plane was due to land, and came back loaded with boxes of things the Red Cross had sent for the trappers: underwear, sweaters, socks, and mittens. It was all turned over to Bill Golley to distribute. Ann Dirks came in from Adak on the plane, too, and the jeep took her home. Her medical examination had revealed nothing wrong.

By Sunday morning the chill wind had dropped to a breeze. The church bells were ringing when I went on my rounds. Ann Lillian was greatly improved and had been a fine patient, never making a fuss when the needle was jammed to the hilt in her body every three hours. Penicillin proved to be a miracle medication. The injections would be continued until the doctor thought it safe to discontinue them.

Birdsong awakened us next morning, and immediately after breakfast I took a little bed jacket, juice, and canned tomatoes down for Mary Snigaroff. As I came out on our porch I saw a soldier leaving one of the houses by the back door. He ran down behind the church to the road. I called Simeon's attention to the soldier. With the binoculars he identified the man. I gathered my medical things and hurried to see my patients before the children came for school. When I returned Bill Dirks, Jr., was sitting at the breakfast table with Simeon. The soldier had had to pass his house, going up the hill on the way back to the base. He and Mattie had seen him. He had called Lieutenant Barker and asked him to come to the village. I cleared the breakfast things away and made a fresh pot of coffee, then went down the hall to the classroom.

We were happy to welcome Ann Dirks back, and I think that the children, after being out of school during the heavy windstorm, were glad to be back on schedule. I know that I was, for I enjoyed teaching these youngsters. There was much quiet movement and whispered help and a general air of busyness as dark heads bent over their tasks. Two of the older girls went into our quarters, as usual, to fix the cocoa and get the graham crackers for the midmorning snack which the school provided. They came back and whispered to me that most of the village Council was there.

At noon, when I went in to lunch, Simeon told me that the Council had met nearly all morning to consider a number of serious matters: a threat made before witnesses against another's life, prostitution, and liquor sold or given to minors. The Council was determined to try to put a stop to illegal activity in the village.

"Most of it stems from having the base on the island," Simeon said. "Bill, as chief, has called a village meeting tomorrow at 4:00 P.M. in the classroom." He told me the reason two of my older boys were absent that day was because they were drunk.

That afternoon a comic book that Ann Dirks had picked up in Adak was put on my desk. It showed some Halloween party activities, and the youngsters wanted to know about them. After my explanation they asked if they might have a Halloween party. I agreed, and for the next three days lessons revolved around plans and preparations for the party. Even the tiny ones were drawn into the discussions.

Next afternoon the children set up the chairs for the village meeting, which was postponed until 5:00 P.M. because Andrew Snigaroff had not come in from fishing. Lieutenant Barker was asked to attend the first part of the meeting. He arrived early and waited with us. The Council requested that Simeon and I remain the entire time. When we entered the schoolroom at five o'clock it was filled with serious-faced men and women. The two schoolboys sat with downcast eyes. They were the only adolescents there.

Bill Dirks, Jr., opened the meeting in English, then spoke at some length in Aleut, for several of the older people did not speak English or understand more than a few words. Then he called on Lieutenant

Barker. Everyone listened carefully when the lieutenant addressed the two boys.

"For the time being, I am forbidding you to come to the base," he told them, "because of the temptations and the vile language. There is nothing good for you there. If you come you will be sent away. Is this understood?"

The boys nodded. The adult brother of one of the boys spoke next. "He's been warned, but he won't listen. We are through with him if he won't straighten up. We'd like to see him sent to a school that would discipline him, or have him put in the Army." He said he was speaking for his mother. She nodded in agreement. The man looked at his young brother, then sat down again beside their mother.

The father of the other boy rose and spoke to the group and his son in Aleut. He stood with his hand on his wife's shoulder. Then he resumed his seat beside her.

Both boys hung their heads. The Old Chief rose and spoke sternly to them in Aleut. Then they were excused, and they left without delay.

The next issue to be brought before the group was prostitution. We knew that because, although young Bill Dirks spoke in Aleut, all eyes turned toward the attractive young woman who was sitting alone, her chin raised defiantly. Then Bill spoke in English, pointing out that the young woman had disregarded previous warnings, defied the Council, continued to carry on her illicit activities, and was corrupting minors. She was not good for the village. Her mother spoke pleadingly and briefly to her. The young woman cursed her mother and turned away.

Bill asked Simeon to read the laws and bylaws from their village charter, granted by Congress. These made it clear that the elected Council was the governing body of the village.

Bill then asked the lieutenant for his cooperation. Lieutenant Barker said that he would immediately issue orders that the village was to be off limits to the GIs, and he would do his best to see that the orders were enforced. He was then excused and he left, but everyone else remained.

Young Bill now turned to the third issue before the people, the threat by one of them on another member's life. He spoke in Aleut. Cedar Snigaroff broke in and delivered a tirade in a soft voice. When he sat down George Prokopeuff took it up. The man who had been threatened remained silent. The mother of the young man who had made the threat spoke directly to her son. Cedar's son Poda sat next to me and interpreted.

"She said to him, 'If there is anything between them let them forgive each other.' "

Then Simeon was asked to plead with the youth. He asked, "Since you have had time to think this over and realize the seriousness of this threat, how do you feel now?"

Scowling, the youth replied, "I feel same way. I catch him sometime, some place, I'll kill him."

"Why?" asked Simeon. "What has he done to you?"

"He fight my dad one time and lick him."

Simeon asked the youth to remain after the others left, and young Bill adjourned the meeting. All left except the Council members and the young man. As his mother left she spoke directly to him. "Don't come home until you've made friends again."

The Council went into session, leaving the youth sitting alone. They voted unanimously to send a request to the Juneau office of the Alaska Native Service to have the young woman removed from the island. Then they turned back to the present problem. The Old Chief spoke a few words to the youth, who burst into tears and said, "All right, forget it."

Old Bill talked gently with him for a few minutes longer, and it ended with a promise to make friends and forget the past.

I was impressed by the straightforward way these people faced their problems and handled them. We congratulated Bill Dirks, Jr., on his handling of the meeting.

He said, "It had to be settled before they go trapping next month. Those two men will be on same island. We don't want anything to happen. And we need 'off limits' for the village. Maybe we get word to send her out on the *North Star* when it comes." Then he continued, "Too bad nothing for young boys to do in village. On base lots to do: pool tables, jukeboxes, cards, and drink beer. I'm sorry, but they're too young."

Simeon said that he would appeal again to the Red Cross at Adak for materials for the youth center. Bill nodded and left.

A clear bright day followed the meeting. The sun rose over the mountain peaks at the end of Amlia in a blaze of glory. Birdsong greeted the new day. How unusual and delightful to hear birds singing on the very last day of October in Alaska!

While I was getting breakfast I heard the truck rumble off over the hill to get another load of coal from the abandoned pile at the base. The hum of outboard motors in the bay followed as the hunters and fishermen took off. From my window I saw several women in bright kerchiefs hike along the beach with their fish buckets. The village was back to normal. The new mothers and babies were all doing so well that Annie Golley had gone fishing, too. She brought us fresh cod for supper when she came for her knitting class later that afternoon.

The schoolroom was a happy, busy place, in sharp contrast to its appearance of the previous afternoon, as the children worked on preparations for their Halloween party.

In the evening four little boys came running up from the beach with a live kittiwake; it was a beautiful small gull-like bird with a yellow-green beak, bright eyes, and its head was half white, half pearl gray. When it was put on the floor we found that it had lost a foot long ago. The boys wanted to keep it for a pet, but were persuaded to take it back to the dock and release it.

Halloween day arrived on a fierce, howling gale. It was awesome to watch the furious gusts lay the grass low and whip the bay into a white froth, with waves dashing high upon the rocks and breaking into a smother of foam on the beaches. Some gusts brought snow and sleet, some rain and hail, and all carried arctic chill. It was impossible to heat the classroom. School was dismissed for the afternoon so the older children could put up decorations for their party. The little ones would have theirs the next afternoon.

Nadesta Golley, Sophie Dirks, and young Annie Golley went to the kitchen to make doughnuts. After they had pushed chairs and desks against the walls the boys brought in a tub, half filled with water for apple-bobbing. Then they left, but the other girls came to our quarters for their knitting class. Alfred Prokopioff brought Annie Golley over, for the wind was too strong for her. Dimitri, her son, took her home after knitting class. The girls had made great progress in their knitting and had several pairs of socks and mittens to show for their efforts.

The party for the older children was a huge success, noisy and gay. When the last ghost story had been told, the last apple dunked, the last doughnut eaten, and the last party-maker had gone we put out the lights and tumbled wearily into bed.

A violent earthquake about midnight was a fitting climax to Halloween and brought October to a close.

Julia Golodoff and baby Stephanie, baby Janet and Lydia Dirks

❋NOVEMBER 1946

kimadgim tugida

(month devoted to hunting)

If October went out on a gusty wind and an earthquake, November came in still and white. A swallow sang from the roof of the priest's house. Bill Dirks, Jr., came in at breakfast time, closely followed by Larry Nevzoroff and Davy Zaochney.

With dancing eyes Larry asked, "You feel that earthquake last night? It make noise like baby's cry. The house afraid."

Davy said, "That cry was the devil or *idigidi,* I think."

Many of the village families burned a light all night to protect their homes from the boogeymen called *idigidis.* I had noticed that many of the lamp chimneys were so patched with adhesive tape that little light came through. Ann Lillian Nevzoroff had a lantern chimney upside down on her lamp, for the store had no lamp chimneys in stock.

After a while the little boys accepted a couple of doughnuts and raced out to play in the snow until time for school.

"My family doesn't keep light all night unless someone sick," said Bill.

The little ones had their party in the afternoon. Gregory Golodoff, in big boots, "marched like Japs" around the room, a heavy scowl on his little round face. Then all of them, even four-year-old Joseph Nevzoroff, did a Russian dance. They played a game or two, but the food was the high point of their afternoon. My high point came when one of the two absent boys came and asked me to help him make up his work.

The boy's desire to return to school was not the only result of that meeting. Bill and Mattie Dirks came Saturday evening for a card game. We had just started to play when one of the middle-aged men who had gone to school with Simeon as a boy came in.

He said, "I've come some little trouble to talk about. Glad this fellow is here." He indicated Bill. Then he dropped a bomb. "I'm asking this woman who made all the troubles to be my wife. Maybe I can save all her troubles."

We were speechless.

"What you think, Simmy, Ochetla, Bill, Mattie?" He turned to each of us.

Bill spoke up. "Go home and get sober, then come back here Monday at four o'clock and we'll discuss it."

Simeon gave the man a cigar and gently ushered him out. Our game continued. Not another word was said about the new situation, but I'm sure it was uppermost in all our minds.

The Old Chief came to breakfast with us after church. We always enjoyed his visits. That morning he told us of an earthquake he had experienced as a lad, out on the water with his father.

"The water was calm one minute and bouncing wildly like tiderips the next." He cupped his hands to show us. "Hard to handle boat."

He laughed uproariously about the startling proposal of the previous night. "I told him he's old man now. No one wants him now." He told us that the Council would probably oppose the man's offer if it came down to that.

Four o'clock came and went on Monday, and although Bill Dirks, Jr., turned up, the other man failed to appear. Bill said, "He was pretty shocked when he sobered up."

The first barge of the month came in, bringing much mail. The furnace had gone on strike; with no heat in the classroom there was no school. Simeon and I worked in the kitchen on reports and letters. We sat beside the windows where we could watch the constantly changing weather and hear with joy the full-throated song of the sparrows. Toward evening Annie Golley brought us two ducks, cleaned and ready to be cooked.

A promise of movies that evening spread like wildfire throughout the village. The boys came to set up the chairs and get the room ready. The audience sat in outdoor clothing in the chilly room and thoroughly enjoyed themselves. They walked home under a quarter moon which shone on the ruffled waters of the bay.

Mike Lokanin came immediately after breakfast next morning to work on the furnace. The bay was still and blue, and Bill Dirks, Jr., stopped in on his way to his father's to tell us that several of the men were taking advantage of the calm to run over to Amlia Island, across the pass, to harvest their vegetables. We went back to our never-ending paper work. After lunch we took time out and hiked over to Korovin Bay. It was beautiful on that side of the island. A bright surf was rolling in on the beach where a blue fox had played. Hundreds of ducks, like flotillas of small boats, rocked on the water. Huge razor clam shells, tossed up by last week's storms, covered the beach. At last, refreshed and invigorated, we walked home in the darkness and rain. Mike had the furnace going and the apartment was warm. He stayed for supper with us, but left soon after.

Although we were back to the rain, hail, snow, and generally gusty weather, some of the men and older boys went deer hunting the following morning. Simeon took the movie camera and went along.

The girls and the little ones came to school as usual. Above their soft voices I could hear the swallows singing in the rain. Nadesta Golley asked for crepe paper for her mother, to make flowers for the church.

After school Philip Nevzoroff sent Larry up with a chunk of white salmon. I had never heard of white salmon. The piece looked exactly like a center section of king salmon except for its color.

By seven o'clock that evening it was dark, and the hunters had not returned. Annie Golley came for flour to bake bread next day, and when I looked out of the window for the third time she smiled and said, "They are OK. They wait and come home by moonlight."

She was right. A bright, nearly full moon lighted their way, and a rising wind sent clouds scuttling across its yellow face.

The ground was white with snow when we awakened November 7. The thermometer stood at twenty-six degrees, the coldest day so far, and the sky was clear and blue. While we ate breakfast we watched some happy little boys, out before school, drag their sleds up the hill in back of Philip Nevzoroff's house and coast down. Ducks flew low over the blue waters of Nazan Bay. Many little birds darted about and sang near the village houses. The men were out early, doing chores and tramping new trails in the snow between houses. George Prokopeuff brought us new potatoes and turnips. Bill Dirks, Jr., came with "apples," as he called his turnips, and some reindeer from the hunt of the day before.

In midafternoon Colonel Mossman flew in with Captain Blizzard and Lieutenant Rogers. They brought mail and took a jubilant Mike Lokanin back to Adak to visit Pari. Bill Dirks, Jr., appointed Cedar Snigaroff to care for the sheep in his stead.

The day's mail contained no word with regard to the removal of the young woman, who was continuing to disrupt the village. A despondent Bill Dirks, Jr., came one evening to talk about the situation. He said that when he finished the building in the village he planned to sell his home and move his family away because that woman had turned the young men against him. Being chief was a thankless job sometimes.

"I'm trying to line up work in Adak for those fellows after the trapping season," Simeon said. "They need something to occupy their time and energy, and a chance to make some money."

Bill acknowledged that it was a difficult situation for the young un-
married fellows. "We all need a chance to make some money," he
added.

During the phase of the full moon we had three days of beautiful
weather. The air was crisp and cold. Some pipes in the village froze. The
little boys enjoyed the snow that remained on the ground, but there was
a feeling of unrest among their elders. No word had come from the
North Star. The Attu trappers had to abandon their hopes of trapping
Attu and Agattu Islands. There were no supplies and time had run out.
They should have been on their trapping grounds before this.

Ten days after the Council's request about the removal of the young
woman a terse answer came; "Appeal to nearest commissioner if unable
to handle." This left a frustrated Council wondering what their rights
were. Simeon offered to get in touch with the Juneau office for legal
advice.

One evening, about eight o'clock, Alex Prossoff came to ask if we
would like to go clamming by moonlight. We bundled up and hurried
down to his boat. It was dark, for the moon was behind the clouds, but
the snow on the hills made them stand out as though they were lumines-
cent. A light spit of snow stung our faces as the boat sped through the
dark waters. On reaching Chuniksax and the clam beds we found the
tide still too high for digging. Alex could hear the clams, and when we
stepped out of the boat we could feel them with our feet, but we decided
to go back to the village and wait for low tide. An hour later Alex came
to tell us that the tide had not run out, so clamming was postponed to
another time.

Alex stayed to visit, and as always we enjoyed his company and his
anecdotes. This time he told us of trapping with his father for the first
time when he was eight years old. He caught fifteen foxes. That year he
was sent to Unalaska to go to school. He put his money in the school
bank and spent it on skates, skis, a sled, and shows. Then with gestures
he showed us how a young Norwegian girl in Unalaska filled thirty-five
barrels a day with herring. He turned serious and said, "When we come
to San Francisco I wanted to get Elizabeth diamonds, but no money.
Young girls like pretty things. When older they find it's not things that
count."

When Alex left that night the wind had risen and it was storming
hard. The storm blew itself out during the night. The next day was

bright and pretty, but a heavy surf was running. Bill Dirks, Jr., came in before church to report that three boats were missing—his own power dory with its inboard engine, and two skiffs. He thought that they were sunk in the bay. What he minded most was the loss of his fishline. "That is hard to get," he mourned. "I got four more motors." Then he said, "Last Friday men stringing wire at AACS found bedding, a Coleman stove, dried fruit, and a barrel of brew. They dumped the brew and brought the stove back. I know young fellow it belongs to. If he wants it he'll have to buy it back from me." (The AACS to which he referred was the Alaska Army Communications System hut.)

The anxiously awaited word arrived on Monday, November 11. The *North Star* would be in any day. The first group of trappers were to be ready to go immediately. They held a trappers' meeting after school to firm up their plans.

On the day after we received word of the impending arrival of the *North Star* we had no school. I spent the day packing first aid materials for the trappers. The older girls thoroughly cleaned the classroom while the little boys worked in the basement. The older boys worked with the men, trying to finish laying the electric wires.

Max Nevzoroff came over to tell me that his mother, old Mrs. Nevzoroff, was very ill. I found that she had a temperature of 102 degrees, and I relayed that information to Dr. Thode. He sent back instructions to start giving penicillin shots every three hours. It could be pneumonia. We started the shots immediately and took her the last of our lemons and some orange juice.

Three of the Snigaroff girls came in the late afternoon. Anfusia had a toothache which we doctored. Then the five of us bundled up and hiked over the hill to see if the *North Star* was at the dock. It was not, but the hike was exhilarating in the windy dark and rain.

The girls set the table while we went to give our dear old lady her shot and try to make her comfortable. The girls had supper and spent the evening with us. Affia sang a little song about *pootchky,* and they told us about how all the little girls, when they played house, hung the dried open pods of the lupine on racks for their dried fish. They tried to teach me some of the more simple string figures at which they were adept. "Monkey me, now," my instructor would say as her pretty little fingers manipulated the string. We walked the girls home at ten o'clock before we went to give Mrs. Nevzoroff her next shot and take her some hot broth.

Excitement reigned in the village the next morning. A boat had been sighted out at the entrance of Nazan Bay. Hopes ran high that it was the *North Star* at last. False hope—it turned out to be an Army tug with three barges in tow; a fourth had been lost in the storm that had raged for three days. They came into the bay seeking shelter, bringing nothing but four trappers from Unalaska and Umnak.

Late in the afternoon Annie Golley brought in fresh warm bread, and Bill Dirks, Jr., dropped in to tell us that Dan Prokopeuff had seen his boat at Atxalax. The four of us were having coffee and fresh bread when the new trappers came in. Two of them were former schoolmates of Simeon's—Nick Peterson and Simeon Pletnikoff. The others were a young Zakarof, son of a former Unalaska chief, and John Taylor, a white man who owned the trapping rights on Great Sitkin Island. They stayed for supper, and several of the village men came in for the evening to swap trapping tales.

On Friday the fifteenth the wind shifted to the south and brought more rain. Mrs. Nevzoroff was much better. The men were making progress in laying the electrical lines. With luck the lines should be completed in a couple of days. No one was going far from the village to hunt. All waited expectantly for the *North Star*.

A telegram came, requesting a copy of the annual school report that Mrs. Greene had sent to Juneau in May. It had not reached the office, and I was asked to send another immediately. Since it was Friday I would not have to take school time to do it. There was a whole weekend available, unless the boat came. We were also sending out four of the children on the *North Star,* and their papers had to be prepared.

Annie Golley came in the next morning while I was working on the report to ask me to bring some things and come dress Elizabeth's hand. It had been badly cut when she accidentally struck a window pane in the dark. Elizabeth, Annie's daughter, had been doing my laundry. She was a real help to me. I would miss her services.

By Saturday evening the report was finished and ready to send. Bill and Mattie Dirks invited us up to play cards. When we came home Mattie gave me a copy of Helen Wheaton's *Prekaska's Wife*. She said, "Maybe about one-half of this book is true."

"Looks to me," said Bill, "only about one-fourth true. Picture doesn't look like community boat, either."

We had read the book before, but we reread it in snatches before going to bed. We could well understand the people's objections to the picture that it painted of them.

Sunday was a beautiful clear day. I went early and dressed Elizabeth's hand. After church we borrowed Philip Nevzoroff's boat and with Annie Golley we went fishing. It was delightful on the water. Myriads of ducks and cormorants flew about us. We went to a rock near Tutusax, and as soon as we lowered our lines we each caught a *kaluga* (sculpin). The tide carried us along so swiftly that Simeon had to give up fishing and man the oars in order to keep the boat in position while Annie and I fished. I caught my first cod. That was a thrill. When we returned we learned that a barge had come in and taken the four visiting trappers out.

Two lovely Aleutian rosy finches on our window sill greeted us on Monday morning. The day had barely begun when Dr. Thode flew in from Adak, bringing a box of fresh fruit and vegetables sent by Colonel Mossman. Mike Lokanin came home on the plane, too, dressed like a GI, tie and all. Pari was fine, but no baby yet.

Dr. Thode went with me to see my patients. He examined Elizabeth's hand and took her to the clinic, where he gave her a local anaesthetic and took five stitches to prevent a bad scar.

"Give her sulfa if her temperature shoots up," he advised me when I took her home to bed. All of us at Atka were grateful for his interest and care.

Poda Snigaroff brought up the store reports and went over them with us later. We worked on them all evening.

Clara Snigaroff sent a note with Affia when she came to school next morning, saying that Julia Golodoff's baby had arrived at five that morning. At noon recess I went to put drops in the baby's eyes and to weigh her. Alice Stephanie Golodoff was pretty, but tiny. Julia had ordered clothes for her long ago, but they had not arrived. Clara had found some things to serve until they came.

Both Mrs. Nevzoroff and Annie Golley's Elizabeth were running fevers that evening. I started Elizabeth on sulfa and took her some fresh fruit and vegetables. An orange brought a happy smile to Mrs. Nevzoroff's gentle face.

The sun rose in glory over Amlia's peaks on the morning that the *North Star* finally arrived. Alfred Prokopioff had been up on the lookout hill, and he came running to the schoolhouse to tell us that it was at the dock. A few minutes later Simeon and I were at breakfast when we heard the beat of excited feet and Davy Zaochney burst in.

"*North Star* tie up at dock!" he beamed. "No school today, eh?"

"No school," I beamed right back. "You boys all go help Bill." I really need not have added the last, for no one could have kept a boy away from the dock that day.

We hurriedly finished our breakfast, and before I put the apartment to rights I put Larry Nevzoroff and Nick Golodoff to work sweeping the snow from the steps and porch. There was a remote chance that someone from the Juneau office would be on board, and we knew that trappers from Unalaska and Umnak were. They trapped in the western islands, as our men did. The little boys would want to be on hand when visitors came.

Mrs. Nevzoroff's temperature was still 102 degrees, and I hoped that there would be a doctor on board the vessel to look at her. As I left her house I saw my two little boys escorting a young woman across the bridge, and I hurried to meet them. It was my friend Jeannette Stewart, the botanist from the *North Star*. Arm in arm we came back to the school. There I gave her the set of flowers which I had gathered and pressed for her New York Botanical Gardens collection. I left her with Simeon, having a cup of coffee and exclaiming over the flowers, while I went to dress Elizabeth Golley's hand. By the time I returned the jeep had come for Simeon, and the village was filled with strangers coming and going between the houses. Children were sent to borrow coffee from Ochetla for the guests. The older boys had all gone to the dock to help unload the store supplies, sort them, and set aside and reload what was needed for the trappers.

Jeannette and I hiked over to the dock, going along the beach. The day was glorious—sunshine, a breeze, and rolling surf. We had almost reached the dock when the village truck passed us, returning to the village with a load of supplies and men. Simeon was among them, and he wore a grin a yard wide.

"See our gun!" he shouted, holding up a shotgun.

"Who sent it? Where did you get it?" I called.

He shrugged. "I don't know. It just came, addressed to me." Another answer to a prayer, I thought, for we certainly had been wanting a gun. The ducks and geese had been coming in greater numbers every day.

Jeannette and I went aboard, where we were greeted by various members of the crew and taken in to lunch. For an hour or so we visited. Nurse Keaton told me that there was no doctor on board, and that she could not leave, for she had in her care a little Eskimo girl and a tiny Aleut baby, recently orphaned by a murder at Nikolski. She assured me that the penicillin treatment would do all that was possible for Mrs. Nevzoroff. She, like Glenn Greene, was surprised and delighted that Mary Snigaroff was still with us. Arrangements were made for the four children who would be coming on board later, three for hospitalization for TB and one for school at Seward. Then Jeannette showed me her flowers and some interesting old ivory and jade things which she had purchased in Nome. Before I left the boat she cleaned out her locker and gave me knitting needles, yarn, crochet hooks, thread, a knitting book, a small lantern, and other odds and ends.

The men and boys were busy as a nest of ants, working on the pile of freight heaped on the dock. It was a mess. This stuff had been shipped in early September, coming up on that Liberty ship two and a half months earlier. The Army boat was used because of a strike in Seattle. Things had been broken open, strewn around, and pilfered. Fresh foods had rotted, and things in general were in a deplorable state. The men were subdued, but the boys were in a state of wild excitement, leaping about and shouting. They were all wearing new caps from the store supplies. All of the Atka men had a penchant for caps with stiff beaks, reminiscent of the caps worn by Coast Guard officers.

Everything in that heap on the dock had to be taken to the warehouse about a mile away, checked, rechecked, and re-marked for one of the three islands where the trappers were going, or left to be taken to the village later. The trappers' supplies had to go back to the ship and be loaded into the hold. Captain Salenjus, impatient as always, wanted to leave immediately. Simeon told him our men could not possibly be ready before midnight. The captain agreed to wait until midnight, but no longer. Furthermore, the booms would be taken in at six o'clock, according to seamen's rulings, so the men would have to load their packages before then or load them by hand.

When the men were ready to go back to the village for the rest of their gear Jeannette, Simeon, and I went with them. We went to give Mrs.

Nevzoroff her penicillin shot, got the children ready to go, had dinner, and entertained some of the men from Unalaska, whom Simeon had not seen in years.

Then at 10:00 P.M., as we returned from giving Mrs. Nevzoroff her next shot, we heard the church bell tolling and we knew that a special service was being held. The three of us slipped into the back of the candlelit church. The church looked lovely with its soft lights and the flowers the women had made. The entire service was sung by three choirs instead of the usual one. The whole church vibrated with sound and was most impressive in its simplicity. The prayers of the entire village went with their trappers.

Shortly after eleven o'clock the truck stopped outside our quarters and, dressed warmly, we three scrambled aboard. The four youngsters and their suitcases were lifted aboard, and others climbed in. Trappers, with their wives clinging to them, all laughing excitedly, shouted good-byes to those unable to get on. At last, packed like sardines, we were off for the dock, singing and swaying under a brilliant canopy of stars. There was a bit of pathos about this last gay evening, for seldom a year passed but some trapper failed to return in the spring.

The dock swarmed with people. After I had kissed the children and seen them going off happily to bed with a packet of little gifts in their hands I looked for Simeon. He was waiting to introduce me to a number of his friends whom I had missed during the day. They were as delightful as their names sounded: Peter Schamakinski, Ivan Berikoff, Grigor Bezizikoff, Sergei Dushkin, and Alexei Zaharoff. Russian? No: Aleut.

Finally we shook hands with all the trappers and bade them "good-bye and good luck!" The ship's bells sounded at midnight. We nearly burned our throats, gulping down a last mouthful of coffee in the galley where we were having a last-minute chat with Nurse Keaton, Jeannette, and some of the crew. We scrambled over the rail, and the ship slowly pulled away from the dock and headed out into the bay. Bill Golley's wonderful smile gleamed back at us from the rail.

For a few minutes we stood there, watching the dark hull with its lighted windows as it moved slowly away. Then we all made a dash for the truck and were soon speeding back toward the village, just in time to catch a last glimpse of the *North Star*. Then we were back in the village, dropping people off at their homes; mostly women and children, but a few men, too. Danny Nevzoroff and Bill and Mattie Dirks came in for sandwiches and coffee. Then we went to give Mrs. Nevzoroff her shot. She was improved, but there was a houseful there: Vasha Zaochney and her four children, three in a bed, and young Vasha, and Peter Nevzoroff and his wife, Annie. We stumbled home and dropped wearily into bed. We slept through the alarm three hours later, but fortunately Simeon awoke soon after. We dressed and got the shot ready and walked through the dark and the lightly falling snow to the old lady's house. Only Peter was awake. I woke Mrs. Nevzoroff; we gave her the shot and made her comfortable, then headed home to bed again. Lights were still bright in many homes.

The next three days dawned clear and cold, with snow on the ground. Sparrows and rosy finches fed on the window sill and sang from nearby rooftops. Our days and nights were broken into three-hour sections. I taught school in that time frame, and Simeon helped sort out our supplies at the dock for transfer to the village. Many were in very bad shape. The men and boys trucked the store and school supplies, and our own, over to the village, working long hours each day.

Mary Snigaroff was rapidly growing weaker and was suffering great pain. I gave her morphine as instructed, and wired for APC and codeine and more penicillin for Mrs. Nevzoroff. She, too, was weaker; too much family around. Peter spoke to Vasha, who took her four children and went home. Mary Prokopeuff came in to sit with the old lady during the day while Peter Nevzoroff worked with the men; Peter took over at night.

During this time we experienced some of the compensation that enables a doctor to go out on call at all hours of the day and night. We bundled up as though for a trip to the Arctic, took our flashlights and medical things, and plunged into the raw beauty of the blustery Aleutian night. The hills and islands looked like monstrous haystacks lightly dusted with snow. Dim lights, safeguards against the *idigidis,* burned in some of the windows; others were dark. Stars sparkled in the sky and slowly the Big Dipper circled the North Star. We noted its changed position each time we went out. Snow and sleet, borne on the wind from some unseen cloud, stung our faces as we shuffled cautiously along the slippery trail, crossed the bridge, and climbed the hill past Philip Nevzoroff's silent house and came at last to Mrs. Nevzoroff's. Here a dog barked sharply, once or twice, at us and our moving lights. Peter, ever alert, opened the door and we entered the warm bright room. His mother lay there, eyes closed, breathing laboriously. I would shake her gently and a sweet little smile would light her face as she looked up at me—reward enough for leaving my warm bed.

The day after I wired for medicine a plane soared in from Adak, on a howling wind, with Captain Blizzard, Dr. Thode, and the medicines. Because of a cross wind they had had a bad bumpy ride, although General Lynch had sent his own plane and it was comfortably appointed. They probably would have to spend the night because of the storm. Dr. Thode went to see our patients. Later the officers came back to spend the evening.

Dr. Thode told us he was taking back to Adak an Army boy who had been staying out at the range. He had come into the base that morning, armed with a knife and looking over his shoulder wildly, shouting, "Someone is after me!" He was mortally afraid of the dark and loneliness.

"I hope the people here don't hear of this," Simeon said. "It would be certain proof of *idigidis.*"

That weekend we were treated to the awesomely beautiful sight of great green waves dashing high against the cliffs along the shore and falling back in a smother of white foam and spume. It was difficult to make our way through the storm to care for our patients. Our old lady was better, but very sore from all the needle punctures. I fixed something hot and nourishing for her each trip. Sunday night the stove ran dry and we went to bed dinnerless. We got up a couple of hours later, and Simeon finally found the pump and oil to start the stove so that we could keep the instruments sterilized. I went alone at 6:30 A.M. and found Mrs. Nevzoroff's temperature down. She was stronger, but not getting much sleep, due to the soreness from the many injections. Simeon was ill and stayed in bed until noon that morning. Everyone had been working harder than usual. The men remaining in the village wanted to get the supplies and coal brought over to the village so that the remaining trappers, those who were going to trap Amlia and Atka Islands, could be on their way.

The youngsters started on "old-timers' stories." The little ones and I worked on what Larry Nevzoroff called "Atka ABCs."

A telegram came saying that Pari Lokanin's baby had arrived—a girl. Mike was a beaming papa again. It was our fifth girl in five weeks.

When Peter Nevzoroff's wife Annie, who was pregnant, heard the news she said, "Again! I wish for boy."

Alex and Elizabeth Prossoff came up for the evening. As usual, Alex told stories. He had gone fishing in Otaru Bay one time to show the Japanese how the Aleuts fished with a gig.

"All I caught is an old boot," he laughed, and Elizabeth laughed with him.

He told us how good the Japanese interpreter on Attu had been to them. He had advised them to take all the food and necessities that they could to Japan. Alex told how the guards at Otaru took their sugar, salt fish, seal, and sea-lion meat from them, and how he traded a tent for fifty pounds of rice to keep them alive. Alex promised that when he had time he would come and tell the whole story of when the Japanese captured them on Attu and later took them to Japan and made them work for them.

Next day Simeon borrowed Philip Nevzoroff's skiff and went duck hunting with his new gun. He got two harlequin ducks, beautiful birds, black with white on their heads and golden brown near the wings. He turned back when he saw a plane land. When the ducks were ready to serve four Army officers from the Alaska Army Communication System in Anchorage arrived on an inspection trip. They brought our own guns, which had been sent by our friends, Rolf and Sylvia Wittmer. They said that there was lots of mail.

That night we had another earthquake, accompanied by sounds as of a musical saw vibrating. Larry Nevzoroff and Davy Zaochney again said that it sounded to them like a baby crying.

Eighteen big bags of mail were trucked over the next morning; another school day disrupted. Much of the contents were the long-awaited packages and the ever-increasing number of magazines for Clara Snigaroff. We, too, received much personal mail and many packages, as well as three telegrams just relayed from Adak. The most important of these was one from my older sister, telling of her husband's recent death. Our agent in Chicago wanted additional information, as he had already started to plan next year's lecture tour. This brought home to us as nothing else could how brief the time remaining for us with these courageous people who had won our hearts.

That night Simeon showed a reel of the movies we had taken on Atka earlier that summer. The delight of the people in viewing themselves and each other was wonderful to see. They supplied a running commentary for an otherwise silent film. They said that they never knew their flowers were so beautiful.

The next day was Thanksgiving, and we all had much to be thankful for. Our dear old lady was well on the way to recovery; the penicillin Dr. Thode and Captain Blizzard had brought on that stormy day had saved her life. Now her two older sons, who would not leave while her life hung in the balance, would soon go trapping with the others. We spent the entire day checking and stowing away school supplies and our own supplies that the men had trucked over.

The youngsters set up the classroom for movies again that night, a double feature from the base which ran from seven until eleven o'clock. Simeon and I left after the murderer was exposed and enjoyed our first oyster stew in ages.

It was good to note that all of the youngsters wore new shoepacs. The knitting class would work on socks and mittens for themselves and the little ones.

The last six days in November were clear, bright, and beautiful. A light snow lay on the ground, with the temperature hovering between twenty-five and thirty degrees; the air was crisp and fresh. We would have liked nothing better than to take our guns and go to Korovin. Duty called, however, and instead we spent the entire Thanksgiving weekend answering business and personal mail. When my part of that was done I got the new books and paper work ready for the children for Monday.

We were not the only ones working. Most of the supplies had been trucked over, and loads of coal had been dumped by each house. The seven men who were to fan out over Amlia Island to trap were hoping the good weather and calm sea would hold until they had crossed the treacherous pass between the two islands. They were busy now, making sure that their homes and families would be secure while they were gone. Andrew Snigaroff would trap on Atka so that he could get home frequently. Some of the families had moved in together. Vasha Zaochney's family was staying nights with Annie Golley. When Pari Lokanin and the baby got back from Adak they would stay with Mattie Dirks. Matrona Gardner would be with Vera Snigaroff.

Bill Dirks, Jr., came in, the last evening in November, to announce another birth: Cedar Snigaroff had a grandchild! We finally guessed what he meant: one of the sheep had had a lamb—the first one born on Atka.

Anfusia Snigaroff and Ethel Ross Oliver

✳ DECEMBER 1946

1. agalgugaq 2. tugidigamaq

(chief month or long month)

December first was a red letter day. It had taken seven months, but our own piano had finally arrived. It was uncrated and installed in our quarters, and the little piano we had found there was shifted back into the schoolroom. Simeon immediately set to work to put the piano in tune. One of our purposes in coming to Atka was to collect Aleut folklore and folk music. Already I had started the children on the *onikas*, (bedtime stories) told by the old people. Simeon would try to find the music and transcribe it for piano.

His first opportunity came the next evening when Alex Prossoff, Elizabeth, and the baby came up for the evening. Alex and George Prokopeuff were leaving the next morning for Amlia. Alex wanted us to keep an eye on his family in his absence, which we promised to do. Early during the conversation we asked if they had old lullabies for their babies. "Oh, yes," they chorused. "An Aleut baby is always lulled and sung to sleep."

As a result, later in the evening when the baby became sleepy and Elizabeth took him into the dark and quiet of the next room, we listened for the native melody she would sing. To our surprise the soft notes of a familiar strain came to us: Elizabeth was humming "Red River Valley"!

One of the things we enjoyed about Alex was his penchant for telling humorous tales on himself. That night while the baby slept and we visited over coffee and fresh fruit Alex asked, "I ever tell you about the time I shoot my stove?"

"No," Simeon answered. "How did that happen?"

"It was on the Rat Island one winter. I was going from one end to the other and when I got there I was going to cook some geese I have in my pack and make some coffee before I go back. There is little barabara there and a Mascot stove. We trap the eight miles from one cabin to the other. Everything is ready for cooking. I feel in my pockets but I got no matches. I don't smoke that time. Then I think what to do? Someone I hear say one time that you can start fire by shooting cloth. So I have shotgun. I get dry cloth when I turn my pockets out; I cut it up, take a piece and pound it into seal blubber until it's full of oil. Then I put it in shell next to two wads and put other wad in and put shell in gun.

"Now I want to shoot where I can get cloth when it burns so I look for something hard to stop the cloth. Only thing I see is Mascot stove. Good! I think that will stop the cloth. It will fall on floor by stove. I pick it up and put in stove, start my fire.

"So I step outside door, lift my gun, and fire. I look around. No cloth drop. I sure surprised to see I shoot clear through stove!" We all burst into laughter, and we never did find out how he cooked his goose.

Shortly after the story was ended they picked up their sleeping baby and headed home. Alex left with a carton of cigarettes and a whole box of kitchen matches as well as our wishes for a successful trapping season.

Alex and George Prokopeuff left for Amlia next morning in a cold, windy rain. They were the first of the seven men who were going to trap that island. The others would follow at the next weather break. Their eagerness to be on the way was increased when Andrew Snigaroff brought in two foxes he had trapped the day before on Atka Island.

Bill Dirks, Jr., and some of the older boys hauled thirty-six barrels of oil to the school and brought some gas for the light plant that day. The Old Chief forecast stormy weather so outside work was speeded up.

With the arrival of needed school supplies I found it possible to accomplish more individualized teaching. This brought greater satisfaction to the youngsters and to me. The age range in the group was so great that it was most practical to allot individual assignments and check the work with the pupil alone; this enabled each to advance at his own speed. It also permitted more freedom for the boys to fish and hunt when necessary and still keep up with their schoolwork. Needless to say, we had group work each day. For instance, early in the month the children began planning a Christmas program in which everyone would have a part.

Simeon tested the children's voices in preparation for a regular music class. He found that shy Titiana Creveden had the truest voice, but all were good. Many had sung by rote in the church choir all of their lives. Simeon had taught his piano pupils to read music. Now he would teach the children to sing by note. Through his skillful direction he soon had the whole group singing Christmas carols.

One afternoon as Annie Golley left after her knitting class she said to me, "Trappers gone. Now is time to weave baskets. I come over tonight and we start you making basket. *Ang?*"

"*Ang*," I answered. "Good! I'll be glad to learn how to make baskets at last."

In July, August, and September we had worked with the grass—gathered it, cured it, and separated it into warp and woof strands. For the last two months it had lain under the bed in the guest room, rolled in clean white fifty-pound flour sacks. Our energies in October and November had been employed in knitting for the trappers. I was eager to work with the grass again.

After dinner I dragged out a roll of the grass that Annie called the *khla* (boy), which would be the warp. When she arrived she told me to get a small bowl of water. We set up a card table in the living room and set to work.

"First we twist many grasses to make strong. Have to wet fingers so grass don't break. Do like this." Annie dipped her fingers in the water and ran them down the length of the strand, then very carefully twisted it. She placed the twisted piece to one side and picked up another. I followed her example. We twisted over a hundred warp strands that evening.

"Tomorrow night we start weaving after we make few weaving strings from other grass, the *anaq*," she promised.

Annie came the next night to start my basket. This time we twisted a number of weaving strands from the longer, stronger "mother" grass. Then Annie picked up several warp strands of equal length and a long strand which she called a weaver. With an intricate stitch she wove the warp strands together and spread them in a circle to begin the basket. The circle formed the center of the bottom of the basket. She tied in a second weaver. Then she separated the individual warps and, holding a single one between the thumb and forefinger of her left hand, she intertwined it with the weaver in her right hand. Then she took the next warp and continued the process, always firmly gripping the assembly as each strand was finished. From time to time she inserted new warp strands, thus enlarging the circle. This would be the bottom of the basket.

She put it in my hands when it was a mere half-inch in diameter. "Hold it firm like this so stitch doesn't slip, but don't pull," Annie instructed me. "That break the grass. Keep little bit damp, not wet, and twist weaver little bit each stitch."

She laughed and added, "In Juneau some peoples say they hear we weave baskets under water. How they think we do that?"

At first my fingers were all thumbs, until I caught on to the rhythm of the work. Annie showed me how to insert new warp by extending it half an inch under and weaving it in as usual, then bending the extension against the next warp and tying it in with the next stitch. Annie kept an eye on my slow progress, indicating when a new warp should be inserted. After a couple of hours she said, "That's enough for one night. Get one of Simeon's big white handkerchiefs to wrap this in and you can put the grass away."

Earlier in the summer she had told me that no one had embroidery thread to weave in for the colorful designs. I told her I would try to get some by the time we needed it. I wrote to my mother, and in the big mail last month Mother had sent not only a generous supply of different colors of thread but also a couple of her crochet pattern books with ideas for new designs.

When I went back to the living room I took the package and showed it to Annie. She spread the embroidery thread on the table and fingered it lovingly. Her face was beaming. "My basket ready to put in design now," she said.

"Take what you need," I offered. She chose two skeins, one pink and one pale green.

The first week in December came to a close with the storm that the Old Chief, Mr. Dirks, Sr., had forecast. A wind came howling out of the north, bringing a freezing rain and heavy forbidding clouds. Lights must be on by three-thirty in the afternoon, and the earliest we turned them off in the morning was nine-thirty, and then not in the classroom.

The storm was too savage for Annie to come over to continue on the basket, but her daughter Elizabeth came and we knitted together while Simeon designed a simple Christmas card for us to send out in the next mail. Elizabeth told me how, as a tiny girl, she had watched Annie knitting. One day she got some big matches and sharpened the ends. She was busy knitting when her father saw her. He made a set of needles for her, and when they were finished and polished he gave them to the delighted little girl, saying, "Now you may knit socks for me."

By Monday the storm had blown itself out, and although it was still cloudy a plane came in, bringing Pari Lokanin and baby Helen home. Dr. Thode and three Red Cross women came, too, as well as Nurse Cummings from Unalaska. Dr. Thode and I visited Mary Snigaroff, and later I made cotton rings to protect her pressure areas. The doctor brought more medication for her. Before they left the Red Cross women promised to send Christmas decorations on an early plane.

The youngsters came for play practice and I read aloud to them for an hour or more. Before they went home we promised to go clamming the next night.

Davy Zaochney, raucous as a raven, rounded up all of the older boys and girls, and they gathered in our quarters by eight o'clock, although we were not to leave until nine-thirty. At the right moment he shouted, "Let's go!" Everyone donned warm outer garments, shouldered a shovel or rake, and off we went to the dock, sacks in hand. Clouds hid the moon. Out on the water we could hear, but not see, a boat engine warming up. We hailed it and two boats appeared. We all piled in, engines purred, and we were off. Behind us lay the tiny village, bright windows gleaming. As we cut through the water phosphorescence burned in our wake, and along the beach a light flickered, appearing and disappearing among the rocks: Olean and Clara Snigaroff gathering sea eggs at low tide, as for centuries their grandmothers had done at the time of full moon.

Once we reached the clam beds around the little island near Chuniksax we scattered and started raking and shoveling for the rich, fat cockleshell clams. Excited voices rose and fell on the crisp night air, and dark shapes bent and straightened. There was the silken swish of the waters and the sound of sleepy geese somewhere on an island beach. With our own sack filled, we helped others until every sack bulged. Then the boys brought the boats around and walked them up little channels, as close to the beds as possible. We loaded the clams and moved out to meet the incoming tide. Our engine was cold, so Simeon rowed while George Nevzoroff, our boatman, pulled on the starting cord, trying to crank the engine. It was midnight when we reached the dock where the others waited. We all fell to and carried the boats high up on the beach. Simeon and I dragged our own clams home and weighed them: forty-nine pounds. We gave Affia Snigaroff twenty pounds and would share the rest with Mike Lokanin, Bill Dirks, Jr., and Annie Golley. At 1:00 A.M. we finally went to bed.

We woke to a lovely clear day, blue sky, and birdsong. Moses Prokopeuff came running up the hill to the school to say that someone had sighted deer near Atxalax and some men were going hunting. "Could the boys go, too?"

When I answered "Yes," off he ran. He had no sooner gone than Mattie Dirks came to ask if Ann Dirks could help her, because Bill and Mike Lokanin were leaving next day for Amlia with the other trappers.

For some reason Moses had not gone hunting with the men, but instead chose to go over to Korovin Bay with Simeon and me when school was closed early so others could help at home.

More than a month had elapsed since we had last hiked over to Korovin. The coming of winter had so changed the landscape that when we reached the bay we walked right into some artist's version of the craters of the moon, eerily beautiful. A weird greenish light lay on the water. The bay was strangely calm, and myriads of ducks and geese rested on the water or flew high overhead. We walked down along the beach, which was strewn with razor clam shells. All along the beach foxes had patted down trails, weaving in and out among the rocks. Over on the far shore where the ancient burial caves yawned in the dark cliffs a group of old squaw ducks called, "Ah-ha halik, ah-ha halik!" over and over again. Just at sunset a flight of beautiful gray emperor geese flew low over the water, so close that we could see their white heads, yet so far out that if we had killed one we could not have retrieved it. The ebbing tide had already robbed us of two ducks that Simeon had shot. The southern sky burned red behind the snow-capped volcanic peaks, a cloud of steam rose from the nearer hot springs on the slope of one, and the northern sky was black with impending storm when we left our bay of enchantment and headed home for a fresh clam dinner.

Early the next morning the rest of the trappers embarked for Amlia. It was cloudy and a storm threatened, but the men were certain that they would be across the pass before it broke. A group of us gathered to see them off. Mike Lokanin entrusted Pari and the baby to our care, and then they were off. We stood on the dock and watched them until they were out of sight, then silently went our own way.

The village, without the men, settled down to quiet living until they returned. The older schoolboys shouldered more responsibility for family concerns. In the evenings our quarters were a gathering place for many of the women and children—the women to work on baskets or to knit, the children to work jigsaw puzzles or to look at books. One evening Davy Zaochney looked up from a picture of a camel in a *National Geographic* magazine and asked, "Mr. Oliver, what part of the camel do they make cigarettes from?" Often while we worked Simeon played the piano for us.

The expected storm arrived with wind and rain, and much of the snow disappeared. Flocks of little birds foraged for seeds in the dead grass all over the village. Mattie Dirks and Vasha Zaochney came in one Sunday morning while we were having breakfast. Vasha had a bad toothache and asked Simeon to pull her tooth. We gave her novocaine and he pulled it. Mattie told us that dogs from the base had killed six of her chickens.

With the change of tide the little birds ceased caroling. The wind grew stronger and brought in snow and sleet. The temperature began to drop. Simeon drained Mike Lokanin's hot-water tank and Annie Golley's. For three days the blizzard raged. Pipes froze all over the village, and the blowtorch was in great demand. Snow lay deep on the ground, and we thought winter had at last come to stay. Before the blizzard the hills and islands looked like great brown haystacks with a light sprinkling of snow. The blizzard had turned them completely white except for a brown smudge outlining their shapes, where the constant wind blew the snow away.

In spite of the weather most of the children came to school. They particularly enjoyed the play practice and the Christmas selections. We tried to have all of the women and children come to dinner with us, a few at a time, and stay for the evening when others joined us. The evening that Mattie Dirks and her boys came she told us that Cedar Snigaroff had found two dogs in the sheep pen. They had hurt four sheep, one so badly it had to be killed.

Four or five women came nearly every evening to weave on their baskets. Annie Golley kept a close eye on my progress. One evening as she inspected my work she took out a few stitches and laughingly said, "Too soon to put in design!"

The day after the storm was over dawned clear and very cold. A beautiful big moon sailed in the morning sky, with Venus sparkling like a diamond nearby. The sunrise over Amlia was particularly brilliant. Angel Snigaroff had not come to school for several days. She came with her sisters that morning, proudly wearing a new pair of mukluks her father had made for her. Andrew had used the esophagus of a seal for the leg and foot, with sea-lion flipper for the sole. The short stiff hairs on the flipper enabled her to walk safely on the icy road. She took off one mukluk and showed me the pad of soft short grass which served as an insole to keep her tiny feet warm and dry. All four of the Snigaroff girls were very proud that their father knew how to make "old-time Aleut mukluks." The shortages during that winter brought back to use several Aleut crafts. Another example was the pair of short, wide skis George Prokopeuff made, with seal-skin bottoms. "No need for ski wax," he said. "See when I go up hill hairs go like this." He showed how the hairs would dig into the snow when going uphill. He smoothed them with his hand and said, "Then I go like wind down hill!"

When I went in to fix lunch at noon I found a note from Simeon saying that he had gone goose hunting, and postponing the singing lessons until evening. The youngsters approved this, and since we could leave school early I decided to take them for a walk. We ran and slid on the icy road and jumped in the snow drifts. On our way back home we stopped to watch a plane coming in. I had just started to prepare dinner when the jeep drove up and four men climbed out. Among them was Simeon, carrying his gun; others had ducks, and one carried a huge white bird. When they entered the living room I saw that the white bird was a large snowy owl—a monstrous one.

Simeon had hunted all day without success. At Korovin both water and sky were full of birds. He counted six hundred geese in one flock, and he saw as many as fifteen huge flocks in the air at one time. There were thousands of birds on the water, but no way to retrieve any he might shoot. Disappointed, he left Korovin and came back by the dock on the Nazan Bay side. As he turned homeward he saw two mallards drop down into the mouth of a small stream which emptied into the bay. He followed them and shot as they rose, hitting both. One fell back into the water and swirled around in an eddy. The second fell dead and landed in a snowbank across the stream. He stood surveying the situation and planning a way to retrieve his birds. Suddenly from behind him, and so close over his head that he instinctively ducked, something white hurtled past and plopped down on the duck in the snow. Then this huge bird, its talons clutching the mallard, turned and stared unblinkingly at Simeon. Simeon had worked too hard to allow this fellow to get away with his duck, so he shot it then and there. Then he went down to the shallow mouth of the stream to wade across, meaning to retrieve the bird in the water on his way. He took only a few steps before he sank to his boot tops in quicksand. Down and down he went. With all the strength he had he turned and, leaning forward, worked his legs as hard as he could, literally churning his way out. He said he was badly frightened for a bit, and he had good reason to be, for every now and then quicksand or a bog claims a victim. That night when the

youngsters came for music Moses Prokopeuff told of losing a brother
who fell in a bog. He was in to his armpits when rescued. He had
worked his way out of his packsack and had kept himself afloat by
resting his arms over it, but he was in a bad way when he was found,
and he died a week later.

The two officers who were with Lieutenant Barker were coming to
borrow our snowshoes. Captain Slusher and Captain Smith were stationed in Anchorage. They had been sent to inspect the beam station
equipment, about seven miles out on the range from the base. This
station was vital to planes flying to the Orient, as well as to those flying
out along the Aleutian Chain. The unexpected heavy snow brought by
the recent storm had not yet been cleared away, so the men decided to
snowshoe out if snowshoes were available. We lent them ours.

Two days later a warm chinook wind blew in from the Pacific, bringing rain. In a matter of hours the snow was gone and the hills and island
were again brown. That evening Lieutenant Barker came to ask Simeon
to mimeograph menus for the GIs' Christmas dinner, to which we were
invited.

A few days before Christmas another plane came in, bringing not
only mail for us and more magazines for Clara Snigaroff, but a whole
bag of mail that we had sent away a month earlier.

One of the pilots told us that they had spotted a small herd of reindeer
on the hills back of the base, so two days before Christmas Simeon and I
took the older boys and girls to see if we could get reindeer for Christmas dinner. It was a clear, beautiful day. We started early and each took
a sandwich, and with guns and a camera we headed up the old trail back
of Andrew Snigaroff's house. When we reached the tableland we spread
out in three groups. With the disappearance of the snow the deer had
climbed up into the higher hills again; no deer were in sight. When we
were all together again we hurried across the island, urged on by the
chill wind that blew in the upper lands. Soon we looked down into
Korovin, where the sea was smoky with fog which the wind was blowing into Nazan Bay. We passed the old lookout tower, now deserted,
and dropped down to Korovin. Here we got some ducks and Simeon
bagged our first emperor goose, a beautiful bird. Now we would have
our belated Thanksgiving dinner. It was a tired bunch of hunters who
trudged home that night, but they all wanted to go again soon.

On our return we learned that five of the Amlia trappers had brought the Old Chief in because he needed medical attention. We hastened down to see him, taking a little medical kit with us. He had considerable abdominal pain and needed the services of a doctor. We gave him medication for the pain and went back home to send a message to Dr. Thode. As we left the Dirkses' home Sophie told us that the trappers had brought twenty geese back, too. Every family would have goose for their American Christmas dinner.

Aleuts belonging to the Russian Orthodox Church celebrate Christmas twice each year—the American holiday on December 25, and the Russian one two weeks later, on January 7. Since we were free to choose when to take our holiday vacation we decided to close school during the week between New Year's Day and Russian Christmas and celebrate with our Aleut friends.

After breakfast on the day before Christmas Simeon went down to see the Old Chief, bringing additional pain medication and the word that a message had been sent to Dr. Thode. When he returned we spent the whole day making up bags for Santa to deliver to each family on Christmas Eve. Fortunately we had plenty of government mail bags on hand, so every family could have one. The Red Cross at Adak had sent us two boxes of Christmas tree trimmings, favors, and napkins, and these we divided. In red and green paper we wrapped our simple gifts for each individual. We took some of our surplus canned goods and put them in, too. We topped the bags with candy, nuts, and fresh fruit for the children and cartons of cigarettes for the adults. The cigarettes were a surprise gift from a friend at Adak. Major Schleuder, in charge of the PX, had found nineteen cases of wartime issue cigarettes. He knew that they were old and he wanted to dispose of them, so he sent them to Atka. Because they had been so well packaged they were in excellent condition, moist and fresh, and they were most welcome.

It was around 10:30 P.M. when the last mail bag was ready, and we were about to sit down to dinner when one of the youngsters came to get the can of cigarette "crumbs" which we always saved, following the crucial shortage of last October. I broke out the red Santa Claus suit and he put it on and took his family's bag home. Then he returned with two helpers. The three boys, Billy Golley, Davy Zaochney, and Peter Prokopeuff, delivered all of the Christmas bags. The boys had a lot of fun surprising the different families and telling us of their reception here and there.

As a fitting finale to that busy day we had Simeon's first emperor goose for our late Christmas Eve dinner. When I tidied the kitchen Simeon played old favorites on the piano before we called it a day. A knock on the door signaled the arrival of Mike Lokanin bearing gifts. So pleased and happy that we had remembered his month-old baby daughter, he had brought us the precious little icon which he had carried from Attu to Japan, hidden in his shirt. It had served the homeless group as their religious center during those bitter years, and it had come back to the Aleutian Islands with them. Mike made a lovely little speech as he handed this treasure to me and showed me where he had written on the back, "To Ethel Oliver—Mike E. Lokanin." My eyes were full of tears as I thanked him and gave him a hug. Simeon was as touched as I.

On Christmas morning birdsong floated in through our window to awaken us. We looked out on a brown world; every bit of snow in the village was gone again. Breakfast was not yet over when our neighbors began dropping in to wish us Merry Christmas. The children came to tell us how happy Santa's visit had made them. One little tyke had hung up his stocking before going to bed, and his sister and brother had filled it after the bag arrived. Their eyes sparkled as they told of his delight when he awoke. "He was so happy!" Vera Nevzoroff said.

A couple of the boys from the base arrived to borrow glasses and some of the decorations and candles for their Christmas dinner table. "Somebody put water instead of gas in the jeep," one said, "but we'll probably have it running again soon, and we'll be here for you around two-thirty." We were going to be their guests at dinner.

"Oh, we can walk over," we assured them.

"No, we are going to come for you. The road is pretty muddy," they insisted.

After checking on Mr. Dirks, Sr., Simeon made and ran off menu placecards for the base dinner and I made a big batch of divinity fudge for the group at the base. We entertained Christmas callers all morning. We dressed and were waiting at two-thirty, but no jeep appeared. A little later we heard a heavy rumble and, looking up the road, saw the ten-ton bulldozer lumbering into view. When it drew up before the porch we saw that the boys had attached a trailer in which was a box covered with an army blanket. We climbed in, and our strange chariot lumbered clumsily back the way it had come. From their windows our laughing neighbors watched us go off to our dinner. All the way to the base the cat treads kicked muck back at us, seated on the box in our best bib and tucker. Fortunately we were able to dodge most of it, and when we drew up with a bumpy flourish at the door of the mess hall we were still presentable. We had both gone to dinner in all sorts of conveyances, from taxicabs and airplanes to dogsleds, but this was the first time either of us had gone by bulldozer! Simeon told the sergeant that had I been heftier than I was I might have taken it as an affront; instead I was delighted with the new experience. The long table was festive with the candles and Christmas decorations. The dinner was fine: roast wild goose, duck, and chicken with all of the usual trimmings. It was followed by an hour or two of stories and visiting, and when it was time to leave the jeep was ready to take us home.

We were not surprised the next morning when the plane buzzed the school, for we were expecting Dr. Thode in answer to our SOS. School was in session and the children were having milk and the cake we had brought back from the post when six officers arrived. Simeon took the doctor and his helpers down to the Dirkses' home and I continued school until noon, then fixed lunch for our seven guests. Simeon told me that the doctor had found a stricture and done something to relieve it, and although the Old Chief was in great pain he had presented Henry Thode with a silver-fox fur, holding the fur in his hand as he said, "Doctor, you give us plenty medical help. Community wants to give this skin to you."

Young Bill Dirks chimed in, "From whole community." Before the officers left to return to Adak Simeon gave Dr. Thode and Jack Mann autographed copies of his recent book, *Back to the Smoky Sea.*

That night we went down to take Mr. Dirks some morphine as the doctor had prescribed. He told us the Aleut names for a number of our plants and the medicinal uses of some. Many have aptly descriptive names. One which delighted us and caused the girls who were listening to giggle was the name for the Alaska cotton grass, *aglax lim itch woosie*—land goose toilet paper!

Except for Christmas Day school went on more or less as usual. The big thing in all our minds was the Christmas program to be given during Russian Christmas holidays, beginning January sixth. After school, the last Friday in December, the children gave the schoolroom a good cleaning and did the hall and clinic, too. The older ones came back in the evening and started decorating the room, working until 10:00 P.M.

On Saturday afternoon Simeon and I walked over to Korovin. A heavy wind was blowing. No eagles sat on their perches above the lake, but salmon still swam in the shallows. Billy Golley was at the old cabin, picking a goose for the family's supper. Simeon got a goldeneye, or merrywing, duck in the creek. We went on out to the beach to try for a goose. Lots of them were out on the water or high overhead. We met Cedar Snigaroff and walked back to the cabin with him. He gave us a nice fat emperor goose and we started home. Back at the upper end of the lake we met the jeep. The men were looking for us; their sergeant was ill. They brought us home and we sent the requested medicine back to the base with them. When the duck was cleaned that night I noted that it had been feeding on salmon eggs. I should have known better than to cook it, but I roasted the two birds next day. The duck was fishy, but the goose was excellent.

The last two days of December were stormy, with rain and wind. The thermometer stood at thirty degrees both days. The youngsters finished the Nativity mural and a Christmas air pervaded the building. Affia and Olean Snigaroff came one evening to do the front of the room. I stayed with them while Simeon entertained the two sergeants who had returned our snowshoes.

On New Year's Eve Annie Golley came over, playing Santa. She brought three pairs of beautiful hand-knit socks, a scarf, and a kerchief. She went home with some mincemeat, a carton of cigarettes and, to her delight, some raffia. She said she had paid one of the women a quarter for two strands last year. The raffia is occasionally used in basket weaving.

Late in the afternoon Simeon and I walked over to the base to hear the New Year's celebration as it crossed our nation—New York and Chicago—and then we came home in the jeep. The mess hall cookstove was out so we rounded up some gasoline camp stoves. At midnight the villagers fired guns into the air to welcome in the New Year.

Atka Village children with the Russian Christmas Star

❋ JANUARY 1947

anulgilum tugida

(month of the black cormorant)

January and a New Year! When I asked why January was called the month of the black cormorant I was told that the early Aleuts used to hunt the cormorants then to supplement their dwindling food supply. The birds were hunted at night on the low cliffs where they nested, and captured by hand. Their snake-like necks were wrung and the birds were bagged. Archaeologists have noted cormorant bones in the middens of the western Aleutians. Since guns and ammunition have been available ducks and geese have replaced the black cormorant in the winter diet, except for rare cases on the trap lines.

Because the Russian Orthodox Church followed the old-style Julian calendar, the church New Year was still two weeks away, and we were deep in preparations for our second Christmas celebration this winter.

One of the interesting Christmas traditions in the Aleut villages was star caroling, or starring, as they called it. During our holiday preparations we heard many expressions of regret that all of the stars had been destroyed. We had little in the village with which to make a star; nevertheless we told the youngsters that if we could enlist one of the older men to show us something of its creation we would try. The girls offered to make crepe paper flowers for it and for church decorations. By pooling the assets of the entire village we gathered the materials. William Dirks, Sr., still recuperating, worked with the boys to make the eight-pointed star, four feet in diameter. Then it was brought to our quarters to be covered and finished. We used a sheet for the back covering, and Simeon painted sprigs of Aleutian flowers on white bond paper, in lieu of glass, cut to fit the eight large points and an equal number of smaller points. He spent an entire afternoon drawing and coloring the lovely Nativity scene on cloth for the stationary center about which the star revolves. Around this center the flowers were fastened—the crown. Rosettes tipped each point and ribbons joined the points together. It was indeed a gay and colorful affair, and many came from all over the village to admire its growing beauty. "Ai ya ya!" they exclaimed.

On Sunday, the fifth, more of our Amlia trappers came in. We had looked for them earlier, but at full moon the tides run very high and strong in Amlia Pass; wicked water for small boats. Those with outboard engines did not dare brave the crossing except under the most favorable conditions. Two groups had inboard engines in their dories, so they came in. They brought disappointingly few blue foxes for their season on Amlia. George Prokopeuff was convinced that the silver foxes were killing off the smaller blues.

For some days the boys at the base had watched the growing moon, and that Sunday evening five of them came to go on a moonlight clamming trip. Moses Prokopeuff had promised to take them, but on this particular night he and Sophie Dirks were working like mad to finish the star for the church service the next afternoon, so he begged off. However, he ran down and asked his uncle, George Prokopeuff, to take us. Accordingly, at 9:30 P.M. we left four of the children in the kitchen working on the star, and we went clamming with George and the GIs. We worked fast once we reached Chuniksax, and very shortly we had our sacks and buckets filled. The Army boys were as delighted as youngsters with this new experience. We all laughed as they told how they had been going down to the beach at the post and running along the edge of the waves, expecting the tide to bring the clams in to them. They were amazed that here on the beds they could dig with their feet and kick out the big fat clams. We were gone less than two hours.

On our return everybody crowded into the kitchen to watch Simeon open and clean the clams for a feed. The boys were from Texas, Colorado, and Wisconsin, so they were having their first experience with this type of food. Rather gingerly at first they took the firm white muscle, which holds the clam to its shell, and tasted it raw. Soon, however, they were stretching out their hands for more. I fried pan after pan of the luscious fat fellows and at midnight a crowd of us sat around the table in the living room, drinking coffee, eating fried clams, and sampling the fruitcake which the girls had made to serve to our guests following the Christmas program.

It was good that we had gone clamming that night, for a storm blew in the next day. This was the time that the overdue baby of Annie and Peter Nevzoroff decided to make his appearance. I was working on angel wings when one of the girls, in a housecoat and galoshes, ran in to say that Annie Golley wanted me at the Nevzoroffs' right away. I went as soon as I could slip into my boots and parka, and I found two very frightened women trying to deliver the baby, who was still reluctant to come. There was little that I could do except reassure them and the suffering mother and arrange to wire our good doctor in Adak for advice. On my way back to the school I picked up a boy and Simeon wrote out a message which the boy carried over to the base. Soon an answer came back that the Navy was responding. No planes were available in Adak. A little later Vasha Zaochney appeared to say that the baby, a boy, had arrived. I went back with her to take care of its eyes and see how the mother was. A plane flew over the village and not many minutes later a young Navy lieutenant drove up in the jeep, prepared to take our patient to the hospital in Adak. Lieutenant Norris said that his plane had been en route from Dutch Harbor to Adak when the emergency call reached him. Despite the storm he gave the engine the gun and broke some speed records to drop down here forty minutes later. We thanked him sincerely and told him that the stork had arrived first. Everything was under control, but it was wonderful to know how eager the Army and Navy were to lend a helping hand when the village needed it. Then I went back to my costumes.

Costumes for the entire play had to be very simple and made from available materials. Angel wings—what could we use to make them? We cudgeled our brains, trying to figure out what we could use that would stand up under the strain. At last we hit on the idea of a lace curtain, doubled and starched stiff. When it was cut to shape a little frill of fringed crepe paper pasted around the edge completed it. Sometimes we had really felt the need for a scrap-bag or rag-bag, but as yet the village did not possess one to draw on for emergencies like school programs, masquerades, and like occasions.

All day on the sixth I worked on costumes and last minute preparations, with time out only for the baby's arrival, so we missed the first church service, which was held in the early afternoon. At 7:00 P.M. Simeon and I joined the rest of the villagers for the evening service. How nice the little church looked! Danny Nevzoroff had used the flowers that the girls had made to good effect, on the altars and over the doorways. Chairs were brought in for us, as usual, but the rest of the congregation stood, except for our dear little old lady, Periscovia Nevzoroff, and Mary Snigaroff. Andrew carried Mary over through the snow. This was probably her last Christmas, and her participation was so devout that it made tears start in the eyes of many of us. During the service I held one or another of the new babies whose mothers stood behind me. It was very cold in the church, for it had no stove. The Old Chief sent one of the boys out for a gasoline camp stove. When it was brought in the boy pumped and pumped, and when he lit it, it immediately went out. Mr. Dirks came from the choir loft, picked up the tank and shook it, and then with a severe look thrust it at the boy, who immediately went out with it. He was able to start the stove when he returned, and soon its warmth was pervading the women's section of the church. All of the men and boys were up in the choir loft.

The service, chanted or intoned, lasted for two and a half hours. At its close all the worshipers went forward, crossed themselves, and kissed the holy picture on the altar; even our newest babies had their tiny faces pressed to it by mother, aunt, or godmother. Then we all exchanged Christmas greetings.

On Russian Christmas morning we had not yet breakfasted when Captain Blizzard's plane brought Dr. Thode to look at our new mother and baby Paul. The doctor was pleased to learn the baby's name, for his own middle name was Paul. After our calls he came back to share some of our famous 1898 sourdough pancakes with us and Captain Blizzard. Then Simeon made up packages of fresh clams for them to take home with them.

A short time later Mike Lokanin brought us two big emperor geese, and Bill Dirks, Jr., followed with a third.

Without warning we heard a commotion in the hallway and a large group of villagers came in, bearing the Christmas Star. Starring had begun. They all faced the east as they sang their Aleut carols and some Russian ones while the star was gently rotated about its stationary center. The entire proceeding was truly lovely. We gave them fruit and cookies for the party which would follow after they had made the rounds of the village. Each home so honored contributed something. They held their star so proudly as they sang, and all made way for it as they departed.

Our program was for the night of the eighth, and all that day everyone was very busy. All we women and girls were in curlers and kerchiefs. There were endless last things to do. Simeon made the programs and the boys set up the chairs. Our GI guests arrived before the stage was set, so some of them helped with that.

The church choir, with the revolving star, sang the star carols. That made an excellent beginning for the evening. Several children spoke the pieces they had learned. Tiny Angel (short for Angelina) Snigaroff had a long poem which she spoke beautifully. Her name was fitting, for she was born on Christmas Eve six years before. She wanted Santa to bring her a doll, so she spoke clearly and well. All of the little ones did well.

Of course, the *pièce de résistance* was the Nativity play and the Christmas carols sung at the appropriate times—the old, old story, ever new. Simeon and I had seen beautiful and costly productions in New York and in churches elsewhere, where everything was as nearly perfect as artistry and money could make it. Never, however, had we seen it more enthusiastically or devoutly performed than in that little village. Simplicity was the keynote. Costumes for shepherds, kings, and the holy family were the commandeered bathrobes and housecoats of the village, worn with the gayest headkerchiefs obtainable. Affia Snigaroff made a lovely angel in a white satin nightgown with surplice and wings of lace curtain, tinsel twined in her dark hair. Baby Nicky Golley waved his fat legs in the air as he lay in the sweet-smelling hay in the crude manger before the blessed virgin, Nadesta Golley. George Nevzoroff took the part of Saint Joseph and stood nearby. The children's voices blended well as they sang their carols. Simeon played the piano for them. "O Come, All Ye Faithful" was particularly impressive, with all of the yougsters kneeling about the manger in the closing scene. These little ones had few inhibitions and were undaunted by their somewhat ludicrous appearance.

Santa topped off the evening with a big bag of gifts that had been accumulating for days. Mike Lokanin made an excellent Santa, dressed in the red suit and with a pillow to help out his already portly appearance. Naturally jovial, he was never at a loss for the proper thing to say. Angel Snigaroff received her doll. Everyone received something, and Ochetla received many things. A real treasure, and indeed a museum piece, was the exquisite sea-lion-gut wall-pocket which Mary Snigaroff had made for me, though she was so weak that she could work but a few minutes daily. Mike gave Simeon a Gideons' Bible which doubtless came from one of the hotels at which the Attuans had stayed en route home from Japan. After the gifts the girls served punch and the fruitcakes they had made for the guests.

Next morning some of the young people helped straighten up the schoolroom and put things away. The next use to which it would be put would be the New Year's Eve dance.

After order was restored we donned our outdoor clothes and hiked over to our favorite area, Korovin Bay, leaving our neighbors to their celebration, Russian-Aleut fashion. They went to church every day, and a constant party went on during the entire week. Groups wandered from house to house in a joyful mood. This new year, their first at home and in their own homes, was ample reason for their happiness.

At Korovin we dug all day but unearthed little—only two stone knives—but the fascination for digging remained with us. The day was bright and sunny, the air crisp and cold. Enormous flocks of geese flew along the shore or settled among the rocks. When the tide went out we gathered a big bag of blue mussels before starting home. The jeep met us at the lake. At the post a plane was just landing, and we had a short visit with a friend of my son's from Adak. Lieutenant Rupert Welch told us that Ernest was well and would be coming to Atka later in the spring. The jeep then took us home. Young Annie Golley and Nadesta Golley came to share the blue mussels that evening.

The New Year's dance started at seven o'clock. It would last only until eleven, when all would get ready to attend midnight mass. Sergeant Jerry Jackowiski brought over some of the boys from the base as guests. Unlike Jack Miller, who had danced with all of the women and girls when he was in Atka, the GIs danced only with the girls. Because the few Atka men furnished the music, I danced with the older women in turn. The only ones standing on the sidelines were the teen-age boys who had not learned to dance. One young GI, not much older than they, was a very good dancer, and when I had the opportunity I asked him if he would be interested in teaching the boys to dance. He said he certainly would be glad to. It would give him something special to do two or three nights a week. I suggested he offer his services to the boys and get their reaction—let it come as his own idea. Later I saw them in a huddle, and smiles on all the faces.

The dance ran over until eleven-thirty, for Danny Nevzoroff, the lay priest or reader, loved to dance and kept saying, "Only ten minutes more! Time for one more dance!" and Alex Prossoff would start his accordion going again.

We had time for a cup of black coffee in the kitchen, and a few minutes before midnight we heard people going to church and joined them. Soon shots rang out on the frosty air and the hills gave back the echoes. Tracer bullets streaked across the darkened sky, and above and around the shots and shouts we heard the choir singing. We hurried into the church, taking with us the GIs who had stayed after the dance to attend the service.

For nearly an hour this unique mass carried on, the singing and chanting punctuated by rifle shots just outside the windows. The boys came and went, taking turns in the choir loft and playing their parts in the devotions. Then they would quietly slip out to fire a few more shots into the sky.

At last Danny left the loft; the service was over. The choir followed him to the altar where he turned to the congregation and said in English, "Happy New Year!" That was the signal for all to greet one another with handshakes and kisses and for more shots to ring out.

Cedar Snigaroff, when he greeted me, leaned over and whispered, "You come to my house after?"

"*Ang!*" I nodded. "For a little while, we'll come."

After we had seen our soldier guests depart in the jeep we followed some of our neighbors to Cedar's house. Several others were in the big spotless living room when we entered. Cedar brought two big chairs for us. Vera, his daughter, came in from another room with a fruit jar filled with a pale golden liquid, and three glasses. Ceremoniously our host poured and then handed us each a glass. We three clicked glasses and wished one another, "*Snu gu guthum!*" (Many Happy New Years!) and each responded, "*Snu gu cha!*" (The same to you!) The others in the room watched as we drank the cold cider-like liquid. We visited for a few minutes with Cedar, then thanked our host and, wishing the group "Many Happy New Years!" we took our leave.

All night long the arrival of the new year was celebrated, and when the birds wakened us next morning we looked out on a quiet village, asleep in winter sunshine. So beautiful was this second New Year's Day that we ate a hasty breakfast and, taking our movie camera, headed up the hill toward Sand Bay. The Old Chief had told us that he had seen a herd of reindeer heading that way. We took no guns, for the village had had a successful hunt the Sunday before.

For an hour we slowly climbed, keeping the village in sight. Often we turned to look back at it, sleeping below us at the water's edge, the round brown hills like great somnolent animals guarding it. Sixty miles east of us, across the gently heaving blue waters, Seguam's white cone rose from the Pacific. On such a brilliant day, although it was midwinter, the beautiful song of the brown Aleutian sparrow did not seem unusual, as it often did when it sang in the snow.

Once we had crossed the island and reached the north side we again found snow patches in the sheltered valleys and down the slopes. From the crest of the hills on that side Simeon spotted a herd of deer sleeping on a brown hilltop, across a deep valley far below where we stood. A wind blew up from Korovin Bay, whose waters rolled into Sand Bay below us to the right. We dropped under the crest so we were no longer outlined against the sky, and moved downwind to cross the head of the valley and to circle back upwind toward the sleeping deer.

On our way we heard the "rusty hinge" call of ptarmigan and a moment later saw them, up the slope from us under the lee of a rock cliff. Simeon got some good shots of the white birds before they became uneasy and flew away. We continued to stalk our deer, hoping to creep close enough to get good shots of them, too.

We crossed the valley and doubled back around the knoll on which the deer slept. All about us we noted where they had pawed up the tender white reindeer moss on which they fed. A little depression quartered up the knoll, and we followed it, right into the midst of the sleeping herd. We saw the mass of bare antlers rising like bleached dead willows, and the one standing animal feeding away from us. Simeon started the movie camera and its whirr aroused the herd, which as one animal jumped to its feet amid a clattering of antlers. After a moment of startled surprise the deer headed into the wind and thundered away. They ran for about a hundred and fifty yards, then stopped and turned to look back. Their hurried departure had failed to arouse one big fellow who continued to sleep, fifty feet from the grinding camera. We thought that the bull might have been wounded on the last hunt; unarmed, we had no wish to court trouble, so we made no attempt to go nearer.

Finally the old bull opened his eyes, glanced our way, and dropped his head to resume his slumber. Suddenly he threw back his head, gave us a wide-eyed look, and leaped to his feet. Stumbling in his haste, he tore after his fellows who were waiting and watching him. When he joined them the herd rounded the hill and disappeared. We laughed for days when we remembered the start he gave when he realized that we were not reindeer.

We were glad we went for pictures that day, for soon after that we received distressing news. The mail boat, which all the villages along the Chain had anticipated would reestablish the Aleutian mail run between Seward and Atka, had burned on her initial trip. All mail and freight was lost, but fortunately her crew survived. We were fearful that our whole summer's film work had gone down with her, along with clothing and other necessities for all the islands.

Christmas mail came in from Adak right after the middle of January. A cold snap arrived at that same time and all of the water pipes in the village froze. Every family moved into the one room that could be kept the warmest and holed up there. Our furnace was the hot-water type and had to be shut off, so we moved into the kitchen. Close beside the oil range we placed the typing table, and on either side of it two chairs from the living room. There, with the flames roaring up the chimney and the teakettle singing, we enjoyed our many letters and cards from family and friends, and caught up on news from other parts of the world.

School was held in the living room. The children wore their coats, for the gasoline camp stoves did not emit enough heat to more than take off the chilliest part of the cold. Standard tests had finally arrived, so I took small groups and administered them. The results enabled me to ascertain more accurately individual weaknesses, and we were soon making great strides in remedial work.

The living room became a dance floor when Bob Barnes came to teach. There were five teen-age boys in his class, all eager to learn to dance. Simeon usually played the piano for the class, but one evening he had to get some important mail ready to post, so one of the boys rounded up a squeaky old gramophone and a few dance records. We sat in the kitchen, working and listening to "The Good Old Summertime" scratching away above self-conscious giggles, Bob's "Step, step, close," and the shuffle of big clumsy shoepacs.

On the whole we rather enjoyed our return to pioneering. In the evenings when school was over Simeon would fill the kerosene lamp, for our light plant chose this time to balk, too. Then we would bundle up, take our kettles and bucket, and walk the distance of a couple of blocks to the creek to get our water. Our neighbors were carrying their water then, too, so we could exchange greetings and learn how they were faring.

Back once more in the kitchen, and with the lamp lit, we dawdled over our simple hearty dinner, washed the dishes, and then if it was not dance class night we spent the evening reading, writing, or playing cribbage. When bedtime came we filled the hot-water bottles to warm the icy bed, undressed before the kitchen stove, and put on outing-flannel pajamas and hurriedly crawled into bed.

The frigid weather hung on until the end of the month. Although the temperature never went below twelve degrees Fahrenheit, out in the wind it was as bitter as if it were well below zero.

January, usually a long, dark month, seemed unnaturally short that year. This was due, of course, to our extra Christmas and New Year. The trapping season ended with January. Some of the men were already home and the others were due soon. Once more we would take up normal village life with our occasional movies and Friday night dances. Everyone looked forward to that time.

Parascovia Lokanin Wright in 1973, with grass for basket weaving. (Photo by Reg Emmert.)

✳ FEBRUARY 1947

qisagunax tugida

(month when last stored food is eaten)

The temperature began to rise on the first day of February. The wind dropped a little and the sparrows reappeared and began to sing again. We lingered longer to visit at the stream where we went for water. By the next day, water ran in the pipes again, although there was little pressure. As soon as it was safe the furnace was relighted to warm the apartment and the schoolroom.

Annie Golley came to spend the evening and brought her basket to work on. I got mine out from under the bed and she showed me how to put a row of "hemstitching" on the bottom. This weave had the appearance of the openwork stitch done on linen and makes an attractive design.

Sophie Dirks and Nadesta Golley joined us later. They said they hoped that the water would freeze again, because they liked the small classes held in the living room. They had brought a list of words to look up in our dictionary, among them *isolationist, jealous,* and *jeer.*

Simeon had gone to visit with the Old Chief, and when he returned he said that reindeer had been seen near Chuniksax and a hunt was planned for the next day. The early Aleuts had often faced hunger and near starvation at this time of year and so named the month for the shortage of food. Severe weather conditions made hunting on the water extremely hazardous, and there was nothing to hunt on land. With the introduction of reindeer this situation was changed and there was no longer the fear of starvation. However, it kept the few men and boys in the village at trapping time busy supplying meat for the twenty-one families.

Next day the girls and the little ones and I held school in the classroom again. The older boys went hunting with the men. They brought back several deer, and as usual we were given a generous portion. When George Prokopeuff brought it to us that evening he said that one of the female deer had six young in her, the most that either he or Bill Dirks, Jr., had ever found, though not infrequently they had seen two or three. All of the deer killed that day were very fat, even though it was midwinter.

About 1:00 A.M. I got up to get some aspirin for my aching tooth and found the water down to a mere trickle. Simeon got up and we filled kettles, the bucket, and the bathtub so that we would not have to carry water for a while, at least.

By midmorning the water was again frozen and the furnace was shut off. Sophie Dirks and Nadesta Golley got their wish: classes came back to the living quarters again, with more homework assigned and with increased individual attention.

With the cold a snowstorm blew in from the north. Wind and waves played havoc with village property, and the barge from Adak was driven high on the beach. All of the mail and the soldiers' supplies were drenched. Fortunately there was no first-class mail. It was mostly catalogues and Clara Snigaroff's magazines.

Despite the raging storm Bob Barnes came that evening for dancing class. Usually he walked over, but Lieutenant Cavanaugh brought him in the jeep that night. The last time Bob had been over he had said, "I think the fellows are ready to dance with the girls. Can we ask the girls soon?"

"When we can use the classroom again, of course. But while you are using the living room no more than two couples could dance at a time," I replied.

Although the furnace had been turned off, the classroom was not yet bitterly cold, so when the boys came in we suggested that they round up some of the girls and hold their class there. This they did. Simeon played the piano and all of the boys danced. Davy Zaochney, with grim determination, went round and round. Billy Golley danced with a good sense of rhythm. He and Moses Prokopeuff were quite at ease. Both boys and girls enjoyed themselves and asked when they could have another dance. Bob said, "When we can use the schoolroom again, perhaps." I was sure he was as pleased as the young people were with the success of his teaching.

From one of the papers Lieutenant Cavanaugh had brought we learned that Shishaldin and Akutan volcanoes, on islands to the east of us, were erupting. We wondered if they would trigger Seguam and Korovin into action, but they did not.

That wild and beautiful storm of early February raged for three days. When wind and wave abated the last of the trappers on Amlia braved the pass and came home. No sooner had they returned than the families of the trappers who had gone to the western islands on the *North Star* in November began looking for their men to come home.

It was not known what arrangements had been made for their return, but we all assumed that the military would pick them up and take them to Adak, then send them home to Atka on the biweekly mail barge. There had not always been that feeling of assurance. We recalled Mike

Lokanin telling how he and Pari had been stranded on Agattu in the winter of 1941–42. They were trapping for Fred Schroeder, the store-keeper at Attu. He was to pick them up by mid-February and take them home to Attu. He failed to come for them and they ran out of supplies. War was declared that winter and private shipping was restricted, so Mr. Schroeder never got back to the Aleutians. When things were look-ing pretty grim the motor ship *Point Reyes* came and took them to Attu.

One evening Alex Prossoff told us how when he was eleven years old his father had taken him from school at Umnak to go trapping on Segula, an island near Amchitka. Through some misunderstanding the boat that was to pick them up at the close of the season failed to come.

"We ran out of food and ammunition," said Alex. "My father was not worried, because spring was coming. We ate beach foods, sea eggs, and clams. We made tea from the dead brown flowers of a certain plant and dug and ate *sarana,* white root and yellow root and *pootchky.* When the summer birds came we ate their eggs and caught and ate many of the birds, too."

"My father cut a very thin layer of sod, like a blanket, and at night we would lie by a flat rock, all covered with the sod blanket except our eyes, and when the birds landed on the flat rock we'd grab them and twist off their heads. I could get fifty or sixty in one night.

"We had lots of matches so one day my father cut off the white heads and shaved off the red part and filled a shell with it. He made a bullet from lead to fit his rifle and put it in the shell. He put a white match head in the cap and we went to the sea-lion rocks. He killed a big sea lion with his shell, but it used so many matches he couldn't make any more. We used every bit of the sea lion, guts and all. We made thread to sew our mukluks and made oil, and used the sinew for fishlines.

"We had a *bambi* (bathhouse) and could wash ourselves but we had no soap. Our clothes became very dirty. Then my father did something I think is very queer. He had me pee in a can, and he did, too. We saved it. I tell him it will smell very bad. When we had whole can full he washed our clothes. They get very clean but they smell very bad and I tell my father so. He make me take them way up the mountain to a big water-fall and there he throw them in. He leaves them for one day, twenty-four hours. Then he takes them out. They sure are clean, and they smell good, too.

"We think no one is coming for us so we will go to Amchitka and wait for the Atka trappers to come when it's time to trap again. My father makes oars and a sail and a little pair of oars for me, but just when we are ready to start the Coast Guard *Unalga* comes and takes us off. We had been there eleven and a half months!" This was another instance of the resourcefulness of the Aleut people which never ceased to impress us. I thought, what a splendid plot for a book.

On February 8 Major Bill Geyser and another officer, Major Mc-Cormick, flew over from Adak with a thousand pounds of Red Cross things which my good friend Bob Reeve, of Reeve Aleutian Airways, had brought from Anchorage for us. They brought a couple of sacks of first-class mail and a big chunk of delicious Wisconsin cheese. They said that the tug had more mail on it. No radio for us, though. Howard Burhker, the A.N.S. radio technician, had to come from Anchorage to install it himself. Until then we would be without news. Bill Geyser said that more Red Cross things would arrive the next day.

The jeep and trailer arrived, as expected, with boxes and boxes of things. We had them put in the schoolroom and sent for Bill and Mattie Dirks. When they came we opened the boxes. They were filled with clothes, shoes, books, and toys. Among these things I recognized several of my friend Sylvia Wittmer's dresses. Many items were brand new; they had been taken directly off the store shelves and still had "U. G. Crocker" and "Gordon's" stickers on them. I learned later that letters I had written to Sylvia and Rolf Wittmer concerning conditions at Atka had been printed in *The Forty-Ninth Star,* one of the Anchorage newspapers, and they had sparked this outpouring of gifts.

After Mattie and I had sorted everything, which took us three days, the task of dividing the things was turned over to the Church Sisterhood. I was a spectator as with remarkable objectivity the women allotted the clothing, shoes, and toys according to size and need. When all of the family boxes were ready some member was called and the things sent home. Billy Golley came for his family's box; he was carrying a wooden pistol he had made. When Simeon dropped a nickel-plated toy pistol on top of his box Billy's face lit up. "Oh, boy! Thanks!" he said, and he grinned from ear to ear.

One day while this work was going on Dr. Thode and three other officers came. I left Mattie to carry on and went with the doctor to see the Old Chief and Annie Nevzoroff's baby Paul. Then we went to see Mary Snigaroff.

The following day I was again called away. Olean Golodoff had a baby girl, our seventh baby. Ralph Prokopeuff, her common-law husband, was still in bed, but the children were dressing before the stove. Olean and the baby were fine. Julia Golodoff, who was staying with the Snigaroffs, sent word that her baby was running a temperature. I took medicine for baby Stephanie when I took fresh fruit and medicine for Mary Snigaroff. She showed me the lovely little basket she was weaving for Dr. Thode. Clara said that Mary could weave for only a few minutes at a time, but the work was like the finest linen, and flawless. Each time I saw this tiny woman I marveled at her tenacious will to live.

Lieutenant Cavanaugh had told us that there were films at the post which we could show in the village before they were sent back to Adak. It had been many weeks since we had had movies, so Wednesday afternoon after all the boxes were distributed and the classroom cleaned the lieutenant brought the films. The boys put away the desks and set up the chairs. Blankets covered the windows. The jeep brought Mary Snigaroff and the entire village came to see Wallace Beery and Gene Autry. For four hours they sat, enjoying the cowboy pictures and songs. I slipped out and went back to the apartment to work on personal mail. Simeon followed soon after.

Danny Nevzoroff came to ask us to "make a dance" that night. Simeon said it would be all right. I frowned on it, because the next day would be a school day. Danny spoke up, "Not many play weeks left before Lent begins February 23." He wanted to invite the boys at the base, and again Simeon gave permission. The weather was still very cold, and only three came that night.

Annie Golley came in before the dance, dressed in a pretty blue "Anchorage dress." I gave her the necklace that I had been saving for her birthday.

We left our typewriters and joined the dancers. Alex Prossoff, who usually played in the band, told Danny that he wanted to dance with me. Danny struck up a waltz tune and Alex later said to Simeon, "By golly! That the longest dance all night. I think it ain't never going to stop. I get ready to take Mrs. Oliver to her seat and Danny start same wallace over again. 'Bout wored me out."

The next evening Annie Golley came in with something under her coat. After a while she took out the object and, smiling broadly, handed it to me. Wrapped in a clean white cloth was the finished basket which she had been weaving, complete with covered top. It was my first Attu basket, and I was almost speechless with delight.

Alex Prossoff came in, looking for the comb he had left in the schoolroom last night. "It is Elizabeth's comb and she wants it. You give it to her for Christmas and it's only one she has. I take it last night because I want to comb my hair before I play for dance. I lay it on a desk. Tonight she sit up in bed to curl her hair and she ask me for it. I tell her I leave it here. She give me hell so I come for it but it gone." He smiled ruefully.

I went to the bedroom and got a new comb for her and one for him. It was then I learned that Saturday was his thirty-first birthday. Annie Golley's birthday would be Sunday. It would also be Annie Nevzoroff's, and little Annie Snigaroff's. My cookbook was on the table where we were drinking tea. "What kind of cake do you want for your birthday?" I asked Annie.

Alex grinned and, pointing to a wedding cake, said, "She like to have this kind." Annie had been a widow for several years. She told me after he had gone that Alex's mother had been her "wedding mother" (witness).

The next three days turned clear and cold. The temperature was twenty-eight degrees and again we had sunshine, calm blue water, and the village was filled with birdsong. After school on Friday George Prokopeuff came to ask for a generator for his gasoline lantern. All store supplies were very depleted. Talk turned to the subject of the bidarka we had made arrangements with the Juneau office for Andrew Snigaroff and the boys to build. George offered to make a small one for us.

"What will you cover it with?" Simeon asked.

"Eagle throat," replied George.

"How many will it take?"

"Two's plenty. Eagle—dat's a big duck," said George.

Saturday, Alex's birthday, was also Archangel Gabriel's Day, and church was held in the morning. Davy Zaochney came by, clanging the little bell so hard it sounded like a railroad-crossing signal. Our water was frozen again, but Simeon got it thawed so the furnace did not have to be turned off. The Old Chief came up, looking pretty sick. He said he had not slept all night: headache, sore throat, and a bad toothache. He wanted Simeon to pull his tooth, so after I got Alex's birthday cake in the oven I mixed a local anaesthetic. Young Bill Dirks dropped in to watch and to take his father home. Simeon shot in the novacaine. We waited, but it had no effect. I mixed some more; still no effect, so

Simeon gave him some cocaine and pulled the offending tooth. The old man rose right up out of his chair with a yell. Young Bill watched, fascinated, until he saw his dad relax once more, and then he burst into laughter. Old Bill told us later that once on the trap line when young Bill was a lad he had had a toothache and Old Bill had pulled the tooth. Young Bill held onto his father's hand with both of his, going, "Ah, ya ya!"

We kept the old gentleman there for a while to see that all was well, then sent him home to sleep. All that dope must bring some reaction, we thought.

Sunday was another church holiday, St. Simeon's Day, and Annie Golley's birthday. Everyone was all dressed up, and after church they went visiting from one house to another. The captain of the stranded barge came over to see if his men might attend the dance that night. After an earlier incident involving a barge crew all barges had written orders that the village was off limits, except by written invitation from Simeon. On the captain's assurance of his men's good behavior Simeon wrote an invitation for them.

About 4:00 P.M. one of the men came from the post, bringing cake and ice cream. Annie Golley, Bill Dirks, Jr., Mattie, and Danny Nevzoroff came for Annie's birthday dinner before the dance.

The dance was a complete success. The pretty dresses from Anchorage had come at an opportune time, and everyone looked fine. Sophie Dirks had to leave the floor because she giggled so at 'Red,' a tall flaming-haired and bearded chap from the barge who danced by himself around his bewildered partner. Our quarters were turned into a nursery, with babies sleeping all about and someone always in attendance, drinking coffee. Annie Golley came next morning to thank us for her fine birthday celebration. She said that Elizabeth had "monkeyed" Red's dancing when they got home.

The lieutenant told us that Major Bill Geyser was off on his race to beat the stork to his home in Anchorage. He hoped to be there to welcome the baby, already nicknamed "Little Squirt."

After school on Monday we walked down to see the Old Chief. Simeon took pictures of the children coasting and skiing. When we got to the Dirkses' house we talked about the three weeks before Lent, called the "play weeks." (I never did find out how curtailed the children's play would be when Lent arrived at the weekend.) Mr. Dirks described a

couple of the old Aleut games that were once played at that time. One was
the game he had told us about in which two men took turns tossing a
carved fish up into the air in such a way that it came down head first
through a small bone ring held close to the player's body. The penalty for
a player not equaling his opponent's skill was a rap on his knuckles with a
sea-lion flipper bone like the one we found in the diggings at Atxalax in
September. The name of that game was *unghida*.

The other game he described he called *kakanga*. Four men played this
game with ten small ivory discs. A low pile of two or three folded blankets
covered by a dried seal skin was placed at each end of the room. A smooth
window shade was sometimes used if the seal skin was unavailable. Each
pile was called *ichuga*. A small round target was drawn on the skin at the
end against the wall. The four men sat, one on either side of each pile. The
object of the game was to see which two-man team could make the most
points by tossing the little ivory discs across the room at the circle on the
skin. A disc landing within the circle counted one, two, or three points
according to its position. Tally was kept on a string of fifty-one beads,
called *kamish*, stretched where all could see. The center bead was called
kugudax. Each man had a chance to toss his five discs three times for a
game. Mr. Dirks said much betting took place on the sidelines. The
women often bet hand-knit socks and mittens.

"Do the people still play the old games?" I asked him.

"No one have old games now," he answered. "People play cards, play
cribbage, and shoot dice these times. Still can bet," he added.

A day or so later two boats left for the sea-lion beds on Amlia at
about 9:30 a.m. and returned with two big bulls about 6:00 P.M. They
came close to losing one boat and its crew on the return across the
swiftly running waters of the pass when a huge comber washed over the
stern, killing the engine. Fortunately the men were rowing at the time,
and were able to hold the boat true while the engine was dried and
started again. George Prokopeuff said, "I go through Amlia Pass many
times. This hardest time. I scared bad. We run engine and row hard all
same time. Pretty bad!"

That day we had the good news from Adak that after the next mail
barge to Atka our trappers would be picked up and brought home.

On February 19 Andrew Snigaroff and the boys started work on the
full-sized bidarka. Andrew had gathered some material already, and he
put the boys to rounding and sanding some long strips of wood.

Old Mr. Dirks came up to show us one of the sea-lion throats from the last hunt. It was about three and a half feet long and four inches in diameter. He was going to make mukluk tops of it. They would be seamless. He would use sea-lion "slipper" (flipper) for the foot and sole. He said that he used to make and wear them always before the war. Shoepacs and arctics get slippery and are heavy. Sea-lion mukluks are light and one can even walk on kelp and not lose one's footing, he said.

Seal throats were used for mukluks, too, but since they are smaller it took two, seamed fore and aft. Andrew Snigaroff had made Angel's mukluks from seal throat.

Mike Lokanin said, "There's only one thing can cut sea-lion slipper sole that I know. It's the sharp obsidian reef on Attu."

It was snowing again and cold the next day, but a plane came in about noon. Captain Blizzard brought two Canadian military observers from the Williwa Experimental Group. Dr. Thode and my son's friend, Lieutenant Rupert Welch, came with them. Dr. Thode went down to tell the Old Chief and Lydia Dirks that Larry, her husband, was in the hospital with TB. The other officers brought books for Simeon to autograph. Lieutenant Welch told us that the air terminal at Adak had burned, with loss of much mail; some was for Atka. Another bit of news was that the trappers on Semisopochnoi Island had found a plane, containing three bodies, that had been missing for two years.

That evening Alex Prossoff gave me three sea-lion whiskers. He said that long ago when a person was troubled with retention of urine a whisker was smoothed and sharpened and used to puncture the bladder, and bent to hold the hole open.

Excitement reigned in the village all next day. Early that morning the jeep brought four of the trappers home. They had come in on the mail barge: John and Philip Nevzoroff, Innokinty Golodoff, and Johnny Gardner. They reported that everybody was fine, but hungry. Poda Snigaroff and the rest of the men stayed on Amchitka with the furs. There were few foxes on the west end of the island; four men got only ninety-nine. Two men, Spiridon Zaochney and Innokinty Golodoff, got one hundred and fifty on the east end. Bill Dirks, Jr., came in to have coffee with us and said, "You should have seen how everybody crowded into John Nevzoroff's place."

George Prokopeuff came to have breakfast with us and spoke again of his fright coming across the pass on the recent hunt. "That pass is very dangerous when it's rough," he said, shaking his head. A middle-aged man, George was not easily intimidated, we knew. Innokinty Golodoff, Vasha Zaochney, and Annie Golley came in for a few minutes to tell us that Innokinty was high man this year. He got eighty-eight foxes. He told Annie, his sister, that he would give her two hundred and fifty dollars when he received his money. He had lived with her before he and Vasha decided to marry.

We knew the barge had brought mail, and when it had not come over by late afternoon Simeon and I decided to walk over and investigate. However, by the time we got down on the beach it was storming and blowing snow so hard that we turned back home. Great flocks of gray and white snowbirds flew low over the snowy beach all around us.

Next morning was clear and bright, so while the others were in church we hiked over to the base to pick up personal mail from our family and our lecture agent. We also found an important official letter about settling the government claims of the Attuans. There was a big job ahead on that.

John Nevzoroff came in after dinner to talk about trapping. He, Michael Snigaroff, Danny Prokopeuff, and Max Nevzoroff had gone to the west end of Amchitka to trap. He said the tide rips were so bad at one place that they had to take the boat from the water and over a hill. That portage took them nine hours. Then, few foxes—only ninety-nine for the four of them. At one place where they spent the night they found a skull. John recalled: "I said, 'Maybe we won't sleep. This skull might bother us.' Danny said, 'It won't bother us. We didn't bring it here.' We went to bed and that skull didn't bother us all night, but next day we moved to different place." John gave me an ivory spearpoint he had found on Amchitka.

Monday was another beautiful day, and the temperature was rising. However, I spent it in a darkened room, in bed with the most excruciating migraine I had ever had. Simeon got Mr. Dirks, Sr., started with the boys on their carpentry work and Annie took the girls for basket weaving.

The following day I remained in bed. It was another lovely day and the temperature reached fifty-eight degrees. Toward evening I was better able to appreciate the songbirds outside my window.

I found the little boys elated with their woodworking class when I returned to school. They were making sturdy sleds for themselves. The older boys were making baby cribs, a table, a dresser, and a high chair.

Several of the children wore ivory rings carved for them by their fathers at Amchitka. A sperm whale had washed up on the beach and the men had salvaged the teeth. They told us that the Atka men were now the only Aleut ivory carvers.

After school on Thursday Affia Snigaroff, Simeon, and I walked across the hills and down to the dump. Affia found a rock pestle. She said little Aleut girls hunt along the shore for the long smooth stones and dress them for dolls. We picked kelp for jump ropes. Affia told me that the kelp made good pickles and that Clara could show me how.

The last five days of February were all clear and sunny. Andrew Snigaroff took George Nevzoroff and Johnny Gardner out along the beach, hunting for driftwood to make ribs for the bidarka. The boys said that he tested it for flexibility by chewing it. Later he showed us a piece he had sized for a rib and bent to shape by chewing on the wood.

When school was dismissed that last day of February we walked up over the brown hills to Chuniksax to dig clams. All of the boats were out. We enjoyed the walk, though, over the deeply-trodden trails. From the top of the hill we could see several people down on the beds, digging clams. What a picture it would have made, with the gentle waves at low tide lapping the sandy flat, the mountains across Nazan Bay rosy with sunset glow, and flocks of ducks flying low across the blue sky. For a few minutes we stood watching, then scrambled down the hillside and joined the diggers. We stood in the shallow water and with our feet felt for the clams and worked them from their beds. Our little sack was soon full and Philip Nevzoroff brought it and our shovel home in his boat, but we chose to walk back the way we had come. Bill Dirks, Jr., came in while Simeon was cleaning clams for supper and we gave him a batch. Simeon said that at Unalaska when he was a boy they used to keep clams in salt water and feed them corn meal. That got rid of all the sand. Bill Dirks said they did the same, only they fed the clams bread. We vowed we would long remember how good these clams were, fried in butter, with a baked potato and coleslaw and hot tea. Bill had dropped in to tell Simeon that there was to be a reindeer hunt next morning. Simeon promised to come and to bring his camera.

It was hard to realize that night that the first two months of the year were already gone. I, for one, was regretting that we had signed up for a tour of the States. I would rather have spent another year on Atka with these fine people.

Mike Lokanin (standing) and Henry Dirks on fall reindeer hunt

✳ MARCH 1947

qadugix qisagunax tugida

(month of hunger, gnawing thongs and straps)

March came in like a lamb with the same clear, crisp, sunny days that had prevailed for the last few days of February. About ten o'clock on the first morning of the month most of the men, tailed by all of the little boys, struck off up the hill toward the old Alaska Army Communication Service hut. Simeon, laden with cameras and his skinning knife, was with them. By noon we saw them coming back down the hill with whole deer carcasses on their backs, the little boys proudly serving as gun-bearers.

Simeon said that they had gotten into the midst of a small herd and killed thirty-five deer. There was lots of excitement. He got some fine action pictures—reindeer ran, men shouted and shot, and boys scurried for shelter. Every household received a deer, we were given a generous chunk, and thirteen deer were cut up and put in the old cold-storage plant at the base.

Probably none of those Atka men remembered that March was one of the two months most dreaded by their early ancestors, who were often reduced to gnawing leather thongs at that time of the year.

Innokinty Golodoff came in after church next day to visit and to tell us about his trapping. He said that there was oil along the beach on Amchitka. It was too oily for hair seal; he got only two. There were plenty of geese and lots of sea otter. They did not touch the sea otter, even if they found one dead. Sea otter were considered an endangered species, and there were very strict federal laws against killing them, or even possessing the smallest bit of a sea-otter pelt. He and Spiridon Zaochney built a barabara on the east end of Amchitka and set out their traps. The short cut from the last trap back to camp took him one hour and five minutes, full speed, he said.

One day Innokinty got a fox in his trap and when he grabbed it to choke it the fox seized his finger and bit through the nail. He choked the fox so hard it finally let go. When he skinned the fox he took a piece of its fat and put it on his finger, then tore the tail off his shirt and wrapped that around it. Spiridon had to skin and flesh the foxes for a few days. Later Sprirdon's finger became infected. Innokinty lanced it with his pocket knife and applied fox oil to it. (He said that fox oil was an old Aleut healing ointment. Later he brought me a little bottle of it.) After Spiridon's trouble with his finger Innokinty had to do all the skinning for a while. He was pretty fast; he said that he could skin a fox in seven minutes.

Affia Snigaroff, young Annie Golley, and Davy Zaochney came in the afternoon to ask us to go to Chuniksax with them. We hiked over and while there ate kelp stem, which they called *kam o taq*. We collected only six clams, but got a whole sackful of blue mussels. The moon was "in its house" (had a ring around it) when we came home.

Everyone remarked on the unusually long stretch of clear and lovely weather for March. Through our open bedroom windows each morning we heard the plaintive cry of sea gulls, the "ka ta" or "what's that?" of the curious ravens, the chirping of flocks of rosy finches in the grass, and the varied songs of the Aleutian sparrows from the housetops. This was a lovely way to start our busy days.

It was school as usual for the children and me. Most of the men worked on their own homes, putting off construction on village projects until all of the trappers returned home. One day Simeon and Mike Lokanin walked over to the base and wrapped the reindeer which were in cold storage. While they were over there a plane came in, bringing some mail and two officers. Lieutenant Manzer came about the proposed new road, and Lieutenant Bratton to destroy any old planes downed on the island--war casualties.

That evening Lieutenant Cavanaugh called to ask if we would take the two visiting lieutenants clamming. We told him that we had gone the night before, and although the moon was right, for some reason we were only having one tide now, and even at low tide the water was still pretty high. We had to dig the clams while standing in the water. The three officers thought that would be a novel experience, and we agreed to take them. Alex Prossoff, Moses Prokopeuff, Simeon, and I were ready when they came, about ten o'clock. The tide had filled the flats and the sea was as calm as a lake. We stood knee-deep in the water and dug the clams with rakes, shovels, and our feet. Moses and Alex tried to dig them with the outboard motor. They got a few, but the shaft was too short to be very effective.

The officers brought a large package for us, sent from Tomah, Wisconsin, by a former Army chaplain friend, the Reverend Clarence Kilde. After the clamming expedition and a fried clam supper, and after all the others had gone, about 2:00 A.M., we opened the package and found a doll, with a complete wardrobe and a set of little dishes.

The temperature began dropping rapidly next day, although the sky remained clear and the birds continued to sing. Rooster crowing added to the morning medley. Mr. Dirks, Sr., came early for some chicken feed. He said that all of his roosters had died; later he planned to rent one for a couple of weeks from Mrs. Nevzoroff.

When the children came to school and found the doll and dishes they were delighted. The little ones spent the afternoon in our apartment, taking turns dressing and undressing "Simone" and drinking quantities of tea from the little dishes, under the watchful eye of Annie Golley. The older girls and I were having a cooking lesson in the kitchen, and the boys were busy at their woodworking class with Mr. Dirks, Sr.

On Saturday, March 8, Mike Lokanin and Simeon joined the two lieutenants in their search of the hills for the remains of any war-wrecked planes. Lieutenant Bratton's mission was to destroy any remains they might find so as to prevent future searchers from confusing it with new wreckage.

The men took off over the hills above Sand Bay and Korovin Bay, carrying two hundred sticks of dynamite. They hiked the hills all day. When they returned at dusk, wet and weary, they reported no wrecks found, and no reindeer seen, but hundreds of geese and eider ducks and many seals in the bays.

The weather the second week in March remained clear and cold. The temperature dropped to twelve or fourteen degrees at night, but rose to thirty-eight or forty degrees during the day. The water froze every night but was quickly thawed out, and the furnace stayed on, so school went on in the classroom as usual. The girls in Annie Golley's weaving class completed the bottoms of their baskets and were ready to turn them up and work on the sides. Annie had helped me turn mine a few evenings before. We used a full milk can for the basket mold or *kat mus ux*. Annie herself was weaving a grass cover over a small bottle. Her stitches were tight and neat and she was already putting in a colored design.

One evening Affia Snigaroff brought and showed to us two pieces of wood which Andrew, her father, had ready for the bidarka frame. The wood looked like yellow cedar or soft yellow pine. He had planed the strips down to about half an inch in diameter and then chewed them to soften them for bending. Each was covered with tooth marks all along the arc. The wood bent well and evenly and he had tied it with chalk line to hold its shape until it dried. I wondered why he did not steam them and bend them over a frame, as I had seen boat ribs formed on the mainland. Affia said that her father told her that limber and willowy wood is difficult to find amid the driftwood on the beach.

A day or so later Simeon called me to come and see the plane that
Andrew had made when he found he could not use the school rabbet
plane on the bidarka frame. The plane was very small and was worked
lightly with the fingers. It cut a long, clean curl.

Bill Dirks, Jr., said that all the men were enthusiastic about the
bidarka Andrew was building. They planned to gather wood and get
sea-lion skins for two more single-hatched and one double-hatched
bidarki. He talked at length about how bidarki are handled. Getting in
and out of a bidarka takes much practice. It is different from an Eskimo
kayak. One must keep one leg stiff. A very narrow double-bladed pad-
dle is used. They always travel in pairs, about thirty yards apart. If a
fellow tips over he lies still, holding the keel, until the other fellow
comes and takes his hand and pulls him upright. Andrew's father and a
boy had once found themselves in a stormy pass and their bidarka bow
tipped up and the stern sank. Men nearby towed the bidarka ashore and
put its occupants in a steamy bathhouse. Mr. Snigaroff lived, but the
boy died.

The shopwork projects—tables, cribs, and dresser—were nearly completed, and the instructor, Mr. Dirks, Sr., was proud of the boys and
their fine work. Their next project was to be swings, teeter-totters, and
hobbyhorses for the little ones.

The Old Chief celebrated his sixty-fifth birthday on March 13. He
came to have dinner and to spend the evening with us. Simeon told him
that he was now elegible for the territorial old-age pension and helped
him make out an application for it.

Of greatest concern in the village at this time was the failure of the
government to bring the rest of the trappers home. The trapping season
had been over for two and a half months. The men were stranded on the
other islands with little food and hundreds of valuable fox skins. They
were anxious to get home and to ship the furs out for the spring auction
sales in Seattle, when the market was best. Not only Atka men were still
not home, but Umnak and Unalaska men were stranded, too. It appeared that neither the military nor the A.N.S. was making any effort to
bring the men home as promised. Letters and telegrams requesting their
return had brought no response.

The Council delegated Bill Dirks, Jr., and Simeon to go to Adak to see
if personal contact with the military would have the desired effect. They
had other business to conduct for the village, as well. They made ar-

rangements to go to Adak on the next plane that brought supplies for the base. It came in on Friday, March 14, and a GI came in the jeep to pick up Bill and Simeon.

Before nightfall the temperature dropped to twenty degrees and snow was falling. That night the stove ran out of oil and I had a hard time turning off the motor. Alex Prossoff came and filled the tank. Mike Lokanin came later to see if there was anything he could do for me. People dropped in to visit, on and off, all weekend. Several of the women brought the baskets they were weaving and we worked together for a couple of hours on Saturday evening. Their fingers all appeared more nimble than mine.

Sunday, after church, Alex Prossoff asked me to come and see the seal gut he was preparing for me. He showed me two long inflated tubes; one was drying indoors, and the other was being frozen dry. He said that he had thoroughly cleaned the gut, inside and out. Then he had cut the two lengths. Next he had tied one end of each and inflated it by blowing into it, then tied the other end. The piece drying indoors was clear and transparent; the other was soft and white like doeskin. Elizabeth said the latter was used for decorative purposes. Alex said that when they were completely dry he would split them and wrap them on a board, like they did in Attu, and bring them to me. I told them how happy I was that they were doing this for me, and before I left I asked Alex if now might be a good time for him to come and tell me his story of the capture by the Japanese. He agreed, and since his work on his house was held up until supplies came from Adak, it was arranged that he and Elizabeth would come for dinner that evening and we would get started.

When I walked back up the hill to the schoolhouse most of the boys in the village were out playing kick-the-can, a game of which they never seemed to tire. They played it for several hours. From my kitchen windows, while I got dinner, I could see them racing around and hiding.

Alex, Elizabeth, and the baby came to dinner and later I took down, verbatim, Alex's story of their capture and imprisonment, and made a copy for him. The story, as I wrote it down, is on page 241. It was nearly midnight when they took the sleeping baby and left for home.

Next morning it was warmer and the sky was clear. Before school started several of the boys came running to say that they had spotted deer up one of the valleys above the village. All of the men and boys went after them. They got twenty, and when they were divided they brought us two hearts and a ham.

The girls and I spent the day cooking, making cakes and cookies. There had been a run on my shortening and my cookbook. The store had long since run out of ingredients for cakes and other sweet things, but the women knew that they were welcome to anything I had. Each day now the trappers were expected home, and there must be plenty of good things ready for them.

Two men came over from the base to tell me that the barge was due, and so was a plane. Next day a telegram came from Simeon, saying that the mail boat was due the following day. It would bring the trappers home. Everyone, including me, started cleaning house. A lot of mud had been tracked in.

Peter Prokopeuff came to tell me that his brother, John Prokopeuff, had a fever and pains in the stomach. I went down with Peter and found John with a temperature of 102 degrees. I gave him aspirin and did what I could to make him comfortable. I promised to look in on him before school the next morning.

The rough brown hills were patched with snow when I went to check on John Prokopeuff next morning. He was weak, but the pain was gone and the fever down. He said that he would stay in bed all day.

Our trappers, and others from Umnak and Unalaska, came in that night at about nine o'clock. All night long flashlights poked fingers of light into the darkness as villagers went from house to house.

When I got up at seven-thirty next morning the village had gone to sleep. The quiet was broken by the whistle of the *Aleutian Mail* as she came in to anchor opposite Philip Nevzoroff's house. People came pouring from all of the houses. The trappers from Umnak and Unalaska got ready to go aboard. Several sacks of mail and packages which had been thought lost were brought ashore and carried to the schoolhouse, where Danny Nevzoroff and I prepared to sort and deliver them. Among our personal mail were several letters from family and friends, Simeon's watch, a new camera, and some clothes.

The village celebrated quietly all day. When I went to Mary Prokopeuff's to check on John again the house was full of visitors, all come to welcome Danny Prokopeuff home. John was up and dressed and enjoying the excitement.

That night I had a movie show all by myself. Some very good film had come in the mail from Eastman Kodak Co.

Danny Nevzoroff came up from the store to tell us that the village had a total of eight hundred and twenty-six foxes. Each trapper received ten dollars for each fox he had trapped. The skins when sold would, of course, bring more than that. From what Danny said I gathered that the church handled the rest of the money for the benefit of the village. Everyone was pleased with the season's catch.

On Saturday Bill Dirks, Jr., and Simeon came home, bringing with them Lieutenant Currin, a doctor. When he came to the village we took him to see Mary Snigaroff. Simeon said that he and Bill had had a wonderful time. They spent one evening with my son, Ernest Ross, at Major Schleuder's. During the day they conducted the business the Council had sent them to Adak for; they made arrangements to get the trappers home, ordered supplies, sent messages, and transacted other business. In the evenings they were wined and dined in the homes of the various officers who had visited the village. One night Commander Cole took them to the fights. It had been a very satisfactory trip.

While Simeon was going through his mail and trying on his new clothes, little Larry Nevzoroff came in, looking very ill. His "owl eyes" were heavy and he was feverish. I took his temperature: 102 degrees! I sent him home to bed. Simeon said, "Beware of an epidemic. There is lots of flu in Adak now, brought up from the States by the last troop contingent." He had hardly stopped speaking when Max Nevzoroff came in with a heavy cough.

The next day dawned clear, bright, and sunny. Birds were singing when the bell tolled for church. We had had five clear days, but this was the vernal equinox, and the Old Chief predicted stormy weather. He came to tell me that his daughter Sophie was ill. With Larry that made two normally healthy ones under the weather. We took care of outgoing mail and got the schoolroom ready for a council meeting about store and fox business.

Young Bill Dirks came down to ask me to go see his wife, Mattie, while he attended the meeting. She and Annie Golley had been pogy fishing all afternoon. She had eaten some pogy and broken out in hives. I gave her some ephedrine and put her to bed. Then I went down the path to Vasha Zaochney's, where both Davy and Spiridon Zaochney were in bed with high fevers.

I decided to cancel school until we saw whether or not we were in for an epidemic of flu. I asked that I be notified of illness in any family, then took my medical kit and went out in the rain to visit those whom I knew were ill. When I went to see Sophie, the Old Chief said, "Ralph Prokopeuff isn't feeling good today."

After leaving that home I hurried up the hill to Ralph's house. Someone called "*Kongutha!*" (come in) when I knocked, and I went through the storm porch into the kitchen. Olean greeted me. I said to her, "Mr. Dirks said Ralph wasn't feeling good today."

She answered, "Ralph's all right," and nodded toward the table where he sat. He looked around and smiled, and I knew why Mr. Dirks had sent me. Ralph had a beautiful black eye!

All day long new cases of sickness were reported: Teresa Gardner, Mr. Dirks, Sr., George Nevzoroff, Mary Prokopeuff. We knew before evening that we had an epidemic on our hands. Simeon sent a message to the base to Dr. Currin, who had asked to be informed if anybody's temperature rose to 103. Teresa's did, so Mike Lokanin and Moses Prokopeuff went over that night. Dr. Currin was not there.

The predicted storm arrived. It caused some difficulty with the transmission of messages to Adak. They had to be relayed through Fort Glenn at Umnak, and thence to Adak.

All of Philip Nevzoroff's family were now ill, plus two more Prokopeuffs, Nadesta Golley and little Elizabeth Golodoff, both Annie Golleys and Dimitri Golley. Then came a call for Simeon to pull two of Mary Snigaroff's teeth.

A plane flew in just as I completed my first round. It brought Dr. Thode, Lieutenant Lanier, and Major Shrater, General Lynch's physician—all very welcome.

The doctors went with us to see most of the patients and they approved our treatment. When we went to see Mary Snigaroff she gave Dr. Thode the exquisite little basket she had woven for him. He was struck speechless for a moment.

The doctors commented on the sturdiness of the children. There was someone ill in every house now except Bill Golley's. He said that he would put a red kerchief in the window if he became ill.

Nightfall found both Simeon and me very weary, with chills and fever, but we doped ourselves well before crawling into bed. Both of us were sick all night and weak in the morning, but the fever was gone.

Simeon resumed going on rounds with me. Bill Golley could not find a red handkerchief to put in the window so he sent his sister, Ann Lillian Nevzoroff, to tell us that he too was ill.

The epidemic swept like wildfire through the village. So far forty-eight people had been stricken. Five or six were desperately ill, and all were miserable. By the sixth day every house was represented on the sick list; sometimes all members were in bed. Dan Prokopeuff was the only one up in his house. He was doing the cooking and washing the dishes. He complained that housework was hard work.

That night I was frightened to the point of tears over Mary Snigaroff. Her temperature shot to 104 degrees, and she was moaning and not really conscious. I did what I could to make her comfortable and stayed with her until she fell asleep. I went home to bed at 11:00 P.M., praying they would all survive the night.

Dr. Thode was right; everyone was destined to catch the flu. Many were better next day, and hungry. We arranged for Bill Dirks, Sr., to open the store and for Max Nevzoroff, Mike Snigaroff, and Spiridon Zaochney to call at each house for orders and deliver them.

Mary Snigaroff was better, her temperature down to 102 degrees, but her husband Andrew was in bed with a high fever and chills.

Two tugs had come in late the previous night. A fellow came to see Simeon in the morning. He said that they had been sent to try to take off the barge that had been stranded since January. He said that Simeon's friend Nick Peterson, who trapped on Amukta, had got tired of waiting to be taken off the island. He had started out in his dory and had not been heard of since. Two fellows on Seguam were eating foxes and beach food. They were out of grub and ammunition, but could trap foxes to eat.

Dimitri Golley went out to get oil for Bill Golley and water for Danny Nevzoroff. He went back to bed with a temperature of 103 degrees. Johnny Gardner got me out of bed at 3:30 A.M. to look after his mother, Matrona. She had been hemorrhaging since January. She was in pain, and frightened. I got her back in bed with her legs elevated, gave her something for her pain, and tried to calm her fears. I stayed with her until she relaxed, and promised to check on her in the morning.

There was no church that last Sunday in March. Before making my morning rounds I went to check on Matrona and impressed on her that she must stay in bed. I would see that Johnny had food he could fix for the two of them. He went back to the school with me and I opened the school supplies for milk, rolled oats, and dried fruit for their breakfast. The food situation worried us. The store was out of most things, and we had run our own supplies pretty short. When two boys from the base came with a message from Dr. Thode, saying that he would be over as soon as the weather permitted, we asked them to bring down some of our frozen meat from the cold-storage plant. This we would distribute.

Morning rounds found some patients up and new ones down, and some who had been up were down again. A very heavy cough accompanied the lessening fever. Both Simeon and I were sorry sights, coughing like our patients, runny-nosed and bleary-eyed, but on our feet. The men from the base brought over some meat and Simeon and Peter Prokopeuff distributed a big chunk to every household, where it was immediately put to cook.

A plane flew in early next morning. We had taken milk, rolled oats, and fruit to several houses so they could have breakfast, and had just started on our rounds when someone told us that they had seen a GI heading toward the store. Thinking that one of the local GIs had brought a message, Simeon went out to find him. We had not heard the plane because a wild rainstorm was blowing in from the Pacific and we were bundled in rain gear. The GI proved to be Dr. Thode. We took him to see the worst cases. He brought more medicines, which we sorely needed. The Army had also lent us fifteen cases of milk.

The doctor visited both Mary Snigaroff and Matrona Gardner before going back to the base. He approved the treatment I had given both, but his face was grave as he spoke of Mary. He had grown very fond of her.

The storm increased in violence every hour but, dressed in oilskins and rubber boots, we continued to slosh from house to house. We learned later that Dr. Thode's plane was unable to take off. March ended on that stormy note. It had come in like a lamb, and it went out like a lion.

Innokinty and Vasha Golodoff after their wedding, with daughter "Toughie" and Mrs. Nevzoroff

✳APRIL 1947

agalugix qisagunax tugida

(near hunger month)

The storm continued to rage. Snow and sleet, as well as rain, lashed our faces as we stumbled down the paths, visiting every house twice a day. We checked temperatures, gave medicine, changed beds, bathed babies, and distributed food, often cooking it, too. We hardly finished one round before it was time to start the second. The entire village was coughing.

After two weeks those who had come down first were able to be up and about. In order to keep the children indoors I gave them the toys that the Red Cross had sent.

Lieutenant Cavanaugh came one evening between our rounds. He told us that the tugs were unable to budge the stranded barge. It was to be stripped and abandoned and the crew returned to Adak by tug.

On the third of April the ground was white with snow, although there was new grass poking through, which delighted the chickens. The boys reported that only two of the sheep had survived.

That day when I went to Snigaroff's I took a little snowsuit for Angel. Mary was very low. She asked for fruit juice, and I hurried home to get it for her. She was like a flickering candle—a wavering flame of life barely lingered in her tiny body. I realized that there was little hope of saving her, and I was very worried about many others. Most of the older people were worn thin and weak. They complained that they were unable to sleep. With the doctor's approval I was giving seconal to some.

The next morning someone saw deer above the village and a group of the boys went after them. They got seven, and the fresh meat was most welcome.

The Old Chief was running a fever and experiencing pain. He was one of those about whom I was most worried. When we left him we stopped at Mary Prokopeuff's to check on her and John, who were both still very ill. Here Simeon fell while climbing into the loft for something. He injured his back and left hip. I managed to get him home and onto the couch, where I gave him some pain medicine and made him as comfortable as possible.

Mary Snigaroff died that evening, between five and six o'clock. Bill Dirks, Jr., the young chief, came and told us at seven o'clock. Spiridon Zaochney was sent to help Andrew Snigaroff construct a coffin.

While I went to take seconal to some of the patients the barge captain and the diver from Adak came to say good-bye. The barge had been abandoned. After they had gone I told Simeon that I feared we might lose Cedar Snigaroff, too. "Don't worry so. Just keep doing the best you can," he replied.

He spent a restless and painful night. We were awakened early by the pounding next door, where Spiridon was building Mary's coffin.

After Simeon was made comfortable I went on the morning rounds. The Old Chief was worse. His temperature was back to 102 degrees and he had a pain in his chest. Cedar Snigaroff still looked desperately ill. How much was due to Mary's death I could not tell. The whole village mourned her, I knew.

As I came back up the hill I saw Jenny Golley carrying a package to Andrew Snigaroff's house—Mary's shroud. When I went there later I found Andrew and Jenny sitting beside the piece of plywood on which Mary was laid out under a sheet. Over her head in the corner was the family icon, with a candle burning before it. Teresa, the eldest daughter, sat by the stove, her head covered and bowed. Ralph Prokopeuff, one of Mary's brothers, came in and sat with bared head on one of the chairs which were arranged against the wall. All day long people came and went. The young chief came to see Simeon about the necessary messages to be sent to Juneau. He told us that the women of the Church Sisterhood would prepare the body for burial and sit up nights with it, and the Brotherhood provided the wood for the coffin.

On Saturday evening prayers and a brief service for the dead were held in the home before the church service. The unheated church was cold, and the few people who were present coughed throughout the service. It was a dismal evening. All day long smoky fog blew down from the hills, spitting snow and rain and riding out across the water to send whitecaps breaking onto the rocks.

Sunday morning, through squalls of bitter wind and snow, about twenty-five people gathered in the living room of Andrew's home. Mary lay in her coffin, dressed in a white shroud with a blue cap on her head. The head of the coffin was under the icon and the burning candle, and it extended out into the room. Teresa Gardner and Ann Lillian Nevzoroff had taken the paper flowers that were left from the Christmas Star and formed them into a cross. This, with an icon, was placed inside the coffin. Another small icon was fastened on the inside of the lid and a white Russian cross affixed to the outside.

When all preparations were complete Danny Nevzoroff, the lay priest (or reader) entered, clad in his robes. The church choir gathered, standing behind him at the foot of the coffin. The rest of us stood behind them. Danny conducted a simple chanted service. Many wept silently. At the close of the service Andrew led six-year-old Angel to her mother and both of them kissed her tenderly. Andrew wept aloud. Other members of the family and close friends followed them. The coffin was closed and two men carried it to the church. Danny and the choir followed, chanting a dirge.

In the cold, unheated church again we stood through the hour-long service, the open coffin before us, facing the black-draped altars. Other villagers joined our coughing and shivering group until almost a third of the village was present. All showed the effects of this illness that had claimed one of our number.

As the services went on the windows fogged from our breath, yet through them we could see the alternating shafts of sunshine and gusts of snow and sleet.

At last Danny, after an obeisance at the altar, stood beside Mary. He bowed, crossed himself, kissed her forehead and lips and the icon on her breast, bowed again, and stepped back. Andrew Snigaroff and little Angel followed him, first to the altar and then to bid farewell to their loved one. The entire congregation followed; first the older men, then the boys, then Jenny Golley, as the oldest woman present, and finally the other women and girls.

Again the coffin was closed, ropes were put under it, and George Prokopeuff, Mary's elder brother, and Alfred Prokopioff took the foot while Bill Dirks, Jr., and Bill Golley took the head and led the way out of the church. The congregation followed. Danny and the choir climbed the hill behind us, again intoning a dirge.

A sudden burst of sunshine tempered the raw April wind from the Arctic, yet the little huddle of mourners shivered as the coffin was opened for the last time and the last ceremony was chanted beside the yawning grave.

Suddenly we heard the drone of a plane. It passed over us, flew out over the bay and, turning, came back over us for a second look. I thought that it might be bringing the doctor, for it had its wheels down and appeared to land over toward the strip.

The last rites continued. One last kiss from the family, and then the coffin was nailed shut. Gently it was lowered into the grave and Andrew and the young chief rattled the first shovelfuls of brown earth down upon it. Others then took their turns until at last the grave was filled and mounded. Then we all straggled quietly down the graveyard slope to take up our lives again.

I hurried home to see how Simeon was and to find out if the plane had brought the doctor. Simeon was still unable to walk. His hip was numb, but the pain in his back was constant. After making him comfortable as possible I took my medical kit and made my morning rounds. Pari Lokanin had a hemorrhage of both lung and bowel. She was in a bad way, and there were others. Cedar Snigaroff looked wretched and pale. Philip Nevzoroff was down for the third time; he had gotten up too soon to care for his family. My good Annie Golley and the Old Chief were still running high temperatures, and I found Alex Prossoff in bed that day.

It was clear by the time I went through the village and reached home again that the plane had come only on business at the base.

Although he was still confined to bed on Monday, Simeon insisted that I bring some of the overdue monthly reports for him to work on while I was out on village rounds. When I returned I found Bill Dirks, Jr., the young chief, and Danny Nevzoroff, the storekeeper, and Simeon working on the store accounts and books. I fixed us all some lunch, then started work on my own delayed reports. This was interrupted by Davy Zaochney, who had stepped on a nail. Our recent heavy winds had scattered the neat piles of lumber and scraps about the village and the snow had covered much of it, making walking hazardous. We all tried to keep the paths clear, but Davy had taken a short cut. He told me that Dimitri Golley had stepped on a nail, too, so after I took care of him I went to Annie Golley's to take care of Dimitri. Annie was better, but very weak. She was hungry for seafood, so young Annie and I walked over to Chuniksax. We were too late for clams, but we picked blue mussels and sea eggs instead. The walk over the hills was refreshing, a welcome respite from my constant medical duties.

Young Annie took our bucket of seafood home and I stopped to see Alex Prossoff. I had given him a codeine tablet the night before for his eyes. I asked him if it had helped.

"I don't know, Mrs. Oliver. I went to sleep right away," he answered with a smile. This epidemic had affected people in many different ways.

Simeon was resting when I reached home. They had finished the store accounts and that report, together with a couple of others and some messages, had been sent to the base. Word had come back that if the weather improved a plane would come from Adak with mail the next day. Also, the boys who had been called up for military service were to be ready to go over to Adak for enlistment.

The weather next day was no better than it had been during the past two weeks: wind, rain, and spitting snow. It must have been better in Adak, for a plane flew in early in the afternoon, bringing Dr. Thode, Colonel Ware, Captain Harris, and Commander Cole.

Henry Thode examined Simeon, stuck him with needles, and drew pictures on him outlining the numbed area. He said that the nerve band over the left hip was injured from a bump on the spine. He taped him tightly. Had we had transportation he would have flown him to Adak for X-rays. "If he doesn't improve soon that's what we must do," the doctor told us.

The visit of the officers had cheered Simeon considerably, and being tightly bound gave him sufficient relief that we both slept better that night than we had done for the last four.

The mailboat whistled in and anchored off Philip Nevzoroff's location by the time I was up. Captain Petrich came ashore and had coffee with Simeon. He brought several sacks of mail and a batch of month-old air-mail letters. Hastily leafing through the official mail, I learned of additional reports which we were to compile on several subjects. We would have plenty of work for the remaining months of our year at Atka.

As I was preparing medication for Pari Lokanin I saw our young problem woman heading toward Mike's house, too. This was unusual, but I learned the reason when I arrived a few minutes after she did. Pari was in bed in the main room and Sergeant Dicky was talking with Mike. I went to the kitchen for water for Pari's medicine and found the girl sitting on a GI's lap. They both knew that the village was still off limits except for official business or by official invitation. The sergeant was on his feet when I returned to Pari. He called the GI and the two men left. The girl slipped out the back way.

Next day Pari told me that her red sweater and black shoes were gone. She suspected that the girl had taken them. I told the young chief, and he promised to do something about it. Later Mike told me that Moses Prokopeuff had brought the shoes back.

That afternoon two GIs came to talk to Simeon. The one who had been with Sergeant Dicky that morning came to apologize for coming without permission to the village to see the young woman. The other GI wanted to marry one of the girls in the village. The Council would discuss this matter later.

In spite of the miserable weather there was much travel to and from the schoolhouse all day. It was Good Friday and everyone was coloring eggs. They came for school paints and brushes, since we had nothing else to color with. They came, too, to "bum" shortening for their Easter bread, *kulich*.

On my morning rounds Mr. Dirks, Sr., gave me a dozen eggs and Annie Golley gave me six more. I was reluctant to take them, for I knew how badly they all needed this nourishing food, but under the circumstances I could not refuse the gift. Easter is their most important church holiday.

Saturday morning Lieutenant Stevenson and Sergeant Wally Dull, newly assigned to the base, came to see Simeon and to get acquainted. In the afternoon several of the youngsters joined us in the kitchen to color eggs. Simeon could now move to a chair with my help. He had several ideas for decorating the eggs that the youngsters eagerly put into practice. Each took home three or four beauties. Some were quite unique. One of Billy Golley's was inscribed: "Christ is raising."

Nadesta Golley brought us a small frosted loaf of the traditional *kulich* which her mother Jenny had made. Later Annie Golley sent another loaf by her daughter, Elizabeth.

At midnight I left Simeon propped up in bed and went up the hill to the Easter church service, which began with rifle fire. The inner sanctum was open; this was unusual. When the services started Danny Nevzoroff, in his robes, chanting, led a procession—Sergius Golley, Bill Dirks, Jr., Bill Golley, and Ralph Prokopeuff, who carried the Bibles and holy pictures—down the center aisle past the standing congregation and out through the door. Young George Dirks, carrying an American flag, led the way around the church. Most of the congregation followed. Back in the church anteroom a short service was held, and then all reentered. Immediately after the Bibles and icons were replaced the three-hour-long chanted service began. It was very impressive and lovely, but toward the end I began worrying about Simeon, knowing that he could not move without help. I hurried out at the close and ran home to find him slumped down and the pillows on the floor. Later I was told that the service had been combined with the Easter morning service so that the villagers would not have to get up early.

Dr. Thode and Captain Burtner came on Easter Sunday to see Simeon. The doctor said that he definitely must go to Adak for X-rays, and that I needed a physical checkup, too. I told him that I was merely tired. He laughed and said to me, "I think that you are riding on your nerves right now. We don't want you breaking down. When we get back to Adak we'll try to arrange transportation for you both by the end of the week."

After serving them *kulich* and coffee I took the doctor to see my sick people. All who were able were out in their Easter finery, visiting one another's homes. Most of them called on us sometime during the day. Several brought gaily colored eggs as Easter gifts.

On Monday after my morning rounds the older children who were sufficiently recovered came to our quarters to resume schoolwork. The furnace had run out of fuel about the time that the epidemic began, and no one was available to go for oil to refill the tank. Bill Dirks, Jr., told me that he would have someone bring up some barrels from the stock on the beach and get the furnace going again.

While we had classes in the living room, Simeon, propped up in bed, went over the official letters—all marked "Urgent." He selected the one on the organization of the new Alaska Native Industrial Cooperative Association and the attendant loan as the most urgent. He planned to discuss it first with Bill Dirks, Jr., and Danny Nevzoroff. At the instigation of the Alaska Native Service in Juneau a group of native stores was forming an association to do their own purchasing. Heretofore all purchasing had been done through the Juneau office. The A.N.S. was now placing that responsibility on the natives themselves. No one was coming from the Juneau office to explain the new move to the people. It was left to us, as representatives, to do the best we could. We spent that evening breaking down the material for presentation to the villagers.

Next morning the furnace tank was filled and soon the house was warm for the first time since last month. School went on in the classroom as usual for the next two days. In the living room Simeon discussed the new organization, first with Bill and Danny, and later with the entire Council. He patiently read and explained, read and explained again and again and again, for hours on end. I went in from time to time to brew fresh coffee and get more cigarettes for the men. Before these quiet, thoughtful men filed out to go home for their suppers they had decided to call a community meeting for Thursday afternoon to present the matter to all of the people. Simeon went to bed thoroughly exhausted.

Thursday was school as usual in the morning; then at lunchtime the boys pushed back the desks and set out the chairs for the afternoon meeting.

At one o'clock the men got Simeon into a chair in the front of the classroom. Every member of the village who was able to be there was already seated. The young chief, Bill Dirks, Jr., served as interpreter and spoke briefly in Aleut. We explained the papers to the people and answered their questions for two hours. Finally, when they seemed satisfied that they understood, an election was held. Officers for the new association were Bill Dirks, Jr., President; Alfred Prokopioff, Vice-president; Alex Prossoff, Secretary; Danny Nevzoroff, Treasurer, and Bill Golley, Councilman. The meeting was over at four o'clock and everyone left except the councilmen, who stayed to finish up the business. By six-thirty all of the papers were duly signed, the minutes of the meeting reviewed, and the new secretary had prepared the papers for air-mailing back to Juneau. The men took Simeon back to our quarters and to bed and I got our dinner.

We had no sooner finished dinner than Lieutenant Cavanaugh, Sergeant Dull, and the GI who wanted to marry one of the village girls arrived from the base. I rounded up the Council members and the girl was sent for. A frank and open discussion followed, which lasted until 11:00 P.M. The Council finally decided to give the two permission to marry. The GI was soon to be discharged. He would be on probation, working for the community and proving his fitness as a village resident, for five years. Peter Nevzoroff and his wife offered to give them their house; they would move in with Peter's mother. (We learned later that the marriage never took place.)

Time, bed rest, and gentle massage had restored sensation to the numbed area of Simeon's hip and once more he was able to walk, but the pain in his back remained constant. It was with relief that we learned that, weather permitting, a plane would come on Saturday morning and take us to Adak for X-rays.

After school I made my rounds and was relieved to find nearly all of my patients up and around. I could leave for a few days with lighter heart.

Bill Dirks, Jr., and Danny Nevzoroff had spent much of the day with Simeon, going over the village business that he was to transact in Adak. Danny had compiled a list of needed store supplies which Simeon was to try to buy from the PX and commissary.

A plane buzzed the village next morning, so we were ready when the bulldozer, with a little trailer, arrived at about ten-thirty to take us to the base. We had just climbed in when Teresa Gardner ran up to tell us that Clara Snigaroff's baby was coming. I climbed out and rushed back into the clinic for the "baby things." Then Teresa and I hurried to Clara. We found her with two midwives in attendance and the baby definitely on the way. I turned the materials over to them and asked them to wire us in Adak when the baby arrived, then hurried back to the waiting bulldozer.

Dr. Thode was at the plane. We told him why we had been delayed.

"Don't worry! She'll be all right, or they can get in touch with me. You are going to Adak!" he said firmly.

Off we went. As we flew out over Korovin Bay we struck an air pocket; for an instant a foot of space showed between us and our seats. The doctor strapped Simeon in. Glimpses through the fog below us showed a turbulent Bering Sea. Then it became too foggy to see anything, and we flew on instruments. Others said that it was a rough forty-five-minute ride, but my thoughts were divided between concern for Simeon's comfort here and for Clara back in Atka.

After we landed in Adak Dr. Thode took us to his home to meet his wife, Mary. She had prepared a lovely lunch for us and we had a short visit before he took me to see the dentist, Dr. Paul Burroughs. The X-rays for Simeon had to wait until Monday. Dr. Burroughs cleaned and examined my teeth and I made an appointment to have the bothersome one extracted on Monday. Mary Thode, who was about my size but several years younger, lent me an evening dress and shoes for the grand opening of the Cavu Club that evening. Several people informed me that evening that Cavu stood for "ceiling and visibility unlimited."

At the club we renewed acquaintance with many officers who had visited us on Atka, and met their wives, all very friendly and gracious. There were about a hundred people present and we met them all, including General and Mrs. Edmund Lynch. They invited us to their quarters for music the next afternoon. Simeon played the piano and one of the officers, "Pappy" Baker, sang several selections.

We were swamped with invitations, most of which, of course, we were unable to accept for we were after all on a business trip. Everyone was eager to learn about our little village and its fine people. Several said that they had met the young chief, Bill Dirks, Jr., when he and Simeon had been in Adak before. He had been very popular. Most of the fliers expressed the wish to visit Atka before returning to the States.

It was a delightful evening such as we had not enjoyed since our tour the previous year. Simeon was in his element.

Since no business could be transacted on Sunday it was a purely social day. We had brunch with Captain Charles Burtner and his wife, Winnie. Then the captain went to bring my son. I had not seen Ernest for over a year, and the others gave us time for a little visit before Dr. Thode took Simeon and me to General Lynch's home. Ernest spent the afternoon with the others at Major Barrett's, awaiting our return.

Our musical afternoon at the general's was very pleasant, for we were hungry for good music. The general proudly showed us some of the equipment which he had built. He played several selections from his vast library of recordings, among them an oboe concerto and Claudio Arrau's interpretation of Schumann's Piano Concerto in A Minor.

General Lynch showed us his wolfskin-covered couch. He chuckled, "It's especially for my Navy friends in their blues!"

We spent the next three days taking care of the business that had brought us to Adak. At the hospital on Monday the X-rays showed that Simeon had chipped a piece off a vertebra when he fell. Our physical examinations showed that we had both lost considerable weight, but otherwise we were in good physical health.

While Dr. Burroughs extracted my troublesome wisdom tooth, Simeon sent his messages and requests for seals for the fox skins to the Juneau office. Each skin had to have a metal seal attached as proof to buyers and to government authorities that it had been legally trapped.

Together we contacted a chaplain, Major Goering, to see if he would come to Atka to marry our two couples. They had again expressed the hope that they could be legally married soon. Major Goering said that he would be happy to go to Atka with us to perform the ceremonies. Then we sent a message to Atka, telling the two couples to be ready on Thursday.

Our new friends included Ernest in many of the evening social events, so we had a chance to see more of him. The evenings were a constant round of activity—cocktails at one Quonset hut, then to another for dinner and music, and visiting in a third.

Tuesday evening a group gathered at Navy Commander Cole's, where we again saw General and Mrs. Lynch and Navy Captain Harris's wife. Captain Harris joined us later, bringing a special guest, Admiral Noble of Washington, D.C.

Commander Cole invited us to a banquet the following night at the Navy Club, honoring Admiral Noble and the eight full captains in his entourage, all from Washington, D.C. They were making a survey of all of the U.S. Naval bases around the world. Admiral Noble gave us his Washington address and invited us to be his guests there later this year when our tour would take us to the nation's capital.

Late on Wednesday we finished up our business and bought groceries from the Navy for the village store.

The banquet honoring the visiting Naval officers was a gala affair. The Navy Club was filled with beautifully dressed women and smartly tailored men. After dinner, on request, Simeon played the piano for over an hour. Dancing followed. Throughout the evening I saw "short-snorters" being brought out and passed around to collect additional signatures. Some of them were made up of several pieces of paper money, both foreign and domestic, taped end to end and bearing dozens of signatures. Each was a very unofficial certificate that its owner had flown across the ocean during the war; the signers were men or women who had made the crossing, too. Originally, if a flier in a bar could not produce his "short-snorter" on demand, he was obliged to buy drinks, or "short snorts," for all of his companions. And, of course, the signatures of notables were especially prized.

As the party broke up, about midnight, Admiral Noble repeated to us his invitation to be his guests in Washington later in the year.

Our plane was due to leave for Atka early next morning. Colonel and Mrs. Mossman and Colonel Ware came to the field to see us off after we had said good-bye to Mary Thode and Winnie Burtner. Our plane door had been jammed by a truck so our departure was delayed for a bit, but we were off by nine-thirty. Major Goering, Major Schleuder, Dr. Thode, two photographers, and a new sergeant for the Atka post accompanied us.

We all walked over to the village from the post. At the top of the hill we paused to look over the village. We were delighted to see how hard everyone had worked. The lumber, scattered by the recent storms, was again in neat piles. Empty oil drums had been removed. All was in order. Atka village was ready for visitors and for a wedding. While Dr. Thode and I went to see our patients, the two couples were alerted. Clara Snigaroff had a dear tiny baby named Marie, for her mother.

All the village gathered for the wedding. The members of the congregation took their usual places at the back of the church, the men and boys on the right side of the center aisle, the women and girls on the left, all standing. The two couples, Innokinty Golodoff and Vasha Zaochney, and Ralph Prokopeuff and Olean Golodoff, neatly dressed and with serious faces, took their places before the low platform where Major Goering stood between two simply decorated altars. The marriage ceremony was brief and solemn. The young chief gave the brides away. Major Schleuder provided one of the wedding rings. The photographers took several pictures of the ceremony.

Immediately after the ceremony the wedding party went over to our quarters to sign the wedding certificates. Mrs. Nevzoroff, who had been taking care of the baby, and "Toughie," as Innokinty fondly called his baby daughter, were sent for. The photographers took more pictures. A reception for the two couples followed, and their many friends flocked in to drink to their health and happiness in the wine which the officers had brought for the occasion, and to sample the cakes the women had baked.

The memorable day ended with a celebration dance. Again George and Lucy Prokopeuff performed the old native courting dance.

A few days later we received copies of the pictures and the news release that had been sent out following the officers' return to Adak.

I awakened early the morning after the wedding, listening to the birds singing and the raucous croaking of the ravens as they soared over the village, "It's good to be home again!" I thought.

We took up our regular routine once more. After morning class I made a hurried round of the village and found everyone up and about. At low tide Mike Lokanin took several of us out for mussels and clams.

After dinner Alex Prossoff came up for his schoolwork. We studied for two hours. I made a simple outline for him for his secretarial minutes. Over tea we visited. He told us that we were going to have wind. "How do you know?" I asked.

Alex answered, "I feel it in my back. My skin flaps."

Later the Old Chief told me that some Aleuts can foretell the weather by skin reaction. In sea-otter hunting days one old man in Unalaska could predict very accurately the hour of a storm. He had a large following. I remembered Simeon telling me of him long ago.

Alex said that Elizabeth was losing weight and he was worried about her. We tried to reassure him. Many people had lost weight during the flu epidemic, but we would all regain it now that the crisis was over.

The day before had been Elizabeth's birthday. Alex went home with a bottle of perfume for her. As he went out of the door he laughed, "Now I have to watch so no one steals her when she wears this!"

The next day, Saturday, the wind that Alex had predicted arrived with spitting rain and snow squalls. We worked on mail and finished the March reports. Several of the village men spent the entire day putting seals on the fox skins to show that they had been taken legally.

Toward late afternoon the skies cleared, although the wind still blew. I wanted to look in on Pari Lokanin and on the way I stopped at the Dirkses' home to have Mattie sign for her paycheck (for the last several months she had been earning money by teaching sewing to the girls). Vasha Zaochney Golodoff and Annie Golley were there. I joined them for tea and *aladiks* (deep-fried bread) before going next door.

At Pari's I found Mike doing the laundry. Sorted soiled clothes were in piles all over the floor. Pari was lying down with baby Helen. She was still running some temperature, but said that she was feeling better. An hour after I returned home I looked up the hill and saw long lines of fresh clean clothes blowing in the wind.

The barge from Adak came into the village harbor late Saturday evening. It was to take the four boys who were due for military service when it left. Ted Golley and Moses Prokopeuff were sent out to find out why it had come to the village harbor, and reported that it was due to the wind. The barge remained in the harbor overnight but it pulled out before church Sunday morning.

After church George Prokopeuff came to ask if the Sisterhood could have the schoolroom for a village-only dance that evening because the four boys were going away. Several of the women came for sugar and shortening to make cakes to serve. They asked to use the kitchen, as usual.

The evening started off fine, but an hour later several crew members from the barge crashed the dance. At intermission the refreshments were served and the dance discontinued. The boys woke us at 4:00 A.M. to say good-bye.

The last three days of April were cold and rainy, but we were back to our routine again: teaching for me and paper work for Simeon. After school I joined Simeon, who was completing the economic survey.

It was interesting to see what the survey revealed about the amount of native food the villagers consumed between June 1946 and April 1947-- it was tremendous!

Gardens were made on nearby Amlia Island because Atka was rat- ridden. Potatoes grown there and consumed in the village added up to 6.5 pounds per person; we were told that triple that amount might have been harvested, but foxes dug up the fish that were used as fertilizer. The villagers also consumed half a pound of cabbage and 3 pounds of turnips per person, from the Amlia gardens.

Plants gathered on Atka itself added up to nearly a quart of wild crowberries per person, plus 4.5 pounds of *petrusky,* 7 pounds of *sarana* (Indian rice, whose root is dried and eaten like potatoes), and 26 pounds of *pootchky* per person.

Fishing brought each villager (on average) 82 salmon, 43.5 cod, 11 pogies, 10 halibut, 6 trout, and 7 sculpins. Ordinarily, large quantities of all types of fish were salt cured for winter consumption, but for lack of salt only 1,900 salmon were salted and smoked. Shore gathering brought the village 25 pounds of sea urchin, 27 pounds of clams, 15 pounds of mussels, and 9 birds' eggs per person. About 1,200 pounds of black chiton (over 13 pounds per person) were also gathered; this mol- lusk is called "bidarka" because of its boatlike shape. Limpets were gathered in small quantities. King, Dungeness, and spider crabs were eaten when caught.

The survey also revealed that the reindeer hunts had brought the village 152 pounds of meat per person. Other hunting activities brought each villager an average of 59 pounds of sea lion and 32 pounds of hair seal. Lack of salt prevented the preservation of any of this meat. Each person also received 12 Emperor beach geese and 15 ducks, including both fresh-water ducks (mallard, teal, butterball, and golden-eye) and salt-water ducks (pintail, harlequin, scoter, and eider).

Looking over the survey, it was also interesting to see how the village had changed in ten months, as many households were altered by mar- riages, births, and other new living arrangements.

Andrew Snigaroff building frame of traditional bidarka

❊MAY 1947

cidugnim tugida

(month of flowers)

It rained hard all of that first morning in May, but in the afternoon the sun came out. For several weeks illness and the weather had kept everyone close to the village. Recently the boys had been going out hunting or fishing, so when the girls asked me to go hiking with them after school I agreed.

We hiked along the beach all the way out to the Army dock. We raced, played tag, and jumped the waves rolling in from Nazan Bay. When we reached the dock we climbed the bank above it. Here we found fresh green plant life. *Pootchky* was already several inches high. The only flower we found was a lone blossoming shepherd's purse. The girls dug lupine root (yellow root) and parsnip for us to eat. Both were very good.

"If we had our digging sticks with us we could get some to take home," they said. "Next time we'll bring them."

When it was time to leave the bank we took turns sitting on the dead grass and sliding to the bottom. We decided to hike back home on the road, but when we saw several Army trucks approaching from the base we hurriedly took to the beach, like a covey of frightened ptarmigans.

In cooking class on Friday the older girls made Mary Thode's chocolate cake while the younger ones made applesauce to serve at their party in our quarters that evening. We promised to show our movies of the village activities. The cakes and applesauce were a complete success, and so was the rest of the evening.

The village survey took precedence over the other reports that the Juneau office had requested. The young chief and Simeon were to visit each family to gather pertinent information. I worked on the layout for the report. The Old Chief came to visit and have dinner with us, and he made several helpful suggestions which the men incorporated in their plan of work. Bill Dirks, Jr., and Simeon started their family interviews on the first Sunday in May.

Monday morning construction work started again in earnest. The men and older boys gathered before the schoolhouse as they had done last summer. The young chief assigned one crew to carry lumber with which to sheathe Alfred Prokopioff's house. A second crew was to start work on Ralph Prokopeuff's house, up the hill above Andrew Snigaroff's. After assigning the work for the day Bill was free to join Simeon on the survey. I left them in the kitchen, discussing their plans over coffee, when I went to the schoolroom.

That evening when Alex came for his lesson he brought Elizabeth and Alfred, the baby. Elizabeth had a bad toothache and wanted Simeon to pull the tooth, which he did. Many of the people needed dental attention, due to neglect and the malnutrition of the past three or four years. This was true of both the Atkans and the Attuans. I remembered the fine full set of teeth in the lower jaw which I had found when we dug at Atxalax. The normal Aleut native diet had fostered good teeth. When they left that night Elizabeth took Simeon's cigarette lighter so that she could make a seal-gut case for it.

It was good to have the village functioning normally again, to awaken to birdsong and the raucous "adak, edonk" of the ravens, and to see the villagers moving about their daily chores before the construction work and school began. Again, after school and the construction work for the day were over, everyone went about different pursuits. The air hummed with the sound of outboard motors as dory after dory left the dock for the fishing grounds. The sound of saw and hammer also continued, for several of the men worked on their own homes after hours. It was the goal of many to finish the village work and go to Adak to look for work with the military, or to the Pribilofs to work in the fur-seal harvest.

Shortly after lunch on Wednesday Commander Cole of the Navy buzzed the village and appeared a little later with Lieutenant Burnett. They brought a big box of oranges. He wanted to take us to Adak to a farewell party and reception for Captain Harris and himself. We would have loved to go, but our work held us at home. We sent our thanks for the invitation and our good wishes to both couples. The sergeant who had brought them over from the base also brought me some fresh vegetables in return for some baking powder that I had given him.

After school Billy Golley came with some eggs. He said that this was his sister Elizabeth's birthday and he wanted to bake her a cake if he could have some sugar and shortening. I added vanilla and coconut and he went home singing.

Store accounts were due again. Bill Dirks, Jr., and Danny Nevzoroff had dinner with us and then the three men worked on the books until late.

The next day was cloudy and a threat of rain hung in the air. We saw two planes come in from Adak, but no one came to the village. It was about 6:00 P.M. before one of the boys who drove the jeep came to take us over to Korovin to see if the salmon had started to run. We dropped our work and drove to the bay and the creek. There were no salmon yet, but we filled our pockets with *petrusky* and headed back. We stopped at the road cut and dug for a short time. We found some nice pieces, as usual, but the threatened rain came and forced us back home. On the way we stopped to see how the raspberry and strawberry plants we brought up on the *North Star* had fared. All of the raspberry plants had died, but several of the strawberry plants were coming up.

Early Friday morning one of the boys told us that a boat was tied up over at the dock. It turned out to be a Freight Service boat from Adak. Later in the morning Dr. Thode brought young Captain and Mrs. Carol Lund and baby to call on us. While they visited with Simeon I went around with the doctor. The Old Chief smilingly told him that he had needed his services sooner, because his setting hen had died and he had lost all of his chicks-to-be.

Back at the school Dr. Thode said that he wanted to buy enough fox skins to make a coat for his wife. Simeon sent for Danny Nevzoroff, who took the doctor to make his selection. When he returned he had six beautiful skins to display. Annie Golley came in with fresh bread and eggs for him, too. The doctor was a favorite in Atka.

The Lunds asked us to dinner aboard the boat that evening, and we spent a pleasant evening with them. Captain Lund said that he hoped to bring over a group of Adak women in a couple of weeks. Many were eager to see the village their husbands enjoyed visiting.

On Saturday, May 10, Titiana Kudrin gave birth to a five-pound baby boy. She named him Cyril Dan.

Simeon gave Mike Lokanin his gray suit. Mike was delighted with it, though he could not button the coat over his rotundity. "That's all right," he laughed. "I wore Pete Nevzoroff's brown suit that you gave him to church on Easter when Pete had the flu, and I couldn't button the pants!"

All day spots of clear sky were followed by bursts of wind-driven rain and snow. The families came for the promised movie, but the sound was out. We left the chairs set up to try again on Sunday afternoon.

A brilliant sunrise woke us next morning at five o'clock, but shortly thereafter came squalls of rain and snow that continued most of the day. Annie Golley came early to have coffee and fruit with us. The oranges had been distributed throughout the village, but the Lunds had given us a few bananas and a fresh pineapple, which we shared with Annie.

After church the Old Chief came to visit, as he often did. He was accompanied by Sophie Dirks, his daughter, and Nadesta Golley, and followed by Affia Snigaroff and Teresa Gardner. Teresa gave me a hundred dollars to send to her lawyer in Anchorage as partial payment for her divorce. While the Atkans had been at Killisnoo she and Matrona's eldest son had married, but when he chose to remain in southeastern Alaska she decided to terminate the marriage.

That afternoon we showed the movies, and there was enough power to operate the sound. Afterward Bill and Mattie Dirks went to our quarters with Simeon for coffee while I helped the girls clean the school-room and get it ready for classes on Monday. After that, since the Dirkses had gone home, I went for a walk in the rain with Affia and Olean Snigaroff. We climbed up to the point overlooking the bay where Eulalie, the child of an early teacher, was buried. We were curious to see if the daffodils her mother had planted were coming up yet. We were too early. However, great flocks of longspurs had come back. Their return was the main event of the day.

The men were still working on the economic survey, but I finished my part of the report after school on Monday. Simeon borrowed Olean Golodoff Prokopeuff's typewriter, which had a wide carriage, to type the charts.

While I was working Sophie Dirks and Nadesta Golley came with a present for me from Nadesta's mother. Jenny Golley had made an exqui-site thimble basket for me. I marveled at the patience and skill that had produced the beautiful, dainty work of art from the tough beach grass.

I showed the tiny basket to Mike Lokanin when he came in later, bringing us a reindeer ham.

"Jenny Golley is fine grass weaver," he said. "She is Attu woman before she marry Sergius Golley. Attu women best weavers. Pari is silking her basket for you now. Atka grass not so good as Attu, breaks and falls off. When basket is done, keep rice in it to keep it white." I thanked him for his advice and immediately put rice in both of my treasured baskets.

Andrew Snigaroff's forty days of mòurning for Mary were at an end and Teresa Gardner made sourdough liquor for him. A private gather-ing with a few close friends was held at his house that evening.

On Tuesday Bill Golley sent for me. When I entered his house I found a very sick man. He had a headache, sore throat, and a fever. I told him to stay in bed and went back to the clinic for medication, fearing another round of flu.

Some of the properly sealed and tagged fox skins were to go by plane to the Adak post office for shipment to the Seattle Fur Exchange. A plane was to come for them on Wednesday. The Council wanted Simeon to take them. He was too busy with the mass of reports that he was working on. I, too, told them that I could not go. We both felt that it was their responsibility, and they needed the experience. Bill Dirks, Jr., chose not to go because he needed to get on with the construction on the houses. Bill Golley was sick. That left Danny Nevzoroff. He was the logical choice, since he was the newly-elected treasurer of the new native stores cooperative for this village.

Very early the next morning a plane buzzed the village. Shortly afterward a truck came from the base and was loaded with the furs. Danny got in and the truck took off. Then a jeep drove in with Dr. Thode, Captain Kunz, and my son, Ernest Ross! He had come to spend his last two weeks in the Aleutians on Atka with us. His year's contract as a civilian employee at Adak was ended. He would be returning to our home in Anchorage in June to await our return the following month.

Dr. Thode and I went to see Bill Golley while the others visited. Then the jeep took the officers back to their plane, and I got a delayed breakfast together for us. While Ernest settled in, I went to the classroom and Simeon to his typewriter. This was going to be a fine report, but it had taken a lot of nose-to-the-grindstone hours.

In the late afternoon Mike Lokanin came up from the dock to show us his catch. He had brought in the first halibut of the season, a huge hundred-and-fifty-pounder and a small chicken halibut. The big one he carried on his back with an oar through its gills. The small one he gave to us. As he was about to leave with his burden, the large halibut had a final dying spasm and spanked Mike smartly several times with its tail. Ralph Prokopeuff had also caught two halibut that day. Everyone in the village ate fresh halibut that night.

My son had caught us swamped with work. I had two more days of teaching, for school would be out on Friday, May 16. After that I, too, would be doing reports all day long. Ernest selected a number of books from the village library to read for the next day or two, until we were free to show him some of the interesting spots on the island.

Thursday I gave the children the last of the territorial tests and was at my desk, checking them, when several of the girls burst in. Someone had sighted a herd of deer about a mile away and most of the village was going to the hunt, either as participants or as spectators. The girls had never gone on a hunt and would I please take them? I shoved the tests in a drawer and got my boots and parka, and we were off. Simeon and Ernest, with their cameras, were well ahead of us up the trail toward Tutusax. The girls and I found a good viewing place on the hill, over-looking the valley or the draw where the hunt was taking place. The men got seven deer and were very careful to avoid shooting females, who had their dark young fawns running beside them.

While the hunters were dressing the deer the herd retreated up the draw. Simeon took Ernest to our diggings at Tutusax and the girls and I walked on over the hills in search of early flowers. We found three damp, muddy ground flowers. The girls told me the Aleut name for them, but I could neither say nor spell it. When we got back to the schoolhouse I pressed them and added them to the collection.

Wind-driven squalls of rain and snow greeted us on Friday. Ernest read all day and Simeon typed. The children and I had our last day of school together. They turned in their books and I checked them off. They cleaned out their desks. We had some refreshments, and then I gave them their report cards and sent them home. School was over. These children should have had the advantage of a normal school year, with a full-time teacher in a comfortable classroom.

Bill Dirks, Jr., and the other Council members had a meeting with Teresa Gardner in our quarters that evening. She wanted to leave Atka on the mail boat and offered to sell her house. It was purchased by the Council for six hundred dollars. She told us that she wanted to get a job in a cannery for the summer, then go on to Anchorage.

Ever since coming to Atka we had hoped to investigate the coal deposits at Sand Bay. We had read of them in William H. Dall's *Alaska* and the report had been confirmed by some of the people here. Arrange-ments were made for one of the Army trucks to come on Sunday to carry a boat and engine over to Korovin Bay for that purpose. The weather was so stormy that the trip was postponed. The storm had abated by Monday morning, although a light rain still fell. Those of us who were to go to Sand Bay were up early with food, cameras, and sacks for the coal, all ready and waiting for the truck—which failed to appear. Later we learned that no truck had been available for the village project.

The day was not wasted, however, for there were still the reports to work on. The survey, census, and loan reports must all be ready to go out on the mail boat.

Mike Lokanin had received such a drenching while halibut fishing that he had been sick since then with tonsilitis. I spent part of my day taking medicine to him and to Bill Golley. And little Joseph Nevzoroff brought me my first crowflower of the year.

The following day was gray in more ways than one. The weather, rainy and windy, was not unexpected, but the letter addressed to the teachers at Nikolski and Atka was. It came from the acting general superintendent at the Juneau office. We knew immediately, from the tone as well as the contents, that Don Foster, the general superintendent, had had nothing to do with the letter.

A vindictive white trapper who had a grudge against the Aleut trappers and the captain of the *Aleutian Mail* was out to make trouble. He had stopped off in Juneau en route to Seattle and had seen the acting superintendent. He reported that the mail boat was selling liquor all along the line, although he admitted that he saw no excessive drinking among the Aleuts while on the boat. He was among the returning trappers brought to Atka from the western islands. He had left with the Umnak and Unalaska men on the *Aleutian Mail* when she came to Atka on her initial run in March.

In the letter the teachers were given specific instructions for handling the liquor situation involving the mail boat and the village. The letter went on to say that the man was "somewhat concerned about the irresponsibility of the Aleuts in handling the blue fox skins"; some of the skins reportedly had holes in them and were not properly skinned and handled. According to the complainant, the trappers were only concerned about their ten dollars per skin. The teachers were instructed to "make every effort in teaching the Aleuts their responsibility for making their own livelihood."

The sale of the fox skins paid for the store requisitions. The requisitions would be cut if the money did not reach the Juneau office. None of the concern over the blue foxes and their handling applied to Atka.

Every effort was being made to get money to the Juneau office to pay for the store requisitions.

The next paragraph of the letter illustrated how little some of the officials in charge of Atka understood about the island, its people, and their situation:

> For a number of years there have been reindeer on both Umnak and Atka Islands and we have no information to show that they have made any attempt to handle these reindeer regularly, but only kill some occasionally for food. These reindeer should be handled each year. They should be rounded up each year. I do not know if any particular instructions have been sent to your villages, which I believe has [been done]; if so you should explain such procedures to the people and get them to do something about caring for the reindeer and utilizing the meat for food and [the skins for] clothing. If you do not have instructions on handling the reindeer advise this office at once so we may send you complete information.

Atka is a mountainous island, slightly less than sixty miles long from North Cape on the northeast to Cape Kigun on the extreme southwest, and about twenty-five miles wide from North Cape to Cape Utalug, where the waters of Amlia Pass enter the Pacific Ocean. In 1914 twenty pairs of reindeer were put on the island by the government, and now the Aleuts estimated that nearly four thousand reindeer wandered over the entire island, in small herds. Imagine twenty men, on foot, trying to "round them up" and "handle them"!

Reindeer were introduced by the government to serve as food when stormy weather makes it impossible for the people to hunt at sea. Although most Aleutians prefer the flesh of seals and sea lions, they appreciate the reindeer at these times. They use all of the meat, but they do not make clothing of the hides. They have worn Western clothing for over a century, purchased from traders or by mail.

The entire letter demanded a thoughtful, diplomatic reply. To add to our distress, before the day was over a couple of telegrams arrived from the acting superintendent, further illustrating his lack of understanding of the Atka situation.

By the following morning the skies were clearing a bit and we could hear the birds again. We could not get the use of an Army truck for the

Sand Bay trip until Saturday or Sunday, so Ernest made arrangements with Spiridon Zaochney to go down the bay by dory to get pictures of the waterfall near Atxalax.

Before they were ready to start, Dr. Thode and Navy Lieutenant Burnett came with a letter from General Lynch for Simeon, thanking him for the books Simeon had autographed for them. Mrs. Lynch had sent me a letter saying that the trip to Atka for the Adak women had been postponed. Lieutenant Burnett brought us some fresh strawberries and cream.

Mrs. Lynch had seen Mary Thode's beautiful fox skins and she asked me to select six just like them for her, if possible, and also to send the name and address of a firm we would recommend to tan them. Lieutenant Burnett was to select six fox skins for his wife, too, but when Spiridon came for Ernest the lieutenant decided to join them for the trip to the falls instead, and he asked me to pick out the skins for him. Dr. Thode had orders from two other women, each of whom wanted a matched pair of skins for a scarf. Altogether we sold sixteen skins to go to Adak, and I chose a pair of pretty little light ones for myself.

While we waited for Spiridon's boat to return Dr. Thode and I went to check on Bill Golley and Mike Lokanin. Both were improving. Shortly after, the dory came in. Both of Spiridon's passengers were delighted with their trip down the bay, and Lieutenant Burnett was pleased with the skins I had selected for his wife. The officers took off for the base soon afterward.

Everyone in the village was pleased with the events of the day. The excitement was not over, however, for toward evening another plane landed, bringing Danny Nevzoroff and Ted and Dimitri Golley. The two boys, now in the Army, had come to bid their families good-bye, for they were off to the States for further training.

Danny came up later and explained his return. He had not enjoyed his business trip to Adak. He had felt so responsible for the money in his care that he had stayed in his hotel room all day long; he even found it difficult to go out for a glass of beer. In the evening Ted and Dimitri would come for him and they would go to a show, but they were always back by ten o'clock. Danny jumped at the chance to return to Atka when the boys came home.

On Thursday morning Simeon walked over to the base and sent telegrams of reply to the Juneau office. He also picked up a telegram from Mr. Paden, in charge of native stores, telling us to sell all the furs possible in Adak to meet store obligations of about thirty-one thousand dollars. His suggested selling price was thirty dollars per skin. Bill Dirks, Jr., was stunned at that suggestion, for the skins had sold here for almost twice that.

Simeon wired the Adak post office to hold the Atka shipment to Seattle. The Council met in our living room and decided that Bill Dirks, Jr., and Simeon should take the remaining furs and leave for Adak at the first opportunity. There they would contact General Lynch, Major Schleuder, and Navy Captain Harris, and enlist their aid in arranging to sell the foxes in the Army and Navy PXs.

The rest of the day was spent with Bill Dirks, Jr., Bill Golley, and Danny Nevzoroff, bringing the village store accounts up to date. Danny and Simeon had worked on them consistently each month, so they were in pretty good shape.

Ernest took a long walk up over the hills back of the village, and I continued to work on a report for the U.S. Commissioner at Unalaska.

Although by Saturday the weather had improved, no truck appeared for the Sand Bay trip. Simeon took over the kitchen and worked on maps to accompany the economic survey. He used the kitchen counter for the project, so after breakfast Ernest and I stayed out. Ernest used his carpentry skills to fix some windows in the basement, and I packed books. Our neighbors were going about their usual business. Some were out fishing, and we saw a group of boys hiking over the hill toward Korovin Bay. Annie Golley said later that they had gone egg hunting.

After dinner a couple of men from the base came to show movies. They brought with them a Philco Radio man, Mr. Barfield, on loan to the government. Again the power was so low that the movies could not be shown.

We were up bright and early next morning. A GI came with the truck and took the boat, the two Bills, Ernest, Simeon, and me to Korovin, in another attempt to reach Sand Bay. When we left the village it was slightly windy and there were rain squalls, but over on the Korovin side we found great white breakers rolling in on the beach. Disappointed, the others went back to the village, leaving me and my son to walk home later. We went over to the area where Simeon and I had dug last fall and spent some time there. Ernest found a nice stone lamp almost immediately, and a lovely small one later. All I found was that I had lost my digging strength since last fall. On the way home we stopped at the road cut and poked around with sticks for a short time, then walked on home. We had a very good day. Simeon wished he had gone with us, for his work had been interrupted by a visit from the radio man while silent pictures were at last being shown to the villagers in the classroom.

On Monday Simeon sent a wire to Mr. Paden in Juneau, detailing the plans for the sale of the furs at Adak. Then he finished lettering the maps he had made. At long last the *Atka Village Economic Survey* was complete.

With that out of the way we worked on letters for Don Foster. Annie Golley came in for a short visit. She brought fresh bread, warm from the oven. That went very well with the fresh sea-lion liver which Danny Nevzoroff sent us for dinner. Such dear generous people—how we would miss them!

Overnight the weather changed. The skies cleared and the waters of the bay sparkled in the morning sunshine. Birds were singing and we could hear the hum of motors as the dories left the dock. Overhead the seabirds and ravens soared. It was a perfect day to be out of doors. The economic survey, the census, and the loan papers were ready to go out on the mail boat, so we decided to do something out of doors, too. We could not stray too far from the village, in case a plane came to take Bill Dirks, Jr., Simeon, and the fox skins to Adak. We were still discussing the possibilities when Mike Lokanin came to ask if we would like to go for a boat ride.

We headed first for the string of small rocky islets a short distance out in the bay, directly opposite the village. We landed on one of the larger ones, called Uyak. We knew that the earlier Aleuts had come here for a bright red rock that they ground for paint, or used for trade with other Aleuts along the Chain. We found lots of it where it had boiled up out of the basic rock like a spill of blood, and we could see where the ancients had chipped pieces off, but we had nothing with which to take samples. The islet was fascinating with its many clear tide pools filled with all sorts of sea life: sea urchins, limpets, and seaweed. In one pool we found a six-inch-long chiton which Mike called a bidarka, so named because of its resemblance in shape to the boat. We had found many of the eight-piece bidarka skeletons in the digging at Atxalax last fall.

Mike took us to see an old barabara on a bluff overlooking the entrance to the bay. From there we saw several boats out among the islets. The boys were searching for eggs while overhead the screaming sea birds soared or darted down toward the interlopers.

When we left Uyak we overtook Sergius Golley, who was fishing for cod. He had run out of gas, and we drew alongside so that he could fill his tank from Mike's extra can. Several cod lay in the bottom of his boat. When we drew away from Sergius we headed down to Atxalax. On the way we stopped at the beautiful waterfall for pictures, and then we spent a happy, dirty hour pawing through the sloughed-off banks of last fall's pits. We found a few bits and pieces. Then we headed home, feeling greatly refreshed, thanks to Mike.

No plane came that day or the next, although the clear weather held. We went back to our work, and Ernest followed his own interests, walking the beach or the hills, or reading.

On May 30 the rain came down in sheets all morning long. It slackened off toward late afternoon. Suddenly some excited boys ran in, shouting, "Mail boat! Mail boat! Teresa all ready to go!"

A short time later a jeep brought Captain Roy Hough, whom we had met in Seward a couple of years before. He commanded a Freight Service boat and had come from Unalaska en route to Adak. He invited us to have dinner on board. One of his passengers, Colonel Frank of the Alaska Department Headquarters Graves Registration, wanted information about the Attu prisoners. On the way back to the dock Captain Hough told us that the Catrons on Chernovski had lost eight hundred sheep last winter.

After dinner we brought Colonel Frank back to the village with us and sent for Alex Prossoff, Alfred Prokopioff, Mike Lokanin, and Innokinty Golodoff. We all smiled when Alex said that they had come home on "the *General Brewster Rooster*." The men grew quite excited when Colonel Frank said that he might want a couple of them to go to Attu with him later. He quizzed them for an hour before going back to the boat.

Captain Hough told Simeon that he would be glad to take Bill, Simeon, Ernest, and the furs to Adak. He would send the jeep for them about midnight. He wanted to leave with the tide because he had a sick man on board. Simeon said that they would be ready, and they were.

As I set the quarters to rights after they left I thought about a story Colonel Frank had told at dinner. He said that in early 1943 he had landed on a little sandy beach on Great Sitkin Island to install some radar equipment. It was on the Adak and Bering Sea side. There had not been much space to land the PBY. It was only a hundred feet or so from the water to the highest precipice on the shore, where it falls sheer to the sea. Here they found what appeared to be an old village site. The waves were fast demolishing all signs. A red rock with crudely chipped Roman numerals, apparently marking an old grave, drew his attention. The chipping had evidently been done with chisel and hammer. The numerals flat-chipped in the stone were the equivalent of 1620. (I had an idea that those "Roman numerals" were really the Russian letters of a name which marked the old grave, but I had said nothing. It was a good story.)

I was up early the next morning, the last day of May, but already dories and skiffs were out on the water and I could hear the ring of hammers where work on the houses went on. This was supposed to be the month of flowers, according to the old Aleut calendar, but it had not been true on Atka this year. "The month to hunt eggs" would have been a better name, for the boys had found many, both on the shelter islets and over at Korovin. It had been after the first week in June, when collecting with Jeannette the previous year, that we had found the early flowers and watched as the new green climbed up the slopes.

Dr. Thode and another officer came in the morning. The doctor removed baby Stephanie's accidentally injured finger nail. He showed me how to care for her finger before going to check on Mike Lokanin and Bill Golley.

The jeep brought a wire from the acting superintendent saying that Howard Burhker was due in Atka the following week to install a radio, such as the other teachers had for direct communication. This had been promised for months—I would believe it when I saw it. The wire went on to say that all furs would be picked up at that time to sell in Anchorage before any unsold skins were shipped to the Seattle Fur Exchange. He closed with what amounted to an apology for his previous wires. This wire was filed with the others, and I went back to scrubbing the walls and ceiling of the breakfast nook as the jeep took off.

Annie Golley came in later for a visit and had coffee with me. I would surely miss her. Pari Lokanin sent Mike down with a delicious *perugy,* a rice and salmon pie, for my dinner.

View of Atka Village, from Nazan Bay

❋ JUNE 1947

cagaligim tugida

(month seals are born)

The village woke to a fresh breeze and sunny skies on the first morning in June. It was Sunday, and I saw Danny Nevzoroff on his way to the church; a short time later I heard the tolling of the improvised bell, calling the people to worship. Although the weather was unusually good and the waters of the bay very inviting, almost everyone attended church before turning to other pursuits. Soon the village paths were filled with boys and girls and men and women, all in their Sunday best, heading for the church. An hour and a half later church services were over and everyone headed home to change into work clothes.

Mike Lokanin came and filled the oil tank and we visited for a bit over coffee. He told me that the men were going to seine later. Some of them had gone over the hills to hunt reindeer.

After lunch I went to Clara Snigaroff's to dress baby Stephanie's finger, and I saw my first violet of the year.

Planes came and went at the base, but no one came to the village. Olean and Affia Snigaroff and I went for a walk to look for flowers, and we found the promise of many, but it was still too early for blossoms. Affia said that there was an old story about a strong man who sat on a volcano, but she could not remember any of the details. On our way home we watched the men seining. They let out a long net and then, with men and boys at both ends, they dragged it in. They caught two flounders, which Larry Nevzoroff threw back in the water. The deer hunters had better luck. They brought in three nice fat deer which were shared by all of the families.

With the turn of the evening tide clouds gathered and a misty rain began falling. By the next morning the mountaintops were frosted with snow and a strong wind blew.

Mike Lokanin brought a part of a reindeer ham for me; then he joined most of the men and boys, all with packs on their backs, to hunt for eggs over at Korovin. Their departure left the village strangely quiet. The dogs wandered forlornly along the streets.

I had hoped to get started on the Attu reports, but several of the women and girls came to visit. Annie Golley brought her grandson, Nicky, and Lydia Dirks brought her Janet. Everyone enjoyed the babies while we visited over our cocoa and cookies.

Bill Golley spent most of the day in the basement. He tore down the generator engine to work on it so that we could show movies again. It took him all the next day to complete his task, but by evening the engine was running.

Late in the afternoon a truck came in from Korovin, bringing back the egg hunters. They had a six-foot octopus and seals, but no eggs. Soon after their return smoky bonfires burned near several homes. Mike told me that they were burning cottonwood to get ashes to mix with their tobacco for "snoose."

Word came that the *North Star* was due at Atka about June 30.

By midweek the weather was again clear and lovely, with bird-filled skies above and a busy village below.

Affia Snigaroff brought me two presents right after breakfast; Draba, which she called *ai yunum ahmaghi,* and a cluster of pogy eggs. They looked like tiny amethysts, hundreds or thousands in a single cluster, each egg the size of a grain of tapioca. As I tore the cluster apart it sounded like new rubber tearing. The tiny egg cases were clear; the fluid they contained looked like grape juice and tasted like kelp or seaweed, slightly salty.

Moses Prokopeuff came after Affia had left. He told me that he had signed a contract to work on the boats out of Adak. Work was to begin immediately and he planned to send money to his mother each payday.

Four or five little boys came running from the hill back of the village to show me the baby birds, longspurs, which they had taken from their nest. Ten minutes later they were retracing their steps.

Early next morning I started to work on the census data concerning the Attuans captured by the Japanese troops on June 7, 1942. Much more than a list of names had been requested.

Olean Golodoff Prokopeuff brought me a paper of her son John's. It was made out in Osaka at Atsugi Airfield, Honshu, Japan, and dated 21 September 1945. This was where they had become separated from their boxes and trunks.

After she left I went for a walk to find green stuff for a fresh salad: *chilax* and *petrusky.* I found two lovely violets, too. While I was eating dinner Affia Snigaroff and Teresa Gardner brought baby Stephanie to have her finger dressed. Teresa gave me another hundred dollars, the final payment on her divorce, to mail to her lawyer in Anchorage.

They had no sooner gone than Alex and Elizabeth Prossoff and the baby came to help me with the Attu papers. They were very patient with my questions, and I felt that we had made good progress by the time that they left at midnight.

Our men with the furs had been gone for a week when Dr. Thode flew in, bringing a letter from Simeon saying that they hoped to return to Atka the following week. After we visited those needing the doctor's attention Julia Golodoff brought Stephanie to the clinic to have her finger dressed. While they were busy I made up a packet of papers and a couple of personal letters and wrote a short note to send to Simeon. For young Bill Dirks's peace of mind I reported that his crews were on the job every day. They had nearly finished sheathing Alex Prossoff and Ralph Prokopeuff's houses and would start on Alfred Prokopioff's, Lydia Golodoff's, and Mike Lokanin's on Saturday.

Like last summer, the men and older boys worked together on construction eight hours a day, six days a week. Evenings and Sundays, though, each followed his own pursuits. Saturday evening Bill Golley tore down the generator engine yet again; John Nevzoroff started work on a new dory; Alex Prossoff, Ralph Prokopeuff, Mike Lokanin, and Alfred Prokopioff continued to hammer nails at their respective homes. Fishermen were out on the bay and a group of boys headed up the deeply-trodden old trail toward the lake in the hills.

Julia Golodoff came to give me more data on herself and her husband, Willie Golodoff, who was still confined in the government hospital at Tacoma. After talking with Alfred Prokopioff about himself and Mary—his wife, who was also in the hospital at Tacoma—I would be ready to make up the list of Attuans requested by U.S. Commissioner Wingfield at Unalaska.

For five days we had glorious sunshine and soft breezes tempting everyone to drop work and head out of doors to play, but only the children were free to do that. The adults all stuck to the job and hoped that the fine weather would hold through Sunday. It did, and we woke on Sunday morning to another blue, green, and gold day, the sixth in a row. Everyone seemed bent on having a picnic. The village was a beehive of activity very early. Davy Zaochney came by with a pack on his back, from which hung the usual kettle for making tea. He carried two buckets, one of them filled with skinned sculpin ready for the fire. He told me that Cedar and Vera Snigaroff had gone camping.

Family groups climbed into boats and headed down the bay. Others, loaded with gear like Davy, hiked out over the hills toward Chuniksax.

Mattie Dirks came to borrow fishline. Mike Lokanin took some of the boys from the base out fishing. They had brought us four barrels of oil for the engine so we could show movies. After the village quieted down little Annie Golley, Annie Snigaroff, and I took sandwiches and hiked back in the hills to a beautiful stream for our own picnic.

Toward evening the picnickers returned, and Bill Golley started the engine. We topped off the day by showing *Stallion Road*. Alex Prossoff forecast a weather change by the next day.

He was right, for although it was still pretty, early next day ominous clouds began to hang over the mountains and a stiff wind sprang up.

Two sergeants came in the afternoon to find out how much gas and oil we would need to tide us over until the *North Star* brought the village's annual supply. Bill Golley made a guess. When the GIs went back to the base, Sergeant Hackett hooked up a radio to the phone. We still could not send messages out, but that evening I was able to hear the news and an opera. Because of the time difference I heard them while I worked on the Attu papers before dinner. That night we had another movie show: Jimmy Durante and Frank Sinatra in *It Happened in Brooklyn*.

It rained steadily for three days and nights, but that deep drink was just what the flowers needed, for when the sun came out on Thursday the hills and valleys were all abloom. Affia Snigaroff and I went down to the little cove to Angel's Rock for salad greens. On the way back we picked big bouquets of creamy anemones, *slugax amax*, sea gull flower, and long-stemmed purple violets.

Then it was back to work on the Attu papers for me. It had been most interesting to note that the Attu men usually came to Atka for their wives, with only an occasional man going as far as Unalaska. On the other hand, the Atka men might go either west to Attu or east to Unalaska for their wives. Both Annie Golley and Jenny Golley were born on Attu. Mattie Dirks was born on Unalaska.

Annie Golley came one day and told me something about her family. I knew that Innokinty Golodoff was her half brother, "same father, different mother." Willie Golodoff—Julia's husband, still in the hospital in Tacoma—was another half brother. He and Innokinty had the same mother. Olean Golodoff Prokopeuff's first husband, Lavrenti Golodoff, who had died in the Japanese prison camp, was Annie's full brother.

The A.N.S. radio man failed to come at the promised time to install the radiophone. I did enjoy the news and music I could get on the radio Sergeant Hackett had hooked up for us.

When I tired of paper work, letters, and reports, I sorted clothes and did some packing. We planned to take very little from Atka. The Church Sisterhood would distribute what we left behind among the village families.

A plane buzzed the village about three o'clock on Friday afternoon. Sergeant Hackett called to say that Simeon was on board. I was to be ready to go to Adak immediately to replace Bill Dirks, Jr. Teresa Gardner had brought baby Stephanie and I had already dressed the baby's hand, so they left and I began to get ready. A jeep came hurtling down the hill. Simeon quickly changed clothes and repacked his bag, and we were off.

When we reached Adak Lieutenant Merritt gave us his quarters and friends began issuing invitations. It was rotation time for many, and it seemed that almost everyone we knew was packing to leave on the *Thistle*, sailing early on the morning of Thursday, June 19. The power was out on Adak and the PXs were closed. There had been no school for three days.

On Saturday we transacted some business by wire. The post office and the PXs were still closed. We were able to make some contacts to show fox skins, but had difficulty getting around the base. In the evening we attended a farewell party for the Mossmans, Thodes, and Burtners at the Cavu Club. Bill Dirks, Jr., was a big hit, for it seemed that everyone was interested in Atka and the village.

On Sunday morning we were having breakfast with the Burtners when Captain Hough appeared, with Mike Lokanin and Alfred Prokopioff in tow. They had flown over from Atka on Friday evening. As we had discussed during Captain Hough's first visit, they planned to fly to Attu with Colonel Frank, to locate the wartime grave of a radio man, C. Foster Jones, whom Mike had buried. (The story of his death is on page 000.) When Colonel Frank joined us, he invited Simeon to go along the next day.

That evening General and Mrs. Lynch asked us to join them for dinner and dancing. During the evening we saw many people whom we had met previously, among them Colonel and Mrs. Frank Jamison. The Colonel told me that he was flying Colonel Frank's party to Attu the following day, and he invited me to make the trip, too.

At nine o'clock the next morning Colonel Frank's party met with Colonel Jamison's crew at the airfield. After completing certain formalities required of civilians we boarded a DC-3, with its cold metal bucket seats. Here we were briefed on the use of life preservers and parachutes and fitted with them. At 9:50 A.M. we fastened our seat belts and were off. We started climbing immediately and soon shot above the clouds into the blue sky where we leveled off. Colonel Jamison told us we would be flying at eight thousand feet.

White volcanic cones rested on an ocean of cloud billows. A symmetrical cone rose to our right. Farther away against the blue horizon three cones stood outlined. As we neared them we saw that they belonged to two islands. Their tops had been completely blown out, leaving craters. As soon as permission was given we left our seats and crouched on the parachutes and blankets beside the windows. By removing the little round plug in the center of the plastic windows we could take pictures through the hole. The double peaks of Gareloi appeared, with a heavy plume of steam or smoke issuing from the side of the right-hand cone. Mike Lokanin told us that Pari's father had once owned the trapping rights on Gareloi Island.

Now and then an opening appeared in the cloud blanket and far below we caught glimpses of the blue-gray waters of the restless Pacific or the brown and green haze of an island. Abreast of Gareloi the clouds thinned out appreciably, and soon we saw, off to the left, a long, low island nearly obscured by clouds: Amchitka. A few minutes later, just as we reached the island, our radio failed. We flew over an air strip, circled, and landed at 11:05 A.M. A huge sign over the tiny airfield hut read "AMCHITKA—The Florida of Alaska." Major Foley, the base commander, met us as we left the plane and invited us to have lunch while the radio was being repaired or replaced.

We asked him about the sea-otter herd on the island. He said that it was coming back, apparently, after years of heavy pelagic hunting had nearly wiped it out. Every GI had been warned of the severe penalty the government exacted if even a tiny bit of sea-otter fur was found in his possession. Any dead animal found was skinned and the pelt shipped immediately to Juneau. He said that a sick animal had been brought into the infirmary recently, given a shot of adrenalin, and put back into the water, whereupon it swam away.

We took off again at 1:00 P.M., the radio in working order once more. Colonel Jamison flew along the scalloped shore of Amchitka so that we might see the many little coves where the sea otter feed and play among the rocks and kelp beds. At the extreme western end of the island we spotted the brilliant green growth covering a large strategically placed ancient village site.

We rose to six thousand feet and leveled off again. We would fly at this altitude the rest of the way to Attu. The white cones of Little Sitkin, Segula, and Kiska caught the sun above the clouds. A long reef extended out from the end of Rat Island. We could see the tide falling over it for miles and miles.

Colonel Jamison flew over Kiska Harbor to show us the installations and the sunken boats in the harbor, but the clouds were massing below us, so we caught only glimpses. The water below looked like hammered silver. Kiska Volcano rose abruptly to the north. As we left this area we flew into dense clouds and everything was obliterated.

Half an hour later the fog bank cleared and we flew over a Geodetic Survey ship lying at right angles to our course. The ship would spend the summer working in those waters. Five minutes later Shemya Island was spread like a relief map below us. A broad airstrip ran the entire length of the two- by four-mile island. We changed from our northwesterly course to one directly west, and now we were told to fasten our seat belts and prepare for landing at Attu. Excitement built. Mike Lokanin and Alfred Prokopioff, straining at their seat belts, peered intently through the scratched windows for their first glimpses of their beloved island. Alfred sighted Agattu Island first and nudged Mike. A smile spread across Mike's face and he said something in Aleut to Alfred.

As we came in over the Massacre Bay installation, with its rows of warehouses and Quonset huts, Mike turned and said, "Maybe they land wrong place, not Attu!" He had thought that the plane would land at the old village site across the island at Chichagof Harbor.

It was 3:00 P.M. when we dropped down on the airstrip, where we were met by a young lieutenant. After brief introductions we climbed into the waiting jeeps. A light mist was falling as we drove up the hogback ridge above Massacre Bay, past Engineer Hill, and down through Pleasant Valley to the site of the old village at Chichagof Harbor. The jeeps came to rest at the top of the same small hill from which Mike and Alfred had seen the Japanese soldiers pour down five years before. When the two men got out they stood gazing silently across the land to the battle-scarred hills on either side, and out across the water of the harbor. Four or five old Japanese landing barges lay rusting on the beach. All that had been familiar was gone, utterly destroyed. For several minutes no one spoke. Then Mike turned to Alfred, said something in Aleut, and pointed down the hill, off to the right across a little valley. Alfred nodded and the two men plunged down the hill through shoulder-high wild rye grass. On the top of a small knoll they found the outline of where their church had stood. From the southwest corner, and in line with two infant graves, Mike paced off fifteen feet. He looked up at Colonel Frank and said, "Here I buried C. Foster Jones, seven feet down."

It was too late in the day to exhume the body, so Colonel Frank gave instructions to the young lieutenant, with directions for the opening of the grave next day and the removal and reburial of the remains in Little Falls Cemetery at Massacre Bay. Arrangements were made, too, to place markers indicating the holy ground of the church and churchyard, both of which had been blessed.

On our return to the plane Colonel Frank took time to point out the battle areas and retell the story of the Aleutian Campaign. We saw the slit trenches in which the Japanese had lain covered with turf, completely hidden from the sight of the attacking Americans. We were taken to the remarkable tunnel under a mountain, built by General Buckner to house and protect an army: great warehouses, living quarters, offices, heating plant, and railroad—an entire city underground. We found that several markers had been erected at the scenes of battles. One marked where Colonel Yamasaki was buried with his sword where he fell. At this marker we took a picture of Mike and Alfred standing in the rain, their faces wreathed in smiles. We were shown the "Tree of Attu," a small evergreen that had been transplanted from the mainland. From the hogback overlooking Massacre Bay the lieutenant pointed out activities being carried on at the base. Operation Stinky was in progress, disposing of mustard-lewisite gas by dumping it in the bay. Another project was the new permanent weather station the Navy was building.

Whenever we got out of the jeep I managed to collect a few plants. Attu has several that grow on none of the other Aleutian Islands. I found some mountain ash, a Kamchatkan thistle, and a large primula. Most of the plants which are indigenous to Atka I also noted on Attu.

As we left Attu Mike commented with a wry smile, "Gee, I couldn't even understand that village. It's all gone!"

On the plane he gave Simeon a rock from the tunnel. He showed me three small stones he had taken from the church site, one each for Pari, baby Helen, and himself. "They've been blessed," he said. "They'll be buried with us when we die."

It was 6:00 P.M. when we left Attu, and twenty minutes later we flew low over a rock covered with sea gulls and landed on Shemya. We were taken to the officer's mess for dinner and then went on to the club. While the men played pool I had permission to go for a walk. I found some white berry blossoms, *rubus*, and then went back to the waiting room for our 9:40 P.M. departure. Colonel Jamison had delayed our return until after dark in order to get in some night flying. There was a four-hundred-foot ceiling at Shemya, so we were soon in the clouds. The colonel was flying on instruments, with a tail wind helping us along. We rose above the first layer of clouds and soon reached seven thousand feet, the altitude at which we would fly to Adak. Out on the far western horizon a bit of sunset glow still lingered. Red ceiling lights in the plane cast a bloody light over us all. We had picked up two boys going on emergency leave, and all the seats were full. Most of us slept. It was well after midnight when we landed.

Next morning it was back to work for us. The PXs were open and we sold a few skins. Things were going well when a wire came from Juneau, ordering us to ship all the skins through the post office in time for the departure of the *Thistle* on the nineteenth. We worked until late in the day. Dr. Thode and Captain Howard Kunz came for us when the PX closed. They took us back to the Kunzes' for a last evening with the Burtners and Thodes. The Mossman children had come down with chicken pox and the family was quarantined and would not be sailing on Thursday morning.

We went back to the PX to finish up on the furs. Again Captain Kunz and Dr. Thode came for us at closing time. We took the furs to the post office. We stopped for a few minutes at the Kunzes' to bid our friends farewell, then went to our quarters to dress for dinner at Colonel Jamison's. The colonel and Navy Captain Einmo picked us up at 6:30 P.M. We spent a delightful evening with them. Captain Einmo had been in these waters for many years, and had made trips up into the Arctic. He knew Nurse Keaton and all of the *North Star* group. Colonel Jamison had been the commanding officer at Shemya for over a year and was now the post C.O. at Adak.

We missed seeing our friends go aboard the *Thistle*, for it was past midnight when we were back in the area. We decided to be on hand early next morning to watch the vessel sail, but we missed that, too, because we overslept.

We finished up on the fur business by sending to Juneau a draft for the skins which we had sold. Back at the PX we purchased supplies for the Atka store and listened to stories of Major Schleuder's trouble with some of the GIs who worked for him. One boy, working behind the counter, got away with two thousand dollars. We had just returned to our temporary quarters when a note came that Dr. Robert Coates, U.S.G.S., was on Adak with his assistant and would like to see us. When we saw him later and met his assistant, he told us that he had a little free time to investigate the coal deposit about which Simeon had written to him, if he could get transportation. Major Barrett came in while we were talking, met Bob, and offered to fly the two geologists to Atka with us the following day.

We gathered at the airport early the next morning, eager to return to Atka. There was no flight, however, for Atka was fogged in. That was the story for three days. Finally, on Monday afternoon, June 23, we reached Atka. When we arrived in the village we found Bill Dirks, Jr., and Bill Dirks, Sr., both sitting on the schoolhouse porch to welcome us. Annie Golley brought us fresh bread and eggs and George Prokopeuff sent us a halibut. The geologists talked with the two Bills while we looked over our mail. They stayed for dinner with us, then went back to the base where they had quarters while at Atka. We had much company that evening, all very welcome. Pari Lokanin brought Helen, who crawled about on the floor. I told her a little bit about our trip to Attu. Mike and Alfred had not yet returned home.

Our stay in Adak had taken a ten-day bite out of our last month in Atka. It was very good to be back in the village, to wake to birdsong, and to watch eagles and ravens soaring over the village in the updrafts. We missed the happy voices of the children, however, for most of the families had gone to their summer camps. As Annie Golley said, "The village is lonesome."

For three days no truck was available for the Sand Bay trip, but we were not idle. There was more than enough unfinished business to fill our last week in Atka, but we had no wish to spend all of our time on paper work. We wanted more pictures of the people and of their activities.

The first morning after our return Annie Nevzoroff brought baby Paul, a hefty one, when she came to tell me that Mrs. Nevzoroff did not feel well again. "Pain in back," she said. "She go to bed. Her legs are nervous."

I went to see what I could do for the old lady, and when I returned the Old Chief and Simeon were having coffee. He had come to see if we would arrange for Sophie to go out with us on the *North Star* to attend school at Mt. Edgecumbe in Sitka. We had already applied for Affia and Annie Snigaroff. Earlier we had suggested that Sophie go, too, but he had refused at the time. We felt that she merited more than a sixth-grade education, for she was a capable girl and had been doing work beyond that level all year.

A telegram was sent to Juneau concerning Sophie, and another to Adak concerning Mrs. Nevzoroff's condition.

Several new skiffs had been built while we were gone and we must see and admire them. Andrew Snigaroff had finished the frame of the bidarka. It was a beautiful piece of work. He and Bill Dirks, Sr., stood beside the bidarka and Simeon took a picture of it.

Toward late afternoon little boys came running, shouting, "*North Star* coming!"

False alarm: it was a Freight Service boat bringing Mike Lokanin and Alfred Prokopioff and the store supplies from Adak. Our work was not finished, and we did not want to leave before our month was up, so we decided that if the *North Star* came early we would let it leave without us. Colonel Jamison and Major Barrett had assured us that if we were unable to make the *North Star* they would fly us to Anchorage and that Major Davis would get all of our gear on a boat to follow.

Next day Dr. Coates phoned from the base that the *North Star* had been sighted, and again the little boys came running. Again it was a false alarm. This time the boat was a Coast Guard light tender.

The days had been clear and bright ever since our return home, ideal weather for the Sand Bay trip. Finally, on the last Thursday in June a truck was available and Bill Dirks, Jr., took the two geologists and us to Sand Bay.

It was a glorious day for the trip—sunny skies with fleecy white clouds stirred by a light breeze, and the waters of Korovin Bay were gently ruffled.

The dory plowed along, close to the high bluffs of columnar dark gray stone, and finally pulled in to the west shore of Sand Bay. Bill led the way to the coal veins, right on the beach. Dr. Coates said that it was a poor grade of lignite, not of commercial value but of scientific importance. He took several samples and found a few grass and leaf fossils in them.

Then we went over to the east shore of the bay. On the northeast point the coal bed proved to be huge chunks of carbonized fossilized or petrified trees: a most significant discovery, according to Dr. Coates. The two geologists became very excited. Young Thompson, Dr. Coates's assistant, dropped his pack, grabbed his hammer, and scrambled up the fifteen-foot embankment from which the huge chunks of fossilized wood had fallen. He was gone for several minutes, and when he returned he reported that large trees had once stood here. He had found where a heavy lava flow had sheared off fourteen of them.

We all chipped off pieces from the chunks on the beach. Some of the chunks had broad streaks of agate in them. Dr. Coates would not venture a guess as to the type of trees they had been. (We tried to have the type determined after we got back to Anchorage. Alaska Governor B. Frank Heinzelman, former Alaska Regional Forester, suggested that it was a species of yew, probably Japanese.)

Bill Dirks, Jr., had wandered along the shore, and he came back with an eleven-inch-long edible chiton, called a bidarka. Our presence had not disturbed the many puffins, auklets, and seals in the quiet little bay.

We returned home to a fresh halibut dinner at 8:30 P.M. The two geologists had dinner with us, then bade us good-bye. They immediately returned to Adak to continue their study of volcanoes, but we had a promise of future meetings. Bill Dirks, Sr., had dinner with us, too. We picked up word at the base on our way home that Sophie was to go with us on the *North Star*. This made her father very happy.

The next morning the young chief, Bill Dirks, Jr., presented me with the two beautiful blue-fox skins which I had selected earlier. "From the whole village," he said, "because you work so hard to help us."

Dr. Baird, who was replacing Dr. Thode, flew in to examine our patients. He got Mrs. Nevzoroff up; he feared that she would get pneumonia if she stayed in bed. We liked him and his nice way with her. After he left we worked on the Attu papers and our packing until three-thirty, when Mike Lokanin took us down to Andrew Snigaroff's camp to tell him that Affia, Annie, and Sophie were to go with us on the *North Star*, which was due in Atka in three days.

As we rounded a dark bluff we saw white tents pitched beside a barabara. Children, some in shoes and some barefoot, played along the sand and gravel beach where long ago only barefoot children had played. Andrew Snigaroff and George Prokopeuff stood in the doorway of the barabara and girls scurried in and out of the tents. Several ran down to the shore to meet us as our boat landed, and we walked arm in arm back up to the tents. Everything inside was neat, cheery, and warm. The inner space was marked off with driftwood into small cubicles where bedding was spread on grass and mattresses. Three bright-eyed babies lay in their own clean blankets. Affia and Sophie took me to a nearby knoll to show me their secret, a longspur's nest beside a creamy anemone plant. It contained five small mauve-speckled blue eggs.

Mike and Simeon were in the barabara, visiting with Andrew and George Prokopeuff, when we came down the hill. We looked in, and asked Simeon to take pictures of the babies. There was a white enameled stove in the barabara. A mixture of the old and new made life happy and comfortable. While pictures were being taken Julia Golodoff, who owned nothing, slipped into my hand several pretty little stones that she had picked up on the beach. Joseph Nevzoroff gave me one, too.

Mike then took us to visit Cedar Snigaroff's camp, another large tentful. It, too, was marked off with driftwood into small sections for family sleeping. Inside we found babies, puppies, and kittens. At both camps happy people were living as their ancestors had, drying fish for winter on the racks and rocks and eating *pootchky*. Some of the children had *pootchky*-burned lips. Clara Snigaroff gave us a fresh-caught pogy to take home. Then she took me to see Matrona Gardner, who was lying ill here in Cedar's camp. I was appalled at her appearance. She was, indeed, a very sick woman. My dear Annie Golley was sitting with her. As soon as we returned to the village I hastily phoned a message to be sent to Dr. Baird concerning Matrona. Very early next morning Cedar Snigaroff and Davy Zaochney came in from the camp and Mike Lokanin came down to the clinic for the stretcher. Matrona was much worse and they were going to bring her back to the village.

An hour or two later two boats came in, bringing Matrona. Two men had carried her across from the camp to the Nazan Bay side of Atxalax. Elizabeth, Annie Golley's daughter, came for me. Simeon sent another wire to Dr. Baird while I helped to make Matrona comfortable. Olean

Golodoff Prokopeuff cleaned her up and Vasha Golodoff straightened up her house while I ran home for fresh clothes for her. Dr. Baird had sent back word that he was on his way by PBY. The two women had Matrona dressed by the time a truck bringing the doctor arrived.

Dr. Baird shook his head when he saw her. "Practically bloodless!" he said as he examined her nails and eyes and took her pulse. He looked puzzled when he examined her tongue, until he learned that she had just drunk some Koolaid.

"She'll need a lot of transfusions," he told us as he gave directions for placing her on the truck. Sergeant Hackett had put a cot on the truck for her. The men gently lifted her up and settled her securely. Olean and Vasha rode with her to the plane.

Later, Annie Golley told me that Matrona had nearly died during the night. "She lie in pool of blood to her hips. No color in her lips. I keep twisting (massaging) her legs and stomach until my hands ache. My Elizabeth and me laugh and talk so Matrona not get scared. She nearly died. We tear up her blankets, Elizabeth's dress, my underskirt. Too dark and stormy to bring her in last night. Cedar too old, Davy too young."

After they had gone we went back to our packing and papers. The sun was bright and warm, so we made the most of our opportunity and took more pictures. One was of Mrs. Nevzoroff weaving a small rug. She used long narrow strips of old underwear for the woof, and gaily colored cotton from old aprons for the warp. She had no loom but worked with the material in her lap. It was interesting to learn that she was using the basket-weaving method for her rug. Vasha Golodoff told me that her mother had often made rugs that way.

Clouds began to gather toward evening and blocked out the sun, so we went back to our tasks. Our neighbors continued to come in on little errands. Annie Golley brought Nicky over so we could see him in the little parka that she had made. When she set him on his feet he went directly for the piano, as usual.

Overnight the weather changed and rain and fog blew down from the hills. However, the men who had been on a two-day egg hunt around Amlia got into port safely before the fog closed in. Innokinty Golodoff brought us three eider-duck eggs. "Toughie sent them," he grinned. He also brought an eider duck, all plucked and ready for the cooking pan.

All of that last Sunday in June, after church, people dropped in for short visits. Alex Prossoff, Elizabeth, and Alfred had brunch with us. The two-year-old was learning to talk, and he called out, "Papa, Papa!" when we went to the table.

Alex laughed and explained, "*Papa* Aleut word. He say, 'Food, food!' "

In the early afternoon Peter Nevzoroff came in with a badly swollen face and a toothache. I sterilized the instruments and Simeon pulled the offending tooth.

Word came from Dr. Baird that Matrona was still alive but in critical condition. We were grateful for his thoughtfulness. Although many of the officers who had given so freely of their time and talents had now been rotated, we hoped that friendly contact would be maintained between Adak and Atka Village.

Under ordinary circumstances our replacements would arrive on the *North Star*, but word had come that the new teachers would not be on the ship when it came in, so we could not perform the same service for them that the Greenes had done for us when we arrived last year, introducing us to the people and briefing us on the situation in the village. Their help that day had been of inestimable value to us in our subsequent relations with our neighbors. We would have liked to do as much for the incoming teachers.

The storm blew itself out overnight and our last full day in Atka dawned sunny and bright, for which we were grateful. A phone call from the base informed us that the *North Star* would dock at 8:00 A.M. on July 1.

We made a very early start on our own indoor work, for we wanted to be free to spend as much time as possible with our friends. I finished work on the school and clinic filing cabinets, seeing that everything was up-to-date and in order, while Simeon was doing the same thing for the office files. That done, we were free to join our friends out of doors. We got a picture of Olean Golodoff Prokopeuff with baby Agnes and big brother Nicholas. We now had pictures of all of the babies except Titiana Kudrin's Cyril Dan.

Affia Snigaroff and Sophie Dirks came to tell me that at last the daffodils were in bloom on Eulalie's grave. The three of us went up to the point overlooking the village and the bay. We cut the grass and planted fresh flowers on the grave, and then took some pictures there.

Back down in the village we found it humming with lively activity.

Barefoot children played in the water lapping the dock. Men were trying out new boats, and others were building them. We went to watch the progress of Danny and Peter Nevzoroff's boat-building. The women, newly returned from camp, washed clothes and hung them out in the sunshine, and baked fresh bread. Three or four of the older men sunned themselves on the warm grassy slopes. High overhead the ravens and eagles soared. Now and then ravens swooped down to torment the dogs racing along the hillside.

After Simeon and I went back indoors to continue our work, visitors began dropping by. We stopped work to visit and have coffee with them. Many times that day we had evidence that the love and affection we felt for them was reciprocated. Joseph Nevzoroff was in and out a dozen times, bringing me handfuls of green leaves or buttercups; I would surely miss that little fellow.

Angel Snigaroff nearly moved me to tears when she shyly and proudly presented me with the tiny mukluks which her father had made for her so that she could come to school last winter. The soft grass insoles were still inside. They belonged in a museum, and I would see that they got there some day, together with the little rug which Mrs. Nevzoroff finished weaving and sent to me. The beautifully woven grass baskets made by Annie Golley, Jenny Golley, and Pari Lokanin, the wall-pocket Mary Snigaroff had made and given me for Christmas, and the packets of seal gut which Alex and Elizabeth Prossoff had cleaned and dried and split, then carefully and neatly wrapped around pieces of wood, one of frozen gut and one of unfrozen, would eventually go to a museum, too.

Annie Golley and Mattie Dirks came later in the afternoon and took our leftover clothes for distribution in the village, together with some Red Cross items that we had brought back from Adak. The Church Sisterhood would take care of this.

The officers of the Church Brotherhood came in the evening for Simeon to help them make out a substantial order for church goods. Danny Nevzoroff and Bill Dirks, Jr., remained to balance the store books after the others had left.

There was no sleep for us that night. At daybreak we heard for the last time the early morning medley of sounds—roosters crowing, the "rusty hinge" call of the male ptarmigan, and the "little bells" of the longspur's song. I fixed toast, coffee, Spam, and eggs while Simeon finished our last-minute packing.

Bill Dirks, Jr., and Danny Nevzoroff came to get all of our leftover groceries, which they would use in the store. Everything on the kitchen shelves we had already given away. Now the cupboards were bare.

Bill Golley had been up on the lookout point, watching for our ship. He came down at 6:30 A.M. to tell us that the *North Star* was rounding Cape Kaduganax, inside Uyak. We bathed and dressed, and when Sergeant Hackett brought down a truck the boys loaded it and took off with the first load.

After the truck left I went to say good-bye to those who would not be going to the dock with us. I walked up the hill, past Philip Nevzoroff's house, and found Mrs. Nevzoroff sitting on a box in her back yard, watching her chickens. I thanked her again for the little rug that she had woven for me. When I told her good-bye she smiled gently and nodded, and held my hand in both of hers.

Back down the hill I stopped in at Philip Nevzoroff's to say good-bye to his wife, Mary. Then I went on to bid Mary Prokopeuff and Titiana Kudrin farewell and to sit for a moment beside the couch where John Prokopeuff lay.

On the way back to the schoolhouse I met Vera Snigaroff and her father, Cedar, going my way. Vera said that they were disappointed that her brother, Poda, had not come home on this boat. As we passed the church I glanced up at the graveyard where Mary Snigaroff lay and hoped that she would have approved of Andrew sending Affia and Annie out to Sitka for school.

The truck pulled up soon after we arrived at the school. The waiting women climbed aboard and babies and little children were handed up. Sophie Dirks and Annie and Affia Snigaroff stood encircled by their fathers and sisters. We were a close-packed group in the back of the truck when Simeon and I took off on our last ride over the island, ablaze with flowers. We had a final look at Korovin Lake, then swept along the shore and up onto the dock. The truck rattled across the wharf and stopped near the gangplank. Men swarmed on the dock, unloading the boat and stacking the goods. Sig met us and took us and the three girls to our staterooms while the others climbed down from the truck and found places to sit on the timbers near the boat.

When Simeon and I went back on deck the three girls were leaning over the rail, visiting with their friends on the dock below. We headed for the gangplank and there Sig warned us that Captain Salenjus, in a hurry as usual, was ready to cast off as soon as the hatches were battened down. We nodded and went on to the dock. Bill Dirks, Jr., called Simeon over to where he and some other men were checking invoices. Simeon told me later that the balance of our own consignment of supplies had finally arrived on this boat. Simeon told Bill that we would gladly give it all to the village.

Annie Golley made room for me to sit beside her on the wharf. Here I had my final visit with the women, babies, and children. All too soon the whistle blew. The men left their work and came over to the gangplank. Two sailors stood ready to hoist it aboard. The rest of us joined them there.

Aleuts are usually not demonstrative, but our final good-byes were warm and sincere: hugs, firm handclasps, and little personal messages. We reminded a beaming Mike Lokanin that he had taken us on our first boat ride, and our last, at Atka. Pari, at his side, held up baby Helen to say good-bye. Clara Snigaroff, when I hugged her, whispered, "I'll always remember how good you were to my mother."

One last hug for Annie Golley, and then we hurried aboard, amid promises of warm welcomes should any of them come to Anchorage, and an equally warm welcome should we return to Atka.

We stood at the rail with Sophie, Affia, and Annie and waved as the *North Star* pulled away from the dock and moved out toward Cape Kaduganax and the Bering Sea. Our Aleutian year of 381 days was over—a year of rich experiences and warm friendships to treasure for the rest of our lives.

Shepherd Mike Lokanin

✳ APPENDIX 1

Here Is My Lifetime's Story

Mike E. Lokanin

[This personal account was written by Mike Lokanin in September 1946. His manuscript is here reproduced complete and without editing. See page 88.]

When I was a boy I remember there were many people died in Unalaska in the year of 1919. Everyone was at home sick Some of them died, most of the old people and some of the young once died. One evening my mother went down to Larry Nevzoroff's house. She told me not to go away from my daddy. So I stayed home with my daddy. I always know we get our soup from U.S. Coast Guard Cutter mens every meal time so I was watching from my window. My house was very quiet. I heard some one come to open my door. It was Mr. Walter Summerville. He come to give my old man some pills. After he give my old man some pills I tell him I am hungry. I know I am going to say I am hungry. I don't know how to say it but I am going to try so I told him, "Likem eat papa" He was tapping my ball head with his white hand. I know he told me yess. So I watch him when he went out. He went to Peter Samakansky's house and from that house he went home. I know I told him I am hungry. His house did not even smoke at all when I look at the smoke stack. So I look around for food and find a moldy slice of bread. There weren't even fire burning in stove for 2 or 3 days. I went to my stove and fill a cup out of kettle and drink it. I went to my dad's side and told him if he is getting better now and he told me he is just the same yet. I looked out from my window I see the mans coming with bucket so I went to open door for them and let them enter it. Then they was going to give me some soup. I didn't have anything else to put it in so I look around finely I fined a Carolina tobacco can to fill it for me. They fill it with soup and one man gave me a candy. I said to him Tankyo. They went out I try to give my dad some soup he won't take it so I start to eat it. Later the can was empty so I jump in my bed I told my dad that I was gone to sleep so he told me be sure cover myself. If I dont I maybe get sick so I went to bed with him. He was nice and warm when I went by him at evening. We didnt even have light in our house. Around the midnight when I woke up, Oh Jee my side was cold so I turn around and pull myself against my dad. Still was cold. I didnt know if he was dead so I sleep with him til morning. Mr. W. Summervill come to my house and wake me up and pull me off my bed and he take me down to the hospital. I knew my dad was home so I sneaked up to town to see my dad. When I come to my house nobody was home so I went down to

Mrs. Larry Nevzoroffs house. There my mother was on the floor with her face covered with a towel. I thought she was sleeping so I ask if she is asleep yet. Mrs. Larry told me she is dead. I start to cry. I didnt know how I am gone to live in this world so I went to my house and stayed in there untill evening comes. Mr. W. Summervill come and get me again. Only thing I take was my dads gold watches 21 Jewels it laying on table. He take me down to the hospital again. That night I was with little Vasha Nevzoroff. She is only one I know well. If I didnt see her in hospital maybe I couldnt sleep or stayed there. Maybe week later I get along fine but I couldnt forget about my dad and mother. I am 7 years old then. Lots of people died. Court room was full and the jail room was full. Jee I dont know how many was in there. No one else to take care of me so Captain W. Summervill take me to Attu on his trading schooner EMMA. Another boy Afanacie Sokolnikoff went too. We were Capt. W. Summervills boys. We sailed and sailed. One morning when I woke up seem to me the schooner was so quiet so I went out to look. Boy we were in good little harbor. I went in the cabin climb in bunk to tell Afanacie what I saw. He didnt believe me. I pull him off his bunk and he went out and I went out too. I see a skin boat coming by our boat with 2 men in it. I never saw skin boat before I thought it was lots of fun. We ask the Capt. if we can go ashore with him he said Wait for while so we stop on boat. When we get on bow to look at village we saw nothing but barabaras and see the salmon hung on lines. Afternoon capt came on board with mr. Nick Krivden then they take us ashore. Oh Boy the beach sand was very fine and the village was smooth flat. It was nice and clean got long pootchkys. First boy meet me on beach is Alfred Prokopioff next one was Mathew Golodoff whos brother of Innokinty Golodoff. We start to play without known of each others language. At evening I went home to mr. Summervills house and eat my supper and went to bed. We had a bed upstairs. Next morning when I get up 8oclock the boys were out and playing. I was want to go out but we got have a breakfast so I stayed home. When I get through with my breakfast I had to clean my dishes. Of course we always have to clean dish and table thats all our work anyway. Later Capt. W. Summervill tell us to go out and pick some blackberries and blueberries so I went out and Afanasie Sokolnikoff, each of us had 4 bls [pound] can to fill with berries so I had mine about 3/4 Afanasie come along and take my can away from me and put all my berries in his can and my can is empty. I come home with empty can. The Afansie he had can full. When I got home Summervill ask me if I did pick any berries. I said yess but I hate to say Afanasie take away from me so I told him I ate it. He told me to go to bed without any eating because I ate my berries. Maybe I make Afanasie happy from then on I always go out to pick berries but never bring in 1/2 can because Afanasie always take my berries away from me. One day Summervill told me to go out and pick some berries without him. So I went out brought can full. Before dinner next day he sent me out with him maybe he want to fine out I pick almost can full and Afanasie tell me to give him my can I always know he take my berries so I didnt want to give him my can. Then we start to fight. Maybe I wasnt strong enough so he knock me down and start to beat me on my head and I was start to cry. Then I promis him to give him my berries and make another promis not to say word to dad Summervill even if we come home. Nick Krivden was on hill watching us who always work and stay storekeeper for Capt. Summervill. When he saw us fight he stayed untill we went home and when we reached road he yelled for Afanasie to stop. So we stop and watch him coming. Afanasie told me not to say word about he was taking my berries. If I do he said he will give me a good one. I told him I wont say anything about it. Nick came to us and take look in our cans and he say OK so I start home I know in my mind that Nick will say something about those berries. We went in house Capt. take look at both cans and didnt say a word. Supper were getting close. Capt was cooking supper and I know what is going to happen when I see Nick going to store. After while Capt. W. Summervill went to store too. I was on outside of house playing around. When supper ready Capt call me in to set table. That is Afanasies job but this time I was setting the table and dad told me only 2 plates 2 cups. Then he call Afanasie in. Afanasie was very sad when he come in door. Dad told him why he always take my berries he said he never take mine. I was frightened because if I go out he will pay it back to me. Dad asked him why he had fight me. He said he was just playing Then dad wipped him with razor strap wide one all leather. He send him to bed without anything for eat. I always sleep in one bed with Afanasie. It was my time to go to bed I dont know what he was gone to say and do to me. I was going upstairs very carefully without try to make any noise on stair steps. I was standing on long side of my bed for while, and when I heard Afanasie make sound of sleep I went in bed very carefully I was tryin to be feather light but dogon my big belly touch him on his back wake him up. When he turned round my face sure got swet. He asked me if Nick is in house I told him no. He said that Nick tell on us about our fighting at hill. He said he knows it, then I feel little better. Next day dad told me to go out and play and send Afanasie to work on lumbers.

I stayed on Attu with Capt. W. Summervill until 1923. One day dad told me he was gone lieve Attu. He told me if I want to stay or go to Unalaska. I thought Unalaska would be the same so I told him I dont want to go away from Attu anymore. Then he was thinking for a while. He told me to go round the village and look for a mother and dad for myself. In Attu village there was nothing but barabaras which are made out of sod. They are more warmer than wooden house in winter time. I went out and walk around village. I use to know Mr. Mike Hodikoff and his wife and every time I come in there house they trade [treat] me good so I went to his barabara and stick around untill I get call in. He wasnt home but his wife was so I told her why I am coming. She said I will take you and have you for my own boy. So I know then that I have good home and mother and daddy. I went down to Mr. W. Summervill told him I have a mother and father now. He said what is your mother and fathers name now. I told him Mr. Mike Hodikoff and his wife. He said good. He says to me you done a right thing and he take me to his store and give me clothes and shoes and food besides that he left some money for me. I couldnt carry it so I call Mike Hodikoff which is to be my dad. I told him I have lots of things to carry which is given me free by Mr. Summervill and Mike hurry down to store with me and I had 2 big boxs of supplys to last me over 6 months. clothing to last me cupple yrs. So after we got everything in my house we had big time. The kids from all over the village come around and I had lots of friends then.

Now was Afanasies turn to get his mother and father of village too so they send him out to get a good person he can stay with. 1/2 hour later he came in said got father and mother. They ask his fathers name he said he is gone to Martha Hodikoff so the Capt. W. Summervill give him a food and clothes and some money to live on so we got new living again. Afanasie didnt stay long with his mother and father he left Attu 1923 on M/S Eider but I didnt have any trouble with my mother and father they traded me like there own child give me warmest and comfortablest place so I love my dad and mom and my sisters brothers.

I stayed with them untill I was 21 yrs of age then I went down to

Unalaska got married to Mary Tarkanoff and go back to Attu again. Built new house 14x16 6ft high I stayed here with my wife Mary. Later she never stay in her house nights I was wondering what was matter I ask her what she always do nights She said to me she just visit and dont feel like to go home and sleep in house where she visit. So I use to believe it. Later I found she had a boy friend if I was a jealouse man she got to be wipped or punished but I hate to be a jealouse that is meanest thing in this world I seen plenty of peoples get jealouse and use knife and guns. I told her if she cant live with me I will make pappers to Juneau Alaska. She said more better that way because she dont want to stay with me any more of her life. So I made pappers to Juneau office and told what was gone happened between Mary and I. That was in year of 1939. That winter I start to fall in love with Pari and we made up our mind to get married if divose is clear. In the spring the USCG Cutter was at Attu. Judge was there also Marshall was there and they had a court about Mary and I. Mary was married to whom she loved and I got married to Pari and all is good happy cupple from that on. Every winter we go trap the blue fox on Agattu Island for storekeeper Mr. Fred Schroeder which takes Mr. W. Summervils place. 1941 feb 24 I had baby boy named Arty. Sept. 1941 my baby boy Arty died on Agattu Island. 1942 Jan 12 I had baby girl named Titiana. We stayed on Agattu all winter trapping foxes and the boat was to take us off in Feb 15 or 19 and we were out of ammunitions and out of flour sugar tea and milk we were completly out of everything. We were beginning to starve when findly M/S Point Reyes pick us up off Agattu. When we go in Attu everything was blackout and Mr. and Mrs. C. Foster Jones were in Attu. Mrs. Jones was the school teach and Mr. Jones was the radio man. It was plenty snow in Attu then.

When I got in Attu I heard about war, war, but I never did see war so I didnt care much and I didnt think war would be at Alaska. Pretty soon I heard about Japanese are begining to get near Alaska but I still think Japs wont bother Attu because I know Attu is too small for them. We got word from U.S.Govr,t. to pack up all our things. Some time boat will be in Attu to pick us up. So were already packed everything we got. Of course we got the things we need out so we can use it for temporarly on month of May One day we see vessell come to outside of harbor and it was ruff wind was blowing from N.E. and as soon as we saw the boat coming we thought it was Japanese boat. After she got outside the harbor she wasnt anchor because wind was too ruff for her to anchor out there and she couldnt get inside harbor. Maybe about 1/2 hour later we seen launch coming into harbor. Some peoples still think it was Japanese boat. We look through m,Scope. We can see letters on boat U.S.N.T. They had ruff time coming in. Chief of Attu Mike Hodikoff and second Chief Alfred Prokopioff went down on beach to see if thats our transportation. Of course USN or USCG allways visit Attu once or twice a year anyway but people were talking about war. We got exided. When they come on beach the officer got out and shake hands with both chief and chief ask if this is our boat. Officer say he havent got word to pick anyone up off Attu. All they had was 10 army troops with there supply to be taken ashore on Attu but weather was too ruff to take anything over sea in small boats so they said they gone land them on Kiska Island if they can. Officer want Mike Hodikoff and Alfred to go on Tasko for 2 or 3 days so they can show a good landing places any kind of weather. They stayed out 4 days and come back.

The whole community sent out 10 pelts to Dutch Harbor for sale to Navy. because they didnt have a thing in store. All they got was flour few cans salmon corned beef no sugar no butter no milk or coffee so they got some food of Tasko. Mr. Fred Schroeder did not come back from San Francisco with supplys for store. Later last part of May a sub come to Attu a patrolling sub all the men were invided to sub and when we got to submarine capt. took all the men inside and show inside of sub to everyone and then he got on deck and laying against rail on side he ask some qs about how often the Japs come around Attu a year in present time. I was standing back against cabin and talk to one of the crew and I seen the capt was laying against the real and the chain busted and he went overboard in water and everyone on deck start to laugh. He felt backwards. When he reach the water he swim for dory which was ours tied along side the sub. He couldn't pull himself in so some men went down and help him in dorry. When he got on deck he looked at us and smile. He went below a half hour later he come out and said he is ready to leave now. He told us as soon as we see Japs boat please notify Dutch Harbor. We got off and she took off, too. Thats only U.S. boat we seen since 1942 to 1945 at Okinawa we got out of prison camp.

June we had nice all the way. Not much rain, not much wind sunshine all the time. Of course we always standing by all the time for boat to pick us up.

One day we heard Japs bombing Dutch Harbor over radio. We still hear war on radio. One day Attu mens was getting ready for going out to gather drift wood. They get there boats ready and fill up 5 gallon can with gassoline and mixed with lub oil. Everything was ready for next day. all over village everyone was in deep sad looken face. You can tell something is gone happen but they didnt know what is comeng to them. I myself feel something strange gone happen to us.

Some of the other mens say when I visited his house that he got some kind of heart trouble he said maybe too much blood pressure. I asked him what is trouble Oh he said my heart keep bother me I cannot go to sleep my heart is just like it comes up to my throat if it does that I feel awful weakened I ask him if he is gone out for wood with other mens he said I dont feel like to go but anyways I got to go.

I myself dont feel so good but I didnt pay any tention to what I feel Once and while I can feel my heart thump just like it chock me but I dont pay any tention to it. Most everyone look sad to me.

That day the village was so quiet all I can hear is the gass motors of power plant which runs three times a day by the school house All we can hear is PUTO PUTO PUTO even the kids dont like to play. It was really nice at evening all the way out is clear the island seems setin on top of the surface out in Ocean. When I look into mountain everything is green flower begining to bloss. Things look awfull nice. When I sniff in air I can smell flowers and look in to mountains on each side of village look clearer than I ever seen before. Little fog string round foot of mountains looks nice. Hardly little breeze come from the southwest most of the houses are smoking. When I pass some houses I smell the boiled salmon So is my house too, my wife she is boiling salmon for supper. I went down to other end of village to see whats doing and I mett John on road. I ask him if he is going out with his father tomorrow. He tol me he will be out tomorrow if the wither keep like this. He say it will be lots of fun tomorrow going to get seagull eggs and shooting ducks and get wood. He ask me why dont I come in his boat. Iv already got boat to go anyway. Most of the 14ftrs carry 2men and 2 or 3 five gallon cans of gassoline and guns and cooking eqt. They dont have much room if they carry 3 men. I tol him I already got to go in some once boat. Now the sun was get in back of the mountain and the shadow showed on the other side of the bay. When I look toward the school I see Mr. Foster Jones was coming out of his power plant house which is 10 feet away from the school. He was oiling his motor. Of course he always run it midnight too. I keep walking around no wind the ocean in bay was just like a water in pan on the table. When I look out the bay I can see the seagulls and sea parrots flying and little birds waving beside the old ravens flying over the village and crawing. I never see so many crows in my life before as now I thought myself.

I stopt in Alfreds house his wife is my aunt. Sometimes I go visit her house. I had few cups of tea with her. I visited my aunts house untill getting little dark now. When I start to my own house which is 50 or 60 feet away I can hear chipee birds still chiping and still seagulls cloks. I got home.

When I got home my wife had table ready and was waiting for me my daughter was sleeping on the bed. My wife said things look very quiet, lonesome today. I had my supper and whent to lay down on my bed and something in my mind tells me something is gone happened. One thing was in my mind steady, was, Japanese will be here tomorrow but I couldnt figure it out.

My wife was seting by me and said, Darling are you going out with the other men for wood? I tol her I'll be out tomorrow. Bring some seagull eggs when you come home, and I tol her I will if I can. I told my wife that I haven hunch Japs will be here some time she said to me. I hope not they might kill everyone. Every time when my heart thumps makes me feel sick and weak. Its about 11P.M. so I tol my wife I am gone to bed now. She tol me Darling before you go to bed get some water. there is no water in the house for morning. I got up and get water from my aunts house sky nice and clear then I go to bed. My wife was still up washing dishes I didnt have to thats why I go to sleep.

June 7th/42 Sunday in the morning early when I was sleeping some one knocking at my door so I got up and look who was it? he said I am fred with frightened voice. I was wondering what was the matter so I ask him what was the matter. he tol me there is boats out there and they are unknown boats dont have any flag on either. One big 2 chimneyed boat. might be Japs.

I ask how many there are. He was half frightened and shake. He said he dont know it look like more than 4 or 5. So then he got out and went down to his house and I went to my bed again. It was 0300A.M. It was too early for me to get up anyway. My wife she was wake up to she ask me what was matter and who was at the door. I told her it was fred and she start to nurse her baby. I went back to sleep again. I usly get up at 0700A.M. and bld fire and make breakfast eat with my wife. I was just about to get up some one at my door again. I got out of my bed and look out through the window. It is Fred again. I said to him whats trouble, Fred. He said the boats are look like Japanese boats. I said to him why if its Japanese thay could come right in harbor and shoot the village. I said to him why dont he go to the school and tell Mr. Jones about it and maybe he can send wire to Dutch Harbor.

I beginning to think it might be Japs too. I go in my house and Fred left.

I said to my wife Honey Fred said Japanese boats outside the harbor. She lift her head off her pillow look at her baby and said Oh god blesses what we'll do then. I said to her Nothing we can do Honey God knows what we'll do and if our time is come we'll be dead If our hour is there will be dead. So all we can do is think god in our heart that is all.

She said Oh my dear little baby. She gott tears in her eyes as she spook.

I told her I am gone out and see what the others doing. When I got out of my house and start to my aunts house I seen little skiff was gone out to the cannon island to get close look at the boats. When I got to my Ants house most of the Village men were lined long side of house and they all talking and talk. Try to figure out what kind of boats are they what nationality and we seen plane flying, circuling round but didnt seem to bother anything at all. The third time he come to circul round he got close. We saw the red Ball on the wings and on each side the ship single motor and 2 winged and 2 men one on back of pilot. He was gunner. he had machine guns on each side of him.

It was about 830 A.M. evry one getting ready for church that there last time for evr entering there church Before church my brother-in-law Aleck and other person which went out in skiff came ashore. They all said it is Japanese boats. We went to school to talk to Mr. C. Foster Jones and tol him the Japs boat are outside the harbor and we ask him to send message to Dutch Harbor because he got words US Govt to say when he sees Japs or if we seen Japs and tell him. He supost to say "the boys out today and didnt see a boat and come home and they gone to have a fryed codfish" that means a Japanese boats are come here. We ask him to send message. He said it might be marines or navy. He was sending weather reports to Dutch Harbor and I told him he might as

well send message because boys seen Japanese plane. He said if he make
any mistake call up Dutch Harbor it will be his nick. So I just walk out
and I seen Mrs. Jones curling her hair. I stop by her room and tol her I
am afraid they are Japs. She smile and said to me Oh it might by Navy.
If they are Japs why they couldv be in long time ago. I just walk out I
heard the church bell still ring. I did not go to church 4 of us went out to
the Point. The boat was so closs we could see mens walking on deck and
around 20 or 25 small landing barges went back and ford from Holtz
bay to transport. We were walking along edge of hills and plane was
flying round. Didnt seem to bother us so we 4 of us thought might be
Americans too. So we just keep on walking edge of hill and wave at
boat. It was nice and clear sunshine. I thought I hear a sound of talking I
tol the others Hey listen I stood there look around findly I see mens
coming from back of mountain foot. One of the boys I was with tol me
lets go to them they might be Americans. I tol him I dont want to go to
them and we stood and watch them running and crewling on ground.
We look at boats and boats are raising red and white flags and moving
farther out in Ocean. We all made run toward the Village to see what
will be happend. We see mens running down the mountain and hills as
soon as they reach the beach cross the creek and open machine guns and
rifle fire at Village. I though myself My wife and daughter is goner now.
I thought in my mind It will be all right if they are killed without
tourcher and suffer. The way the rifle and machine guns take off we 4 of
us thought nothing was left in Village All we can see is men walking in
Village but they were the men which came to Village. We see Japs
running to Village with guns in there hands. First building they get in is
school where Mr. and Mrs. Foster Jones is. We thought Foster might
send message to Dutch Harbor. I tol the boys its no use for us to go to
Village now the way the rifles and machine guns are shooting. Lets hide
for the night and snake up to village at night and see if anything left. So
we crewl under big rock which could weigh 10,00 [one thousand?]
pound and we heard plane was flying over us and we was gone to take a
peak at it and just about stuck our heads out and big guns went off. Boy
we went back in under the rock we was piled on top of each others. We
stayed ther most whole morning and afternoon. In late afternoon we
heard somebody was talking and it was sound like one of our mens. We
said to each other it might be they hide too. Sudnely I heard they calling
us but I didnt answer because I want to make a sure its our men. By god

I could hear Willie and freds voice so I pull my head out and answer them and I got out under rock with the rest of the boys. Look round but we couldnt see anyone. I answer and said Who is that call us Please show up if you are there. I seen someone setin on a hil It was Willie and fred which the Japs send them to look for us. We all come out under the rock and we start to go home. We ask what was going on. Willie said in low tone them little Japs got us now and fred said We were afraid of Japs before now we got to be afraid of Americans Fred turn his head round with his mad looking face and said We all under Japs instead of Americans. I ask him if anyone got kill He said Evryone is OK accept his wife got hit in her leg but Japanese doctor fix her. I asked him How is my wife and kid He said they all OK I would like to ask more but he look awfull mad I was kind afraid ask him. I told him lets go now. Willie tol me they been lookin for me all over Place and couldnt fine me and the boys with me. Also one boy was missing Sergy Artumonoff. On the way home we find him he give up because he seen us walking all together When he walk up to us he said, Arent the Japs gone to hurt me We tol him Oh Japs wont do any hurt to you. He bagan to smile.

fred tol me I got to go to school. So when we got to school I walk in all the door got guards by Japanese. In the schoolroom I seen Mr. and Mrs. C. Foster Jones setin on one of the school desks. I said Hello to Mr. Jones but one of the gaurds said to me No no no talk to Ameleka He was tryin to tell me not to talk with American Foster anyway said to me Well Mike the world has seem to change today. We are under Japanese rule now. I was gone tell him it was his fault to but I thought it too late now I just look at him with out saying word. Just then the Japanese MP came in with American flag under his arm and come to me and start to read paper which is Proclamation Of course he read in is language He got Intripiter with him. The MP stand in front of me and read paper I couldnt understand the words Intripiter explain meaning of the words that the Japanes capture us from U.S. Gov. now we are under Japanese Gov. Japanese Gov. will keep us under one condition that from now on we must obey the Japanese. After reading the proclamation he tol me to go home not to go round unless I get primission. from Comander Yamadaki. So I went home and my house was in bad looking shape everything was threwin on the floor. My door was spoiled, 8 pullet holes on end of house, 2 pullet holes in my stove which one go through to fire place and my wife wasnt home. All my guns are gone some other things was gone I didnt care much about guns I hate to lose my watch 21 jewels all my papers were scadder on the floor. So I went down to second chiefs house my wife usely stay there if I am not home. By Golly she was there I walk in and look for my daughter I didnt see it so I ask my wife where is Taty She was sleeping My wife was serving tea and she ask me if I like to have cup of tea I sure need it too. I tol her yess She pour me cup and just about I was gone to drink my tea one Japs came in they was looking for me he said I just left the table and go out with him. He tol me to help Mr. Jones move out of school so I went in there. Fellow named Kasukabe, Intripitor, was in school and Mr. and Mrs. Jones was picking up there things. Man had sword. Mr. Jones had big load under his arm. This Jap want him to take some more. He said Aleck and Mike will take them to me Jap said No you take them and he slap Mr. Jones on his face and knock him down on floor and start to kick em on body and picked em up and slap em down again and kick out door. But they didnt touch Mrs. Jones and they didnt touch Aleck and me. After he kick Mr. Jones out he pull his sword out of its case and went after Mr. Jones Of course I couldnt see what happend after he kicked out anyway I was so scared I shake. Seems like I am gone shake the whole Village down I was tryen to brase myself but I was still shake Japs take Mr. and Mrs. Jones to Traders house. Of course trader which is Mr. Fred Schroeder is not on Attu. Lucky hes not on Attu if he was he might be dead or taken to Japan too.

On the way I find Mrs. Jones slipper stuck in durt. Soon as I deliver the things in there to them I just run to my house and I stayed outside try to cool myself from shaking. I didnt want to scare my wife.

I walked into my house my wife looked at me. Whats the matter, Honey you look pale.

Oh I said I just dont feel good maybe from catching cold.

You better warm up Honey she said. She had little supper ready we didnt have much lefted in the house sugar milk also was gone. I had to bum milk from Elizabeth Prossoff for my baby. After I got eaten my supper I helped Pari cleaning dishes and I told her what happend to Mr. and Mrs. Jones She said to me Honey they might do same thing to us. I tol her I dont think so. After we finish dishes it is pass 12 PM day start to break about 1.30AM I went to bed with my wife. I couldnt go to sleep I roll in my bed It was light and bright too. Boy the machine guns go off in the air and I heard plane I went out on my porch and I seen plane was flying very low made a turn go out over Point without bullet touchd. I lite a fire in stove and when I had coffee ready call my wife she wasnt sleeping she got up and have coffee with me she said to me Honey what plane was the Japanese shooting at I said to her It was American plane.

She said to me God bless they might bomb this place.

As I was talking with my wife I heard some one come. I look out It was Kasukabi the fellow who Kick Mr. Jones last night. Jap was in hurry too. I was wondering what was gone on. He come at my door and call me I went out He said Good Morning and I said Good morning to him.

Mr. Foster Jones is dead. Of course I didnt ask him how he died. They had 2 intripiters one was name Imai young fellow and other was Kasukabi He was higher he had 3 stars. Mr Imai had only 2 stars on his collar. When I get down near Schroeder house I mett Mr. Imai for first time.

He said to me Are you intripiter too? Looks to me he is nice to talk with I asked him how Foster died. He said he dont know it either. Later Mr. Kasukabe come to us he start to talk. He was talking in his language I couldnt understand what he says. I see him cut across his wrist with his finger. Someone come out and call him. He go in house and Imai was look round before he spook to me. Then he said Foster cut his own wrist with his pocketknife. I was thinking after they capture Foster Jones I dont see why they left his pocket knife for him.

They call us in he was half sunk in his own blood. They wont let me see his face or body. He was wrapped in blanket. They tol me to bury him without cofin. So I dug a grave by our church. Measure destains from corner of church with my eyes and try to remember wind direction It was burried in SW corner of church grave depth 7 ft. disent from church to grave 15 ft. After that I bury him that was end of him then and I never try to forget where I berried his body. And Imai was by me all the time I work.

Some of us Attuans stay by Mrs. Jones all the time. We dont know what Japs might do to her. She is sick and has bad cuts on her wrists too. But she gets well.

Mr. Kasukabe lost one star. Mr. Imai received 3 stars. He got higher After Foster got murdered.

On June 10, 1942 the Japanese MP called everyone to gathered by the flagpole and Japanese camera man there to take picture under the meat ball. When everyone got lined up the Jap soldiers was lined in right side of Attuans. They all fixed bayonets on there rifles. and raise the Japanese meat ball over captured people, of Attu.

Yamadaki Taicho (it means Cammander Yamasaki) give us an orders that if we want to go out fishing we can go at any time. But the MP will be with us and we must live orders at the No. 1 tent where the Mr. Zebeku is. He is head man for all the boats.

In the next morning we was talking about going out for fishing but none of us able to go to the no. 1 tent and ask for boat. because we didnt know how to say FONI-O-KATSUTI KUDASAI that mean Please let us use the boat. I happend to mett Mr. Imai I asked him to borrow boat from Mr. Zebeku He said to me Why dont I go myself and ask Mr. Zebeku for let me have boat for go out. I tol him I dont know what to say to borrow boat He write me a note on paper ZEBEKU SANG FONI-O-KASUTI KUDASAI

After write the note he read it to me. He gave me the note and tol me to go and see Mr. Zebeku. I went to the school because the tent is near the school When I got to the school the gaurd was standing by the school. He looked at me he said something to me I didnt know what he says anyway. I keep on going without stop by him. I heard footsteps coming back of me I made quik turnround. sure enough that was gaurd. He got gun in is hand. He come up to me and start to talk. I couldnt understant what he says Sounds to me the hungry checken klicking to me the way he talks.I show my note to him and he said no no no ego ego he puss he back I know he wants me to go back. I look for Mr. Imai I tol the Mr. Imai what gaurd did to me and turn me back He ask me if I did see Mr. Zebeku about the boat I tol him I didnt. He said to me Come with me. I follow him to the school. The gaurd was standing in the trail. When Mr. Imai start to talk to the gaurd I stant ther and wait for Imai. After Imai talk to the gaurd took his cap off and bow to me and says KOKORO SANG(it means I am sorry to trouble you) Mr. Imai was stant by the gaurd look at me and smile. This time Imai went to no.1 tent. When we got there the tent was full they were cooking ther breakfast. I was standing outside tent. Imai come out and tol me all the boats will be busy today that I have to wait till tomorrow. So I went home and tol the mens we have to wait till tomorrow.

The Cammander Yamasaki let his troops put the gates round the

village and put off limit to the village for his troops. and off limit for us
where the troops are. Set 4 gaurds inside limits to the village to keep
troops out.

June 12, the weither south wind was still fine. The village peoples are
getting short on wood, short on fish. I went to Mr. Imai and I tol him I
am gone out and get some woods and fish. He wants to go out and see
how we catch fish. He said to me I have to see Mr. Zebeku. I went over
to Mr. Zebeku and ask for boat. This time I got the boat. I tol some of
the others that I got boat to go out for fish and woods and the MP was
to come with us said Imai. Look like Im gone to have to have 2 boats. I
went up to Mr. Zebeku and ask for one more dory. He didnt want me to
use 2 boats. I went down to Mr. Imai and MP I tol We aint got room for
fish or wood. I tol them Mr. Zebeku wont let me have 2 dorys. Imai told
the MP what I said. The MP call the Mr. Zebeku down. The MP was
talking with all of us standing by the dory. The MP slap Mr. Zebeku on
the face 4 times and Imai was looking at us and smile. The MP come to
Imai and talk then Imai come to me and says we can use 2 dorys. We
took the 2 dorys out for fishing and gathering drifted woods. We take
long little Japs flag with our boat. We laugh looks just like target. We
did not get much wood but we catch lots of fishes. When we 2 dorys
come home the japanes took most of our fish away. We didnt have
enough fish for whole village. All I had was one codfish left for myself.

16 June 1942 Nice wither everything was nice and clear no wind. We
didnt have much to do. We cant go away or go any places. We almost
out of wood. We tear off boards inside our houses to burn. No coal, no
wood no oil for our lamps. One evening I fill my lamp with gassoline
and I took my lamp to the bed room where my wife and my little kid is.
Then I lite a match to lite the lamp. BANG my bed room and livingroom
both got on fire and my wife and my kid and I 3 of us blocked in room I
kick the window open but I still couldnt get out. I took heavy blanket
wrap my kid in to it I tol my wife Run through the fire without Breath. I
took my kid and started to the fire. My wife yelled at me She said Give
me the baby. I decided not to give her the kid but she just took kid from
me and she walked right into the flames. I went right after her. She got
out without burn but her hair was on flame also my hair caught fire so
as I step out I grab bucket of water puor it on us then put out the fire.
We didnt have a light that night.

From 7th June to 1st of Sept, 1942 we had been tol to be ready to go to Japan. So we got evrything ready. Imai tell us we better take as much food to Japan as we can. It is hard to get food in Japan maybe. So each family takes flour sugar barrels of salt fish. We dont know how we are going to live in Japan so we take tents stoves fish nets windows and doors also. Good thing we did. One day, 14 Sept, 1942 a coal carrier came and they tol us to get ready we gone to Japan. We take our stuff to vessel. We got aboard at late pass midnight. They put us down in hole where the coal had been. Evrything all black and dirty. Some of the little kids didnt want to leve Attu they cry but Japs soliders pick them up trow them down in hole too. There are 42 of us Attu people and Mrs. Jones. Some old peoples very bad scared. The vessel start off for Kiska and one of our peoples died on the boat it was Alfred Prokopioffs mother and Capt tol us to throw her overboard. So we let her go overboard in between Kiska and Attu Pass. Next morning when we got to Kiska ther were plenty Japs there as in Attu. Some houses are bombed 3 submarines were there 3 sunkin boats were there too and about 12 destroyers were there. Other vessel Big Army transport that was the one to take us to Japan. Everybody was kind of afraid because if American sub or plane come it will be our end.

That evening we take off for Japan. On the way to Japan we were keeped in hatch and not allowed to come out doors. All we had is rice evry meal and salted vegetables not enough water untill 27th Sept,1942 and when we arived at Japan evry one was taken off the boat to Otaro City. We were taken all the way through the city and outside the city. Stop at a house looks like chechen [chicken] or pigs house to me. Looked like nobody had lived in it for long time but anyway Japs made us take off our shoes before we go in. Evryone getting hungry and my kid is hungry for milk. She drinks out of bottle of milk so I ask one of civ. police is to gaurd us he tol me Japanese baby no merko I couldnt understant what merko means so I repeat him again I said Milk he says merko no Japang Baby merko I could understand Merko means milk. Sounds funny to me.

Night was getting late we 42 of us getting hungry so I told Intripiter that we are getting hungry. He tol me we will eat pretty soon Oh half hour later gaurd said super is ready. I thought we was gone to eat by table and chairs, I was thinking about the way I use to eat by the table at home. And I thought I was gone to use forks and nifes and spoons. Gaurd tol us to set down, cross our legs in Japanese style. and I had hard time to cross my legs Oh I was stiff anyways, and he start to pass little squar boxes. I thought myself it might be candie or choclat because I never seen food come in that kind of fancy box.

My wife she was set next to me and as soon as she got box she look at me and smile and open box. I look in it 4 defrent kinds of food was in it. I open my box and look in it. Some rice, some jellystuff salted vegetable and smoked boiled herring small fish boilin sugar and soy and to chop sticks. I didnt know how to use a chopsticks. I try to pick up food with chop stick and evry time when I berly get hold of some food it somehow the food jump off between the sticks fell on the floor. I thought myself look like I aint gone eat like that. So I look round see if gaurd didnt see me. I tol Pari lets eated with our hands. When gaurd wasnt round I just grab hold of some rice in my hand and start to eat it. And it wasnt bad after I been hungry whole afternoon and evening. But when I come to eat that jelly stuff I tryin to swallowed it but come up and down in my throat but Ive got to eat it because gaurd is there. My wife doing same thing and she put hers in paper and put it in her pocket. Didnt have a tea or coffee all we had was cold water. That was enough for me but my baby she couldnt quite eat yet. I had little sugar. I put some sugar in cold water and let her drink it. It was hard for me all ready. The day I got there couldnt get any milk or soap or sugar for kid for uses.

Next day we start to straighten our camp and clean up. Didnt even have a kitchen. We tooked our stove with us when we was moved off Attu. We didnt have place for stove in house so we keeped our stove outside and cook on it. We had some salt salmon and dryed salmon and also salted sealion meat and some cod fish salted with us and some rice which Japanese troop cammander give us before we lift Attu. All that stuff was put away from us when we got to Japan and they had a mesurement for rice 4x4x3 1/2 in. high small box. They use that for mesuring rice. 1 cabbage 1/2 pot onion some carretts to make soup.

After 3 days we were send to clay mining, dug clay out of side the mountain and dry it outside in sun and take stick and mash it and let it dry in powder and then turn in machine, let fan blow threw the 12in. pipe into 4x4ft. hole. I have to stay down there in that hole and keep powder away from hole from pluging. Cover me with canvas and keep me down there untill hole become full. If hole get full I tap on my cover and [they] let me out. My nose and ears and mouth and eyes full with clay couldnt hardly breath. My throat stick together and I have to drink plenty water to clear it. Thats the only way I can clear it with water. I believe I got plenty clay in my lungs as it could be seen in X-ray. While we all stayed in Japan we get pinicilin and x-rayed evry 2 weeks. Sometimes the Japanese doc take blood out of a person vein and put it in other persons. They take blood out of Mike Hodikoff and put it in my arm. I dont know why. They also take blood test after that I have eye trouble sometime cannot see my own writing and read.

Most evryone got sick in 1943 and taken to hospital. Some die from beri beri. Some of them die as soon as they get to hospital.

Evry day mens go to work before they go to work policeman give them lunch 1 ball of rice about size of baseball thats all we get. we have 3 spoonful rice for breakfast.

In 1944 it was hardest time we had. We lost 21 person by starvation. My daughter she didnt eat for 23 days and die. my baby boy born in Japan he couldnt eat either and he die. My daughter die June 23, my boy dies next day and June 26 my wife was taken to hospital.

Evrybody worked and worked evryday. Womens work at camp and mens were at clay mine at hill and mountains, young boys and girls work at factories near where we live. Gaurds wont let little kids go out doors to play.

We had to learn Japanese language even little kids. Japs say they will kill us if we didnt. When we get home from work to our camp at 1700 hrs. PM some womens look awfull. Been crying there eyes are swell from crying just because they dont know what gaurd says and gaurd go after them with stick or stove poker. Make them work. Once Julia Golodoff went 3 days without food to eat or water to drink. She talk back to gaurd when she blame him when her little girl died. She said it was Japs fault. They made her shovel snow in her barefoot but she did not die.

One of the hardest things we could not bery our dead. All got burned and Japs give us little boxes and tell us to put the bones in. This was hard to have to pick up bones and put in little box. sometimes box was not big enough for Aleuts bones.

In the year 1944 evry one of us bigan to starve. When we work at hill clay mine there was one man named SATEO SANG he was forman for us he use to give us some potatoes and dryed herrings and some rice to take home to our wifes but we were not allowed to show it to gaurd because if gaurd seen them he wont let us take to our house. If we get

home sometimes we use backdoor. Backdoor is kitchen which we build
on for cook house roof leaks snow come in through cracks. We put bag
in kitchen and come through the kitchen side. Evryone come home from
work have to report to office of police room at end of our camp. Here
we go for 3 or 4 spoon of rice.

One time I snake out and dig in Japanese garbages get fish heads and
guts and potato palings. Of course I got to clean it very good and boil it
in hot water without salt. Well its better than nothing After that all of us
start to do that. Sometimes little kids cry dont want to eat the palings
but their mothers make them. Thats only way to keep alive.

In 1945 the headquarters at police station change and Hirohito or
Tojo was change. Evrything getting better then. We had new gaurds
fellow named SAKANI TAKIRU SANG. He change evrything Chief of
Police move us from our camp to new house and they also put new
gaurd over us. The things are getting better all the time. Sometimes we
go to Hospital to visit our people in Hospital and we got friends they are
also patients too. Some of them come to us and explain Japanese Radio
program to us and tell us Americans get tuffer evry day and also Germans losing part of ther war. Japs are still holding little better than
Germans. Pretty soon we heard from our friends that Germans are
backed by Russians in to Birlen. 15 day later when we visit our people in
Hospital our friend tol us German are lose ther war. Americans and
Russians got Germans. Most Japanese said they wish Japanese to stop
fight against America so everything would be free and get more food.
Some Japanese says Japanese are strong, Americans are weak. Our
friend in Hospital tol us Americans gone win they tol us some place in
southern Japan are losing already.

Few days after we visit the Hospital and gaurd told us not to go near
other Japs and talk to them. Donnot speak to anyone accept our own
peoples. We know something was happened anyway because we understant most Japanese language now and we listen to radio and people
talking on street to each others. After gaurd left us to go see the doctor
some of them tol us that Japanese lose ther war. Some of Japs dont like
to see us theyr saying all kinds of words on our peoples and our friends
argy with them. Then we know why gaurd wont let us talk to others
because he has a orders from police station not to let us know anything
about the war was ended.

Maybe 4 or 5 days later we were lined up in one row and gaurd was stand in front of us. He got half smile on his face and tol us he is sorry to hide the things away from us for while because he had permissen from H.Q. of Police. Now he is gone tell us something will surprise us. That is war between American and Japan is Over. Nobody didnt win but when Hirohito look up on his side and see if he dont give up he is gone to lose all his nations. So no one didnt win. War is over they might send us home now but we got to wait till Americans come and release us and he tol us we under gaurded yet. He looked little worryed then. Maybe he didnt want us to go away from them. After while he told us plane will bring food and clothing for us. We mark our house P.W. Few days later American and one of the Japanese General were come to our house and Americans were look round firist and then they ask us if we want to go home. Now boy we didnt wait for another word we all say Yess, Yess. Americans write down evry word we says. Americans tol us we are free and not taking any Japanese orders anymore. That we all under U.S. Gov. now because U.S.A. win the war. We didnt wait we ask American mens to give us ride in ther car. All of us went out I was the first one got in car Most of us got in car anyway. We told them some more of our peoples in Hospital so they went up to Hospital with us. Boy when we go in Hospital peoples were glad.

That evening we were gone down to down town. Some of the men went out. They just went right out but gaurd tryen to hold me back. He said we not yet free. I tol him we are not under Japanese orders now. My real gaurd came out to see me argy with this other gaurd. He told the other we are reliesed today. Still he wont let me go. I was getting mad and he see me getting mad too so he also get mad at me. I start for the door then he tol me come back. He said You are staying home. I get so mad I walk up to him and grab his callor and hit him on his jaw, pick him up and hit him with my lift and I was gone to hit him with my right. My gaurd tol me to stop. He come to me and take me by my hand tol me to leve him alone his mouth was bleeding I had my hand brook too. I went out for I put up fight to go out. When I come back he is gone.

For two weeks we do not stay in camp much. At first we didnt have much to eat but a plane comes and drop suply for us and we had plenty food and smoke and candy bars.

At end of two weeks we pack up our baggage and made big box of all our little boxs of dead peoples. One morning 0400AM truck pick us up take us to Chotsi where air base is. In Chotsi MP search our baggage.

Next day when we was gone to fly they take care of evrything for us and put in on plane. That was our first flyt. When we got in plane and put all the kids in Kids had lots of fun Some womens are kind of scared because they never did fly in plane. When motor started my ears couldnt hear thing. After warming up we take off take 6 hours to fly. Got in Osaka sleep there one night take off again. I dont know how many hours we flyed. We got in Okinawa at night. When we are in Okinawa big storm come. We lost our baggage. We stay in Okinawa 21 days then they fly us to Manila. Three days later they take us to boat General Brewster and we are on the way to the States. I think it is Nov. 3 when we get in San Francisco. Just like we was going in new world when we got in under golden bridges. This very beautiful city just like heaven to me. Red Cross and Welfare people are at boat and take us to hotel. They give us money to pay hotel fare and by a clothing.

After 10 days we went to Seattle on train. Dec. 12 got on boat D. W. Branch start to Alaska. 19th got in Unalaska at Capt. Harbor from there to Adak from Adak got on F.S. went to Atka Dec. 21/45.

Now I am shepherd today.

On Attu Island, this sign marks the site of the original village.

✳ APPENDIX 2

Alex Prossoff's Story

[This personal account was dictated to the author by Alex Prossoff on the evening of Sunday, March 16, 1947. It is here reproduced complete and without editing. See page 162.]

We were having church services in the little Russian church in Attu on Sunday morning, June 7, 1942, when boats entered the harbor. When the gunboats got closer to the village we saw that they were Japs. They started machine-gun fire on the village. Some of our boys ran for their rifles to fight the Japs but Mike Hodikoff, our chief, said, "Do not shoot, maybe the Americans can save us yet."

A few of the boys ran away. Japs landed and came running into the village, shooting. Lucky only one woman get hurt. She is shot in leg. So much shooting and machine gun bullets flying all around Japs kill some of their own men. They capture the village. Some Japs take Mr. and Mrs. Jones and all the natives to schoolhouse and keep us there whole day without food and water. Mr. Jones is radio man. Mrs. Jones is school teacher. They very nice people. The Japs keep us there until nine o'clock at night. The Joneses live in schoolhouse but the Japs want the building so they tell them to leave. Mr. Jones try to take little food. The Japs beat and kicked them. They knocked them down. Some of us take a few of their things over to Mr. Schroeder's house and then we could not do anything more for them and the Japs let us go home.

Next morning the Japs tell us Foster Jones is dead. Mike Lokanin buried him by the church. He was just wrapped in blanket. Mike said his wrists are cut. We tried to make Mrs. Jones comfortable. Some of us stay with her all the time. She is sick and has bad cuts on her wrists, too. But she gets well.

Japs have taken down our flag but Innokinty gets it and hides it. I hide the church money. The Japs go through our houses and take many things until one officer stop them. They put lines around our houses and Jap soldiers are not allowed to bother us.

More and more Japs come to Attu. Many of their men get sick. They make their camp all around our village. They pile their things on the beach. One time I tell them wrong thing and storm comes and they lose lots of their things. They get very mad and tell me next time I tell them wrong thing they kill me.

All summer long the Japs stayed on Attu. We did not have much food but sometimes they would let us go out in dory to fish. They made us take little Jap flag on our boat. We used to make fun of it and say it looks like target. We cannot hunt wood so we have to tear boards from inside our homes to burn.

Then one day in September a coal carrier came and they told us to get ready, we are going to Japan. One Japanese man who was kind to us tell us we better take as much food with us as we can for it is hard to get food in Japan, maybe. So we do. Each family takes flour, sugar, and barrels of salt fish.

We are all put down in hold of coal carrier where coal had been. Everything all black and dirty. Some of the little children do not want to leave Attu. They cry but Japs soldiers pick them up and throw them down in holds, too. There are forty-two of us, old men and women, young people and the children. Most all the women and older girls going to have babies.

First we go to Kiska. A white man, Mr. House, is with us here. He was Navy man on Kiska when Japs take it. There were ten American Navy men there. The Japs take all of them prisoners but Mr. House runs away and hides from Japs. He eats things he finds, plants and *pootchky* and along the beach. But finally, he can't find anything more because he doesn't know. So he goes to the Japs and gives up. We never see him after we get to Japan.

My wife's mother gets sick on the coal carrier and died. They make us just throw her into the sea. We could go on deck once a day for fresh air but if we were going by any cities we had to stay in the hold.

After thirteen or fourteen days one night about 11:00 P.M. we landed at the city of Otaru on the island of Hokkaido in Japan. We stayed on board the ship until daylight. When morning came some Japs soldiers, some policemen and some Japs doctors came on board. They examined all of us but did not find any disease. They took us ashore then. We do not see Mrs. Jones again.

I was just wondering where they will take us when they brought us to a house that looked like nobody had lived in it for very long time, fifteen or ten years. It was very dirty but even then Japs make us take off our shoes before we can go in.

They ask us all kinds of questions about Americans. They asked me if Americans are good people; if we have any military outposts on our island; if we know where there were outposts in the Aleutian Islands; how often the Coast Guard and American warships came into Attu harbor. One of our head men told us not to tell the truth to them so we did not tell them the right things. They asked us how many white people lived with us and we told them just two, the teacher and the radio man. I told them the Japs killed the man. They asked us which army we liked best, Japs or Americans. Mike and I are only ones who talk to them. I tell them I can understand American language and that they are very kind to us. As long as Americans are fight for my country I'll be on their side. I told them Japs destroy our homes, make us prisoners and put us on a land where we cannot talk his language. So I cannot say Japs are good people.

All of us are kept in one house. There are forty-two of us in one five-room house. We put our mattresses and blankets on the floor to sleep on. It was getting winter and we did not have enough blankets to keep warm. We had only one stove we brought with us from Attu. The women cooked for all of us on it. The Japs did give us little heaters but we did not have enough coal to keep us warm. They give us only one bucket of coal for all day.

We were hungry, too. At first we did all right because we ate the flour and sugar and fish we brought from Attu. The Japs gave us only two cups of rice for about ten people a day. When our food was gone we could not buy any more from Japs. Then we began to get very hungry.

A month after we get to Japan we had to go to work for Japs. I dug clay for a week and then I went to work in the clay factory. It was hard work. We worked from seven in the morning to five at night and got one day of rest in two weeks. The women, most of them were put to work, too.

I had arguments with the guards over their gods. One of them wanted me to pray to their gods but I told him I would pray to my own God. I asked them where were their gods but they could not tell me. I saw many statues of the gods they pray to. Most were of Buddha, though. They had a funny custom of taking a dragon-like piece of wood into their houses and talking while they open and shut its big fiery mouth. What they say I don't know. Another custom was to send men with big umbrella-like hats and dressed in white to our camp. They held out small cup and begged for money. Finally guards told them it's no use; we did not have any money.

One day I went up to the old Jap who was kind to us and asked him which side was winning and he said the Japs were getting weak. They had plenty men but no guns and things to fight with. I saw some big Jap cruisers, two destroyers while there, but one battleship. The officers had good clothing but the soldiers poor, except their shoes. The officers slapped their men sometimes hard in the face for a little thing, maybe a gun not clean or something. I notice Jap soldier does not have much freedom. On Attu most were young, twenty-five or nineteen years old. In Japan they were maybe fifty or older.

We did not have much clothing. All I had was one pair of pants, two shirts, one pair of socks and one towel in two years.

One old Jap who talked some Russian and English was kind to us. Sometimes we would give him a piece of clothing to sell and he would get us a little food.

We lost twenty-one people in Japan. My step-mother gets sick first. She got TB and Japs take her to kind of hospital. But there is no heat and very little food so she died. Some died of beri-beri. Our chief, Mike Hodikoff and his son, George, eat from garbage can and get poison food. Lots of children and babies die because they hungry and nothing but rice.

When we first get to Japan Japanese seem to have enough food but later lots of Japs hungry, too. We never saw any Red Cross packages of food or clothing while we were in prison. No medicine ever came either.

By 1944 we got so hungry we would dig in the hog boxes when the guards were not looking. Whatever we found we would wash it and cook it and try to eat it. When spring came we would work after five o'clock in some of the Jap gardens nearby for a little extra food. In summer we sometimes helped the herring fishermen. One time I went fishing in the bay to show the Jap fishermen how we fish in Attu. All I caught was old boot. We could not eat that.

Once we killed two dogs and ate them. The men only. We gave our rice to the girls. Next day my stomach is full, I can work. After we dig garden in the fall they let us pick up anything they don't want. So we keep alive, some of us. Some of us died and sometimes I think I, too, would die like the others and never see my home again.

When we were there I used to think Japan must be one of the poorest countries in whole world. In that town of Otaru of about twenty-five thousand people not one painted house did I see. One house only had a coat of tar. Everyone worked, and worked every day. Young boys and girls worked in the factories near the house where we lived.

We had to learn to talk Japanese, even the little children. Japs said they would kill us if we didn't. Sometimes we were beaten and our women whipped. Julia Golodoff once went three days without food to eat or water to drink. This was her punishment for talking back to the Japs and blaming them when her little girl died. She said it was Japs fault. They made her shovel snow when she was barefoot, too. She did not die.

One of the hardest things was we could not bury our dead. There are no burials in Japan. All are burned. When our people died they were burned, too, and the Japs gave us little boxes to put the bones in. This was hard to have to pick up the bones of our loved ones. We kept all our boxes carefully because we wanted to take them home to be buried some day.

I noticed that when a Jap body was burned the bones did not fill the box, but when an Aleut was burned the box was not big enough to hold what was left. I told a Jap guard that his people have small frames, much smaller than Attu people. Must be because his people eat too much rice.

One day, 1945, we learned from hearing Japs talking that Germany has lost the war. So I went to friendly Jap and ask him if it is true Germany lose the war and he said yes. He said the Americans now have Germany. The Japs seem very sad over Germany losing. After that we had blackouts every night. They put us to work digging trenches. One day in August while we were digging a trench in front of a policeman's house we hear noise from radio coming from open window. We know enough Jap to know it is Jap Emperor telling his people that Japan had lost the war. He told them they must now work very hard to live. That afternoon the Jap guard tell us to stop working. They did not tell us war is over but we know it because things change. Japs take their things out of caves where they had them stored. They said it is because of nice weather and they want to dry stored clothing. There are no more blackouts, either. I asked them why did they turn on lights at night and where are the sirens that used to blow when enemy planes are near. They said the Americans are over on the southern side of Japan now so lights don't bother. But not once did they tell us they lost the war.

Seven days later a B-29 flew over very low and saw the PW sign the Japs built for us. They circled it four times and then flew so low we could see people leaning out. They dropped drums of food, candy, and cigarettes, also two bundles of clothing and shoes. The next week they came again and dropped more things. Three weeks later three Americans came. It was then we were really happy! The Japs tried to make the Americans think they had been good to us. They had our camp cleaned up and gave the Americans good food. We told our stories before the Americans and the Japs. We told of the beatings they had given us, of the months of cold and sickness and starvation. We told of our people who died of neglect. When we finished the Japs tore up their stories they had ready. The Americans told us not to take any more orders from the Japs. *We Were Free!* They told us an American plane would take us away in two weeks.

We did not work for Japs now. We went walking all over this city that had been our home for three years. One day four of us went walking and saw a church that looked like our own church at Attu with big dome and a Russian cross. We walked all around the church but could not get in. We knocked at the door for a long time. Then some one come. What a surprise! Gray hair and blue eyes!

"Is this a Russian church?" I asked.

"Yes," answered the old couple in English.

"May we come in?"

"Of course. Where do you come from?" they asked. "Come in."

"We come from Attu, Alaska," I said.

"Where is that?" they ask. "Come in."

We went in and found a map. On it is little dot—Attu. We show them where we come from.

They say, "Oh! You are Americans! What can we do for you boys?"

"We want to go to church," I tell them.

I tell them we have been Japs' prisoners three years. Only church we have is little holy picture Mike sneak with him.

"All right," old couple say. "Come back tomorrow."

So next day we all went back and had church. It was very nice to have church again in a church like ours. The old couple told us their name was Soffieff. These old people came from Russia many years before. They lived in China before they came to Japan. They suffered very much in the war, too.

We went and had church with these old people once more before we left Otaru.

Before we are going to leave Otaru, I go to Japs and say, "We want money for work we do."

They finally give me handful of little paper bills fifty-yen size. I divide among my people. When time to go we ask for kind old Jap man. We take up collection for him and he go home happy.

At the end of two weeks we get on C-47 and fly to Okinawa. We take all our little boxes of dead in one big box, our church books and our trunks. The pilots flew over Nagasaki and showed us where atom bomb dropped. It is very awful! Nothing left of that big city.

At Okinawa all our boxes and things are put inside big wire fence. We had bad tornado there and when storm is over we look for our things, but big box of all our dead people, everything is gone. Some one tell us they will look for our things and they put us on transport boat *Brewster* for San Fransisco. Then I really felt I was going home.

San Fransisco! That is very beautiful city, I think. It looks like heaven to me. Of all the cities I've been in, I like that one best. Red Cross and welfare people are at the boat and doctors and nurses. They take us to Lankershim Fifth Street Hotel and give us money to pay our hotel fare and buy food and clothing. Miss Van Every of Indian Affairs took us round in her car to see things. But mostly we walk. We walk all day, Elizabeth and me, just looking. Elizabeth wear out two pair shoes and heel off one. He [sic] look very funny walking with heel off but we walk till I see sign of little hammer hitting heel and we go there. It's a shoemaker place and he fix his heel. Then we walk some more. Elizabeth always see things he wants. "I want this, and this and this," he say. We were in San Fransisco one week and two days and we were so busy walking and looking we did not have time to go to church.

When we went to Seattle we went to Church of Seven Domes. Some of our people go to hospital in Tacoma. We stay in Seattle many days, then we get on boat *Branch* and come to Atka. We want to go to Attu. They tell us soldiers still on Attu and no more village. We must come to Atka. They will give us new house here.

✳APPENDIX 3

Personal history of war prisoners from Attu

Information taken from tables compiled by Simeon and Ethel Ross Oliver for the village survey, 1947. Except as otherwise indicated, all Attu residents were captured on June 7, 1942, transported to Kiska Island and then to Hokkaido Island, Japan, where they spent the duration of the war in the Otaru War Prison Camp.

Solid brackets indicate marriages. Dotted brackets indicate common-law marriages.

Italics in column two indicate persons listed in column one. Non-italicized names indicate persons who died or left Attu before the Japanese invasion.

Persons on Attu during Japanese invasion (June 7, 1942) or born in captivity	Background (if known)	Wartime experience (June 7, 1942, to September 21, 1945)	Survivors' residence and age in June 1947
John Artumonoff	Born Attu, 1882	Died June 15, 1942 (during Japanese occupation of Attu)	—
Peter Artumonoff	Born Attu, 1921 } children of John Artumonoff and Eva Kosminoff Artumonoff	Died of TB in Japan, August 1944	—
Mavra Artumonoff	Born Attu, 1924	Died of TB in Japan, August 1944	—
Sergi Artumonoff	Born Attu, July 8, 1927	Released September 21, 1945	Mt. Edgecumbe School, Sitka, Alaska (age 20)
Mike Lokanin	Born Unalaska, August 27, 1912; son of Ephem Lokanin and Annie Kostromitan Lokanin	Released September 21, 1945	Atka (age 35)
Parascovia Horosoff Lokanin	Born Atka, November 11, 1922; daughter of Peter Horosoff and Mary Prossoff Horosoff (half-sister of Olean Horosoff Golodoff)	Released September 21, 1945	Atka (age 24)
Titiana Lokanin	Born Agattu, January 11, 1941 } children of Mike Lokanin and Parascovia Horosoff Lokanin	Died of starvation in Japan, June 24, 1944	—
Gabriel Lokanin	[Born in Japan]	Born March 17, 1944; died of starvation in Japan, June 23, 1944	—
Mary Golodoff Prokopioff	Born Attu, April 3, 1896 } children of Mitrofan and Helen Golodoff	Died in Japan	—

Name			
		(marriages of Innokinty and Willie Golodoff)	
Lavrenti Golodoff	Born Attu	Died in Japan, January 15, 1945	—
Olean Horosoff Golodoff	Born Atka, June 11, 1911; daughter of Peter Horosoff and Agrafnia Horosoff (half-sister of *Parascovia Horosoff Lokanin*)	Released September 21, 1945	Atka (age 36); married Ralph Prokopeuff in April 1947
Elizabeth Golodoff	Born Attu, February 16, 1941	Released September 21, 1945	Atka (age 6)
Gregory Golodoff	Born Attu, March 7, 1940	Released September 21, 1945	Atka (age 7)
Valirjian Golodoff	Born Attu, January 22, 1939	Died of beri-beri in Japan	—
Nickolas Golodoff	Born Attu, December 19, 1937	Released September 21, 1945	Atka (age 9)
Leonty Golodoff	Born Attu, June 12, 1931	Died of beri-beri in Japan	—
Helen Golodoff	Born Attu, February 28, 1929	Died of beri-beri in Japan	—
John Golodoff	Born Attu, August 14, 1927	Released September 21, 1945	U.S. Army, Ft. Richardson, Alaska (age 20)
Martha Hodikoff Prossoff	Born Attu, daughter of George Hodikoff and Annie Hodikoff	Died in Japan	—
John Hodikoff	Born Attu, January 12, 1927, son of Moses Lazaroff	Released September 21, 1945	Tacoma Government Hospital, Tacoma, Washington (age 20)
Bladimir Prossoff	Born Attu	Died (of blood poisoning from ulcerated tooth) in Japan	—
Agnes Prossoff	Born Attu, March 13, 1940	Released September 21, 1945	Mt. Edgecumbe School, Sitka, Alaska (age 7)

Note: *Elizabeth, Gregory, Valirjian, Nickolas, Leonty, Helen, John Golodoff* are children of *Lavrenti Golodoff* and *Olean Horosoff Golodoff*. *John Hodikoff* and *Bladimir Prossoff* are children of *Mike Prossoff*; *Bladimir Prossoff* and *Agnes Prossoff* are children of *Martha Hodikoff Prossoff*.

(continued)

Persons on Attu during Japanese invasion (June 7, 1942) or born in captivity	Background (if known)	Wartime experience (June 7, 1942, to September 21, 1945)	Survivors' residence and age in June 1947
Innokinty Golodoff	Born Attu, August 14, 1917 } sons of Mitrofan Golodoff and Anastasia [Grumoff?] Golodoff; half-brothers of Mary Golodoff Prokopioff and Lavrenti Golodoff	Released September 21, 1945	Atka (age 30); married Vasha Zaochney in April 1947
Willie Golodoff	Born Attu, January 14, 1918	Released September 21, 1945	Tacoma Government Hospital, Tacoma, Washington (age 29)
Julia Prokopeuff Golodoff	Born Atka, May 31, 1923; daughter of Andrew Snigaroff and Clara Prokopeuff	Released September 21, 1945	Atka (age 24)
Mary Golodoff	Born Attu, January 30, 1939 } children of Willie Golodoff and Julia Prokopeuff Golodoff	Died of beri-beri in Japan, August 10, 1943	—
Michael Golodoff	[Born in Japan]	Born January 24, 1943; died of beri-beri in Japan, August 10, 1943	—
Fred Hodikoff	Born Attu; son of George Hodikoff and Annie Hodikoff (brother of Mike Hodikoff)	Died of pneumonia in Japan, January 7, 1945	—
Annie Yatchmenoff Hodikoff	Born Unalaska, August 7, 1918; daughter of Eliah Yatchmenoff	Released September 21, 1945	Tacoma Government Hospital, Tacoma, Washington (age 29)
Martha Hodikoff	Born Attu, February 9, 1937 } daughters of Fred Hodikoff and Annie Yatchmenoff Hodikoff	Released September 21, 1945	Mt. Edgecumbe School, Sitka, Alaska (age 10)
Marina Hodikoff	Born Attu, December 13, 1939	Released September 21, 1945	Mt. Edgecumbe School, Sitka, Alaska (age 7)

Name	Birth / Parentage	Fate	Location (Released)
Mike Hodikoff	Born Attu; son of George Hodikoff and Annie Hodikoff (brother of *Fred Hodikoff*); Attu Chief 1926–42	Died of food poisoning in Japan, January 10, 1945	—
Annie Golodoff Berenin	Born Attu	Died in Japan	—
Anecia Hodikoff	daughter of *Annie Golodoff Berenin*	Born in Japan; died in Japan	—
George Hodikoff	Born Attu	Died of food poisoning in Japan, January 10, 1945	—
Angelina Hodikoff	Born Attu, December 10, 1927	Released September 21, 1945	Mt. Edgecumbe School, Sitka, Alaska (age 19)
Stephen Hodikoff	Born [Attu?] January 9, 1931	Released September 21, 1945	Atka (age 16)
Garman Golodoff	Born Attu, May 23, 1888; son of Stepan Golodoff	Died of pneumonia in Japan, January 9, 1945	—
Artelion Golodoff	son of *Angelina Hodikoff*	Born in Japan; died in Japan	—
Elizabeth Prossoff	Born Attu, April 24, 1919; daughter of Anecia Prokopioff	Released September 21, 1945	Atka (age 27)
Alexei M. Prossoff	Born Attu, February 15, 1916; son of Mike Prossoff and Marina Prossoff	Released September 21, 1945	Atka (age 31)

Bracket annotations:
- *Anecia Hodikoff* and *George Hodikoff*: children of *Annie Golodoff Berenin*
- *Angelina Hodikoff* and *Stephen Hodikoff*: children of Anecia Prokopeuff Hodikoff; children of *Mike Hodikoff*
- *Elizabeth Prossoff*: children of *Garman Golodoff*

(continued)

Persons on Attu during Japanese invasion (June 7, 1942) or born in captivity	Background (if known)	Wartime experience (June 7, 1942, to September 21, 1945)	Survivors' residence and age in June 1947
Anecia [?] Prokopioff	Born Mukushin, December 3, 1886; daughter of Steven [?]	Died en route Kiska from Attu, September 13, 1942	—
Alfred Prokopioff	Born Attu, February 9, 1908; son of Stepan Prokopioff and *Anecia Prokopioff*; Attu Chief, 1942–	Released September 21, 1945	Atka (age 39)
Mary Tarkanoff Lokanin Golodoff	Born Atka, January 12, 1918; daughter of John Tarkanoff and Exenia Zaochney Tarkanoff	Released September 21, 1945	Tacoma Government Hospital, Tacoma, Washington (age 29)
Alfred Prokopioff, Jr.	son of *Alfred Prokopioff* *children of Mary Tarkanoff Lokanin Golodoff*	Born in Japan, August 20, 1945	Atka (age 2); the only child born in Japan who survived
Olean Golodoff	Born Attu, November 10, 1939 *children of Mathew Golodoff*	Released September 21, 1945	Atka (age 7)
Fekla Prossoff	Born Attu, June 7, 1935; daughter of Elizabeth Prokopioff	Released September 21, 1945	Mt. Edgecumbe School, Sitka, Alaska (age 12)
C. Foster Jones	Radio operator	Killed June 8, 1942 (during Japanese invasion of Attu)	—
Etta E. Jones	Schoolteacher	Imprisoned at POW Totsuka in Japan, from 1942 to 1945	Unknown

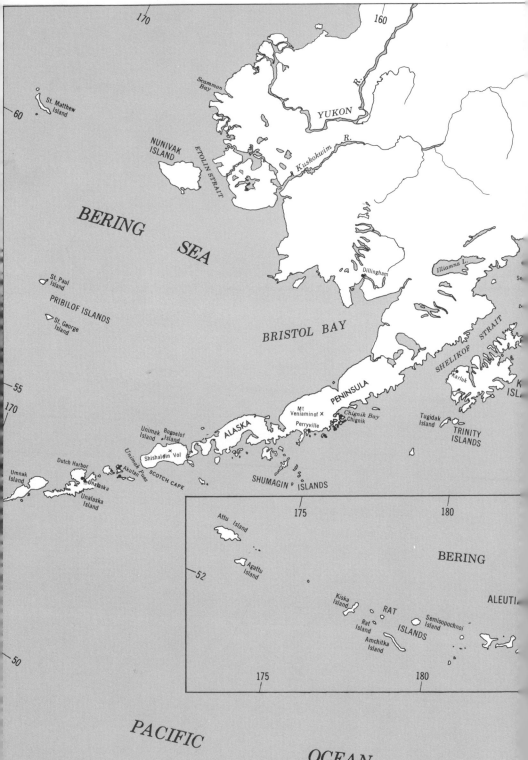

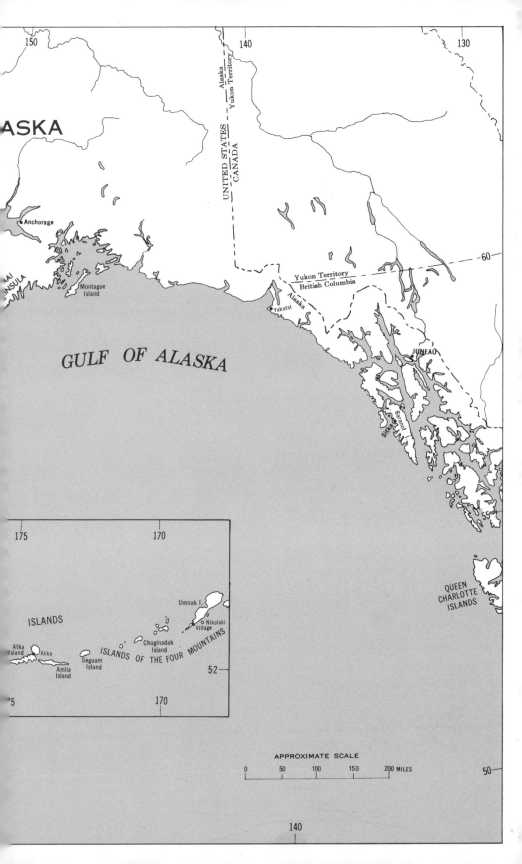

150   140   130

ASKA

Anchorage

Alaska
Yukon Territory

UNITED STATES
CANADA

—60—

Montague
Island

Yukon Territory
British Columbia

Alaska

Yakutat

GULF OF ALASKA

JUNEAU

KENAI
PENINSULA

Baranof

Sitka

55

QUEEN
CHARLOTTE
ISLANDS

175   170

Umnak I.

ISLANDS

Nikolski
Village

Chuginadak
Island

Atka
Island   Atka

ISLANDS OF THE FOUR MOUNTAINS

Seguam
Island

Amlia
Island

52

75   170

APPROXIMATE SCALE

0   50   100   150   200 MILES

50

140